# BRUNO

# A Young Boy's Survival in War-Torn Europe

*Best Wishes !*

*Bruno Reule*

# BRUNO

## A Young Boy's Survival in War-Torn Europe

By Bruno Reule
as told to James Estes

Ger-Russ Publishing of Oregon

Special thanks go to:

Mr. Edwin Kelm and Friedenstaler Heimatausschuss for
permission to use photos from *Friedenstal in Bessarabien* © 1993.

Ger-Russ Publishing of Oregon
2720 SW Montgomery Drive
Portland OR 97201

Publisher's Cataloging-in-Publication Data
(Provided by Quality Books, Inc.)

Reule, Bruno.
    Bruno: A Young Boy's Survival in War-Torn Europe
/ by Bruno Reule, as told to James Estes; edited by
Barbara Christy Wagner. – Rev. ed. p. cm.
    LC Control Number: 00 133096
    ISBN: 0-615-11788-0

1. Reule, Bruno. 2. Germans—Bessarabia (Moldava and
Ukraine)—Biography. 3. Germans—Bessarabia (Moldova and
Ukraine)—History. 4. World War, 1939-1945—Prisoners and
prisons, Soviet. 5. World War, 1939-1945—Children. 6. World
War, 1939-1945—Personal narratives, German. 7. Population
transfers—German. 8. Estes, James F. I. Wagner, Barbara. II.
Title

DK 509.35.G3R48        20009        47.600431/0842 B
                                     QBI00-465

# Dedication

To my mother whose constant love and determination gave us the strength to survive insurmountable odds.

To my father whose spirit and independence gave me the courage to stand up for my own beliefs.

To all the countless others who also found themselves swept up in the politics of war. Many died. All suffered. May their sacrifices not be forgotten.

# Acknowledgments

A very special thanks to Sherrie (Gettman) Stahl, Barbara Christy Wagner, Steven Schreiber, Dr. Raymond P. Koch and Dr. Richard A. Koch for their important contributions. Without them, and many others, this book could not have become a reality.

# Contents

# Preface

When I first heard the story of Bruno Reule and his family, I came to realize a fundamental truth: that neither the terrible atrocities nor the human sacrifices of World War II were limited to one side. How simple it would be if the evil of that killing time could be blamed on only one group of people or political system. What is learned in this true story is that war, in all of its complexities, is the number one disease of mankind. No one is safe or immune from its terrible symptoms. The more our world is caught in conflict or the threat of conflict, the more Bruno's story needs to be read, and read again.

—Rev. James F. Estes

# The Registering

I was a young boy of six when it all began. Wide-eyed and curious about life, I was barely big enough to lead my father's plow horses to the watering trough. What I lacked in size, I made up in eagerness and energy. I wanted to be a farmer just like my dad; to plow the rich, black ground, cutting long furrows across the flat fields, while swarms of birds darted to feast on slow-moving worms. I wanted to plant and reap great harvests of wheat, corn, potatoes and sunflower seeds; but, above all, I wanted to be like him.

Life for us was simple but good. When my dad came in, hot and dusty from the fields, I raced down the road to meet him. No matter how tired he was, he always stopped and let me ride to the barn in the wagon or on the back of a horse. Feeling mighty big and important, I helped him until my mom called us to wash for supper. Toward the end of summer, when the grain was almost ready for harvest, he would break off a head of wheat and bring it home. After we had supper, he'd show us the kernels, proud of what he and the earth had accomplished. He would explain how the grain was "heading out," and how, if the rain held, we should have a great harvest in a few days. "It's an honest return for hard work," he told us, looking at me because he knew how slow I was in getting my chores done. Work and I didn't get along very well.

My dad attended church, but wasn't overly religious. He recognized the creative ability of God, but remained convinced that hard work was the way to heavenly blessings. As harvest time approached, he started looking upward, not in prayer but to keep an eye on the weather. "We could use a little more moisture," he would say, to no one in particular.

Our land was usually a little too dry, but sometimes we had

sudden summer storms accompanied by devastating hail. That's what my dad knew so well. He was dedicated to the soil. I remember him being rather small, but there was a great strength about him, that went beyond physical size. He could lift a bale of hay or a sack of grain with such force that it seemed to fly. But his real strength was some invisible force that made him different from all other men. One day our neighbor, old Mr. Wagner told me, "Your dad only knows how to be himself. He is completely his own man."

It took many years for me to understand what Mr. Wagner meant. It has taken hardships, struggles and life's experiences. I have come to realize that memories of my father have shaped my image of manhood and have become a model for me. During those closing days of the summer of 1940, my life revolved around him driving a horse-drawn wagon to the fields or coming into our summer kitchen with a bucket of warm milk, fresh from the cow. Whatever he was doing, I watched every move.

Just as important to me was my mom. Whether working, cooking or hoeing in the fields, she was always there for us. She looked after my dad, my little brother Egon, who was only a few months old, and me. Another important part of my world was Grandpa and Grandma Funk, Grandpa and Grandma Reule and several uncles and aunts. Our large family and others had left Germany more than a hundred years earlier, creating the small German village of Friedenstal in the Bessarabia Province of Romania. Although not far from the Black Sea, we considered ourselves Bessarabian Germans. Protected by the love and care of my parents, I was convinced of my own importance. In my own little world, I felt safe and secure. But all that we had known and loved, was soon to change.

"Bruno." My mom's sharp voice stopped me in mid-step. It sounded thin and high and got that way whenever she was excited or upset. This was no time to delay or vanish, as I sometimes did. I hurried into the summer kitchen. "You go to the barn and watch for your dad. As soon as he gets here, you tell him to come right in the house."

I had other plans, but this was no time to argue. Choking on frustration, I went out the door and took up a half-hearted vigil in front of the cow barn. Our home and barns, similar to the others of our village, were one long building divided by walls. Across from us on the same piece of land, lived my dad's brother, Otto Reule, and his family. Uncle Otto's house opened out on Hauptstrasse, the main street of Friedenstal, while our home faced on Untergasse. The only other street, one block over, was Obergasse. Along those three straight streets, laid out in lots 150 meters by 25 meters, lived our entire village of 2,245 people. One was Roman Catholic, 45 were Baptists and the rest were Lutherans. The village was divided into two sections. Our home was located in the "lower" part known as Unterdorf. The "upper" section was called Oberdorf. At the north end of our section were two school buildings, the cemetery and the Lutheran Church. Across the roadway into Oberdorf was the "Primaria," the business place of our mayor; and farther up, was the mill.

We were a prosperous people. My family and the other families of Friedenstal owned and farmed more than 22,000 acres of rich farmland, surrounding our village. North of Oberdorf and south of Unterdorf lived the families of the shepherds who tended thousands of sheep that were owned by the people of our village. Well over a thousand cattle, including my dad's, grazed in the surrounding fields. Each evening the cattle were driven down the three main streets. Each cow knew where to turn and came to her own barn and into her stall without urging. On most farms, women did the milking, but not on ours. My dad was particularly fond of good cows and always looked after them himself.

When my dad came in, I gave him my mom's message. Of course, he went right on with his usual chores. He took the harness off, hung it on the side of the horse barn, watered the horses and then, when he was good and ready, went into the house. That was his way and what I had expected, and probably also what my mom expected. He placed a hand on my shoulder as we went through the door of the summer kitchen and gave me that familiar pinch that made my knees buckle, yet caused me to feel close to him. As soon as we came in, my mom stopped what she was doing. Only then did I realize how important this matter was. Not much gets between my mom and fixing supper. "The town crier came by this afternoon," she told him. "He said everyone leaving has to register at the Relocation Office." Supper was always a happy time with us, but the usual curve of his mustache suddenly straightened into a firm line. Seeing that look on my dad's face, I immediately turned into a little mouse, unseen and unheard, but with big ears. The look on my dad's face bothered me. My mom worried over a lot of things; but when my dad got that angry look, it meant trouble.

"What is going to happen, Gotthilf?" my mom asked. Her voice was raised another notch and sounded as it did when she was fearful or completely exasperated. This time, I think she was both.

My dad just stood there in a daze. He finally turned and looked at her, his grayish-blue eyes flashing with a fire of intense anger. I was relieved he wasn't looking at me. "How in this world, or the one to come, do I know?" he said in a flat, lifeless voice. "How does any man in his right mind know what the governments of this world are doing?" Finally, a look of acceptance came to his face. "So the time of registering has come." He turned and walked out of the summer kitchen. He didn't even slam the door, and that was what made my mom and me stare after him.

The "registering" had started a few weeks earlier, June 26th of 1940. That was when the Russian government sent official word to the Romanian government demanding return of Bessarabia and Bukowina regions. Those two areas had hundreds of farm villages settled by Russian, German and Romanian people; and each village maintained its own distinctive culture. Since 1918, at the close of World War I, those two regions had been part of Romania. Now, Russia, a world power with military might, was demanding that they be returned. The Romanian government had been given four days to meet this demand and to also remove all Romanian soldiers from these territories. It took only two days before we heard the radio announcement that Romania had conceded. That was when my dad got worried. "By damn," I heard him say to Uncle Otto, "I know the Romanian army and what they will do."

Uncle Otto looked at him, a puzzled expression on his face. "They can't do anything Gotthilf," he said. "They have no orders."

My dad looked back at his brother and I knew that expression so well. He had used it on me many times. It wasn't that he didn't understand what Uncle Otto was saying. He just couldn't see how Uncle Otto could be so dumb. "I know soldiers and army command," my dad said again. "The troops have been ordered out of Bessarabia and Bukowina and that takes transportation. Since they don't have an overabundance of horses and wagons, where do you think they are going to get them?"

"You think they will make us provide transportation for them?"

My dad nodded, and for once didn't say anything.

"Well, they're not going to make me," Uncle Otto said, along with a few of those choice words my mom would never let me use. "The marshland makes a good hiding place."

My dad's brother was referring to a section of land a few kilometers away. It was a wet area covered with tall reeds and not suitable for farming. I had always been warned not to go there. For the next two days, most of the farmers of our village, including my dad, hid their horses and wagons in the marshland. It was well that they did. The next day a large group of Romanian soldiers came through Friedenstal. Some men from our village were caught on the road and had to furnish the needed transportation. They didn't, however, find any at our farm or Uncle Otto's. That was also when several ethnic German men from Friedenstal deserted the Romanian military service and returned home.

As soon as my mom wasn't looking, I slipped out and followed my dad out of the summer kitchen, but not to be with him. I wanted to be out of sight. This was no time to be seen or ask any questions. I wanted to do some thinking on my own, and this called for deep thoughts. I had always thought our farm was our home. Long ago, my father's family had bought the land, built the buildings and raised the crops. Now, some people, in a far-off country, said our land belonged to them; and the Romanian government agreed? If that was true, did it mean that the land belongs to whoever has the biggest and most guns? Questions with no answers buzzed in my head so fast that I began to see spots before my eyes. I wanted to go ask my dad, but he was in no mood to talk to me. My mom would just tell me to stop thinking such crazy thoughts, and to let older people take care of what didn't concern me. The trouble was, it did concern me, and the older people did not seem to be doing a very good job taking care of things.

The next day was Sunday, September 15th. It was also the day the German Commission on Relocation arrived in Friedenstal to establish their headquarters. Establish as they would, it was Church Day for the families of our village. In spite of our regular Saturday night and Sunday morning routine, life seemed different around our house, as if somebody was very sick. There was no laughter. I didn't see my dad smile, nor did he give me that painful, but welcome pinch on the shoulder. It was obvious that he had his mind on the registration and whether or not we should leave our farm. He had spent his whole life accumulating more land, planting bigger and better crops and raising fine animals. Now he was faced with the bitter choice of living under communism or walking off and leaving all that he had built; and it was not an easy decision.

Unless there was some kind of emergency, such as stormy weather during harvest time, the only work on the Sabbath was usually to feed and water the animals and milk the cows. Some men found reasons to miss the lengthy service and a few families held Baptist services in a home, but mainly we were a German Lutheran village and faithful to the church. My mom sang in the choir and my dad played his French horn in the church band. No special occasion was complete without the band or a number by the choir. It seemed everyone was in church on that Sunday, before the registration.

"These are distressing times," our minister, The Reverend Johannes Miller, said at the conclusion of his sermon, reminding the men how important it was to register. "No German would choose to live under communist rule," he said proudly. "Besides," he added with a big smile, "the German government has invited every family of our village to make their home in the Fatherland." The German and Russian governments had been working out the details for us to leave. Pastor Miller seemed to be looking at everyone at the same time. "Stay strong in the faith," he said, "and know that we are children of our Heavenly Father. He is our Protector."

It seemed easy to believe the words of our big, imposing pastor while he stood before us in his dark robe with white tabs. He was the voice of our village in quiet times. How could his words not be the truth?

Monday afternoon, my dad came in early from working around our farm. Like all the other men of our village, he had made up his mind to register and leave Friedenstal. He had no other choice, he told us. Under communism, the government would own everything; and he couldn't live in any place where he could not own the land. My mom hurried about, laying out our clothes. She could tell at a glance if a button was missing, a shirt was dirty or, for some hidden reason, we were not dressed properly. German families had three sets of clothing. "Going-to-church" clothes were our very best; visiting clothes were our next best; and there were "work" or "play" clothes. What surprised me was that my visiting clothes were laid on the bed, along with my dad's.

"Bruno should go with us to register!" my mom said, as my dad started getting dressed.

When something took my dad by surprise, he always stopped what he was doing, slowly turned his head toward whatever surprised him and blinked at least three times. "Bruno? Why should he go with us?" It was puzzling to hear my mom and dad talk about me as though I wasn't there, when I was standing right between them. "He's only six years old," my dad said, as though stating something my mom didn't know. The look on his face said I wasn't going, and the tone of his voice made it final.

"He's going with us," my mom repeated firmly. "Bruno is the man of the house after you," she reminded him. "He has to learn how to handle business just like you, and it's our job to teach him." Her voice softened, as though explaining and asking permission, all at the same time.

That made me feel good. Maybe I was going after all! My dad was the head of our house. There was no mistake about that. But, when my mom got determined, he usually found a good reason for doing what she said. I could tell by his agreeable smile, the first I had seen since the registration announcement, that he had found the reason.

"All right," he said, laughing and looking at me with exaggerated respect. "If you say he is man of the house next to me, then he can go." Soon after, he found the occasion to walk by and give me that familiar pinch. It felt good. He must have started thinking about the registration and what it meant because he was serious again. I could sense a lot of serious thoughts behind that look on his face. I knew why my mom wanted me to go. I might serve as some kind of restraint. If anyone would have something to say about gun-happy Russians and weak-kneed Romanians, it would be him.

Once my dad agreed, my mom didn't waste any time. There were some things about the two of them that I didn't understand. She said I was going, and had laid my clothes on the bed, but didn't start getting me ready until my dad said yes. It was like hitching up the wagon halfway. Maybe that's how I knew my dad was the head of our house and my mom respected him for it. He knew when to give in.

In no time, I was scrubbed and in clean clothes. My mom was not a large woman, compared to my aunts, but her fingers were bigger than my ears. Holding my head with one hand, she would dig in my ears with the other, claiming to find enough dirt to plant potatoes. I never thought what she said was funny, but my dad always did. He would say I had to spend the next day carrying the dirt back to the fields, or there wouldn't be enough to grow next year's crop. That afternoon he didn't say anything. As much as I hated it, I missed his teasing.

I still remember my family, as we were on that fateful September. My mom was twenty-six and my dad was thirty; I was six and my little brother Egon was a few months old. They had always been there for me, and I expected that they always would be.

"You stay real close to your dad," my mom warned me in a sharp whisper, as she fastened the last button on my shirt.

I had no problem understanding what she meant. There was to be no chasing with other boys, no matter who I might see at the Relocation Office; and no matter how long my dad stood and talked — he was a champion at that—I was to stay beside him. "Maybe, if you're there your dad won't have so much to say," she said, glancing toward the bedroom where my dad was putting on his go-to-meeting shoes. She made it plain that whatever she wanted would be done. "Now you do it," she said. "And that's that."

Despite the restrictions, I felt pretty important about going to register. Although, I later found out that the entire family was supposed to come to the Registration Office, whether or not I got to go was up to my dad. When it came to family, it was he who made the decisions and not some government official. He never hesitated to speak his piece about governments—the Romanian government, the Russian government, and especially Hitler's government—along with a few choice words about officials, generals and men in uniform. Then he'd top it all by saying something about the damn madness of Germany going to war with the entire world that made for trouble. Since women didn't usually speak out in public, there wasn't any way my mom could stop him. If there were several families gathered at the Relocation Office, she would be with the other women and wouldn't be in a position to reach out and grab his arm. My mom had a right to be worried. My dad didn't know what it meant to be silent, and that always concerned our family and friends.

Leaving our house, we walked across Uncle Otto's land and up the road to where the Commission had set up headquarters. Even though it was late afternoon, the sun was still high in the sky and it was hot. I could tell by the way my dad walked that he was anxious to register and get it over. To soften my dad's choice of words, it was all a big irritation, as far as he was concerned. When we reached the office, a few buggies were tied outside. Flies were buzzing around the patiently waiting horses, but most of the men walked, as we did. Since all of our homes were clustered close together in the village, almost everyone walked to meetings, unless someone had a new team of horses and wanted to show the other men.

When we entered the inner door, the room was already crowded. My dad, head up and shoulders square, stopped and looked around. Even though I was only a young boy, I thought how much people could be like a flock of sheep. Perhaps that was also what my dad was thinking. His very posture made it clear he was not one of the flock. Instead, his whole attitude seemed to say, "I'm here. Let's get on with it." That was his way.

In our village, as in every German settlement, there were three men that commanded great respect: the pastor, the mayor and the schoolmaster. These men represented religion, government and education. I knew, or had seen before, several families that came to the Relocation Office when we did. Most of them had been at the Sunday church service, but this was vastly different than when they collected on the church lawn or when several of them chanced to meet at the mill. At those times, the men laughed and joked and had a great time. Now, everyone looked serious, as though they had forgotten all of their funny stories. Standing beside my dad and looking around the large room, I saw our mayor, Mr. Lutz, seated at a table with two other men from our village. He wasn't any taller than my dad, but weighed a lot more and stuck out in the back and in the front. At a larger table, four men were seated. Two of them were Russian soldiers, while the other two were dressed in civilian suits. Their faces and appearance made me think they were Germans. The mayor and the two men from our village were busy examining papers, as if they had to verify whatever was written there. Over at the big table, two of the men were busy while the other two had that disgusted look on their faces like "let's hurry up and get this problem over". One of them, as I was told later by my dad, was a major in the Russian army. He had a sharp face that appeared to be molded of iron. He tapped his fingers impatiently in rapid little jerks on the table. All of that was doubly enforced when he looked at us and I saw his eyes. He was looking at everyone, yet no one, and seemed mad at everybody.

At the other end of the big table from the Russian major was a man from Germany. Even though he wasn't in uniform, it was easy to see he was, or had been, a soldier. Most of the men in our village, including my dad, had been soldiers. A German man, even if he has served in another nation's army, never seems to lose his military bearing. As we were to learn, he was the head commissioner, Franz Liebl from Dresden. He looked just as determined and mad as the Russian officer did. The man seated toward the middle of the table and doing all the work was his assistant, Werner Liedke from Domnau. Next to Mr. Liedke was a lieutenant in the Russian army who was also busy working. As we were sadly informed a few days later, there was good reason for the two men at opposite ends of the big table— the Russian major and the Head Commissioner—to be angry with each other. What they knew was that the German assessor, Albrecht Haverich from Sigmaringen, had started his evaluation of our village farms and was already at great disagreement with the Russian assessment. Eventually that difference would reach the staggering proportions of 110 million leus by the Germans and only 8.8 million leus by the Russian assessor – about 92 percent less. This was exactly what my dad had expected. He didn't know what would go wrong, but, as he had said a dozen times to my mom and me, "Mix three governments, including their armies, along with a large group of hard-headed German farmers and what can go right?" Seeing the looks on the faces of the men behind the big table, I appreciated even more my mom's concern about my dad saying the wrong things.

"Gotthilf, I am glad that we came at the same time as your family."

My dad and I turned around. Standing right behind us were Mr. and Mrs. Wagner and their son Konrad. Mr. Wagner was an old man and sort of stooped when he stood, and his fingers were twisted from arthritis. He and his wife, Magdalena, were very proud of their son, Konrad, who wasn't married and farmed their land with them. My dad shook hands with Mr. Wagner and Konrad, but didn't say anything. Instead, he gave a nod of his head toward the big table.

"So they are taking our land and everything we own," Mr. Wagner said with a sigh as he caught my dad's meaning.

"They'll give us some papers," my dad replied, in such a critical tone of voice that some of the people standing in front of us turned and looked at him. My mom moved close and laid a hand on his arm. That didn't stop him. "Then we can plant the papers and they will grow into big farms, all stocked with strong horses and fat cows," he said loud enough for all to hear.

Several laughed at what my dad had said, but it wasn't a happy or funny laugh. Everyone, including my dad, was pleased that Germany had offered us the privilege of making our homes in the Fatherland. But, the thought of being forced to leave our homes and lose everything we had to the Russians, created a deep bitterness.

In the group, but not really a part of it, my dad finally stepped before the large table, with us right beside him. "Name?" the assistant to the Head Commissioner asked, without looking up from his papers. My dad waited. "Name?" the assistant asked again, his voice sharp and demanding. And again my dad waited. Of course my mom knew what was happening, but that didn't make it any easier for her. I was feeling more nervous than those times she had called me and I hid out, but not my dad. He just stood there with that little smirk on his face, and waited. If the assistant to the Head Commissioner wasn't going to look up and meet my dad person to person, the meeting wasn't going to take place. That was one of his big objections about government and army life, as he had told us a hundred times. They stop you from being a person and make you into a dumb machine that talks when told to. By this time, the Head Commissioner and the two Russian officers were looking at my dad with even more anger in their faces. They were there to get a big job done and not to have the flow interrupted by someone who had a mind of his own. "Name?" the assistant barked again, but this time he looked up as he spoke.

"Reule, Gotthilf," my dad answered, leaning down to the table and looking the assistant straight in the eye. Somehow or other, my dad had won. What had happened, I didn't know. It was that world of adults and I hadn't learned the rules or even how to add up the score. But I knew by the different feelings radiating from my dad, that he was ready to go ahead with the registering. He stated how much land we had and where it was located, and identified each member of the family by name and age. We were given name tags bearing the number 34001 that designated Friedenstal. "Do we go by name or by number?" my dad asked, as we finished up at the big table. Ever since my dad had stepped to the table, there had been silence in the room. His question was innocent. His intent was not. That intent was not missed by the men at the big table or by the people of our village standing behind us. Everyone was watching.

It was also obvious that the assistant was expressing a different attitude toward my dad. "The number will help in keeping all the villages intact, so the people will not become separated from each other." He looked up at my dad as he spoke. "It is the best way we could devise to help everyone stay with their neighbors and friends in the relocation."

My dad nodded. It was a sad little nod as though he was agreeing, but he wasn't. He took the set of papers that listed all of our equipment, animals and farm. "I'm used to numbers," he said. "They're the gift of government."

# The Leaving

On Friday, September 27, the church bells rang. In a short time, our entire village gathered at the cemetery near the church. The band was there and my dad played his French horn. Then the mayor and the pastor made speeches. Two days later, the first group of 737 people was to leave for Chilia (Kilija). The differences between the Russian and German evaluations had not been settled, but military might has a way of taking care of bothersome details. The Russians had issued their demand and the Romanian government was in no position to refuse. It seemed appropriate that our last meeting as a village was near the church and in the place of the dead. A funeral was taking place. We were burying any future life in Friedenstal.

I had loved our life in Romania. Leaving was something I hadn't really accepted, even after the registration, and now the first group of people was to be carried away by trucks and buses.

During the century that the Reule family lived in Friedenstal, there had been many changes. In the early years, our people had been under control of the Russians. Then, after World War I, new boundaries put the villages under Romanian rule. During all of that time, we had remained a village of German culture with strong loyalty to the Fatherland. Not a single German man or woman of our village had married an outsider. We were also loyal citizens of Romania. My father had served as a soldier in the Romanian army, but had always remained a German at heart. Even our farmhouse, a long building that included our living area and barns, was of German design. We lived at one end. That area was large, and, thanks to the endless work of my mom, spotless. I especially remember my soft mattress filled with inner cornhusks. And what a time we had filling those mattresses at harvest time. When the cornhusks wore out, we replaced them with straw. That wasn't as soft, but far easier to get. Through the end of our living area was a door opening into the summer kitchen, where my mom cooked and served meals to our farm workers during the hot summer. Attached to the kitchen was the stable for our horses, then the barn for my dad's cows, his pride and joy. Beyond the cow barn was an open, fenced area and a building for pigs and chickens. The chickens could come into the fenced area to scratch for worms. After the chicken and pig building was an open, roofed building for the storage and repair of equipment.

Our home and our lives reflected the orderly procession of streets and houses in our village. From our house, it was three blocks to the center of town. That was where my dad's cousin, Herbert Stadel, worked in the general store. The school buildings, our church and a few businesses were all close. On every side around us were the fields. Our lives were centered in the village and fields. When we were not in church or observing a national holiday, we were working. Every day, from early spring until after harvest, my dad and the other men of the village were a part of the earthly drama of planting and reaping. There was a zestful eagerness about them. Out of that dedication to the land had come a happy prosperity. Through the years, my family and the other German families continued to purchase more and more land until it took an hour or two coming and going to our fields. Little did I know then that no matter how hard you work or how much you pay, no one on this earth really owns the land.

"Bruno." My dad's voice brought me to an abrupt stop. I was going through the side door into the summer kitchen. For the last several days, we had been packing and getting ready for the trip to Germany. When my dad spoke to me with that edge to his voice, all of the shuffle went out of my legs. I quickly went into the front room where he was working with my mom. He looked up from where he was kneeling among some boxes. His blue eyes measured me up and down, indicating what was going to happen if I didn't start doing a lot more work. "Put this box with the others," he snapped. "And be quick."

"Gotthilf," my mom was asking, as I picked up the box, "how soon do you think we will be on our new farm?" She may have been different from my dad, but she was just as stubborn. I actually thought she was a little smarter, since she could get him to do whatever she wanted. That is, she could, unless he got that certain look in his eyes and began swearing in Romanian. He knew some really bad words in that language. When he did that, even she gave up and let him have his way.

"Olga," my dad answered in that frustrated voice he saved for all things foolish, "who knows what this government will do or when they will do it? Even God must think of our government, and all governments as big sores on the behind of this world." He answered that way because I was still in the room. My mom always attempted to calm down his way of saying things. She either hushed him up or hurried me out of the room. My dad was a talker. Words great and small flowed from his mouth as freely as any wind that blew across our fields. He had a quick tongue, a quicker mind and, when he wanted, could tell a funny story or come up with a sharp answer to any question asked of him. He rose from where he had been kneeling. The large box he had been packing with kitchen items was almost full. I felt his critical eye fall on me. I had learned to move just fast enough to avoid their yelling, or worse. At the same time, I usually managed to do what I wanted. In this case, I was watching for the soldiers to come. I sure didn't want to miss that. Stretching to get the kinks out of his legs and back, my dad looked out the window with an unhappy squint to his eyes. "Don't get your hopes up," he said softly to my mom, almost as an afterthought. "It will be a long way and a long time before we reach that Promised Land." There was silence, but I knew he wasn't through talking. He turned from the window to face her. "If we ever do!"

It had been a week after the first group left Friedenstal and now it was our turn to leave. The plan, as we learned from the town crier, who rang a bell to make sure everyone was listening, was that the soldiers would come October 8th, a Monday. All women and children remaining in Friedenstal were to be taken by buses and trucks to Galatz (Galati) on the Danube River. The men would drive wagons, pulled by their best horses, to that small border town and join us. Why we didn't all go together was beyond me. It wasn't beyond my dad. He had a few of those choice Romanian words, not only to explain what was happening, but also to describe the government officials who had set it up.

Again it was stressed that we were forbidden to take equipment, animals or any furniture with us. In spite of those restrictions, everyone was busy packing what they could and selling the rest. My dad seemed to be the busiest of all. The question for my mom, and I could see it every time she looked around, was how much could be put in a wagon that was only fourteen feet long and five feet wide. Also, knowing her, I am sure she was thinking of the horses. They would have a long, hard pull. Despite all that, there were my mom's prized dishes, linens, clothes, and an endless array of things she had come to love. Many of our special possessions had belonged to our family for generations and had become a part of us. My dad also had his collection of tools and other special things. And, of course, there was my little brother Egon and myself.

Quicker than I thought possible, most of our things were sold. The Romanian people, a great number being of Russian heritage, were friendly, but not foolish. They were also poor and knew that we were forced to sell for what little we could get, or walk off and leave it. I never thought of German people as superior, but we were thrifty, hard working and overly clean. We had much more in the way of land, food and animals than most of our Romanian neighbors. One reason my family had so much was that my dad was good at trading. Even in the hardest of times, he had a way of getting what he wanted. That was what caused him to resent the restrictions on what we could take, especially the amount of money. He figured what he had in his pocket was his business. Why we had some extra money later, I am sure, came from what my dad carried out of Romania. "Rules are made by the rich and have to be broken by the poor," I heard him tell my mom. "Run to sit," I also heard him tell her in a loud, irritated voice, as we spent another day waiting for the soldiers. "That is the way it is with all governments, all armies, all big shots." He walked around our almost-empty house in quick, rapid steps, flapping his arms against his sides in great disgust. "This damn war," he said, stomping outside to walk through the empty barns or to go over and talk to Uncle Otto.

The reasons for delay, as we learned from a mixture of facts and rumors, were varied and complicated. Some, like my dad, said it was the money. The German assessors and the Russian assessors were so far apart that they would never get together. Others said the longer we waited, the better farms we would have in Germany, since it takes time to make such a large land transfer. For reasons I didn't understand, my dad laughed when he heard that one. Then, there was the talk that we weren't going to Germany at all. My dad didn't laugh when he heard that. Germany had invaded Poland a year earlier. They controlled Austria and the Czech Republic. The Fatherland had become more than just Germany. While the officials did whatever they do in far-off places, my dad paced the floor. It was being forced to do nothing while waiting, when he could see no reason for it, which was especially hard on my dad. Yet it wasn't just wasted time that was bothering him. Everything he had built into his farm was being taken away, piece by piece. The cow barn that had been filled with good milkers was almost empty. We had made arrangements with a Russian farmer to keep one cow so we would have milk. Our horse stable was empty except for the two we kept to pull our wagon. I watched my dad wander from place to place. He no longer looked with pride as he went in and out. His face was as empty as our farm. That emptiness was more than the loss of things. He had a compulsion to be busy, believing he owed life as much as life owed him.

"Someone should be working the fields," I heard him say to my mom, at least a dozen times. It was as though he had a need to tell her over and over. My dad felt that the secret of spring planting was to prepare the fields in the last few weeks before winter. "The weeds will be knee-high before the trees start to bud," he said, walking briskly about the empty rooms, flapping his arms like some giant bird about to take off. My mom didn't know what to say. She just agreed with him. I had some questions, but knew enough not to ask them. The weak slump of his arms against his sides said as much as his words about the frustration he was feeling. At a given time I could count on, he would storm out of the house and go for a walk. Sometimes, if he wasn't too angry, I tagged along. We would visit one of our relatives or a neighbor. The usual place was Mr. Wagner's.

"What in the hell is going on?" I heard him ask Mr. Wagner one afternoon. "It doesn't make one damn bit of difference," he shouted at our old neighbor who wasn't hard of hearing. "One government doesn't pay another for what it takes anyway. They find it a lot easier to go to war than to pay honest debts."

The way my dad talked and acted scared me. Then, on that bright sunny afternoon of October 7, the soldiers came. The sky was clear and the day was slow in warming. It was a sure sign that winter was soon to come. Despite my dad's attitude toward the army and all that was happening, I had spent every free minute watching for the soldiers. I was playing on the front steps using my toy horse, which was actually a knee bone of a horse, to pull different wagons made from the knee bones of cows and pigs. Then I heard the roar. There were not many motor vehicles in our region. All our noises came from wagon wheels and horses. This was different. It was exciting. I ran across Uncle Otto's land to the main road, along with a lot of the other kids. That was when I saw the trucks and buses as a long, dark shadow, moving toward our village. In the excitement of what was happening, I forgot that their arrival meant our departure.

Beyond our village, the dirt road made its way across the fields. I didn't know how far the road went. The farthest I had been away from home was eight kilometers to my mother's sister, Aunt Martha Ziebart. She and her husband, Gustav, along with their three children, Leonide, Annemarie and Paul, lived in the larger village of

Arzis. That was the general direction my dad and the other men went to work the fields. Upon reaching the edge of our village, the convoy had clearly separated into trucks and buses. The vehicles were so covered with dust that they looked black. The trucks with their high wheels came first, followed by the long buses. Being used to horses and wagons, it seems to me that they were coming pretty fast. As the noise got louder, I got more and more excited. Then I forgot the trucks and buses when I saw the soldiers. They were sitting high up, tall and straight in their uniforms. They looked straight ahead, but saw everything. I had heard of Hitler's soldiers, but this was the first time I had seen them. I completely forgot what was happening to us as I felt the tense thrill of watching them drive by.

"No more," my dad said half angrily, as my mom set out more boxes. "It will be a long way and I would rather get there with a few of our things than not get there with nothing."

As usual, my mom understood what my dad was saying. "Yes Gothilf," she answered. "I know. You are right." Then, also as usual, she did exactly what she was going to do and carried out another box, finding room for it in the wagon. I guess my dad felt better because he had told her what to do; my mom felt better because he was being the head of the house. They seemed to understand and were happy with each other. My mom spoke softly and reached out to touch him when he came close.

Our wagon, heavily loaded, was near the front of the barn so we could come out of the house or the summer kitchen and load over the tailgate. Late that evening, I watched my dad rearrange the last few boxes and close up the wagon. I saw him looking at the cowbarn, and even though it was getting dark, I knew what he was feeling. The pride of most German farmers was usually their horses, but not my dad. His great love was cows. Some European farmers, even Germans, used cows to pull plows, but that didn't happen in our village, and especially not with my dad.

The next morning, we got up before it was light. Because our bed covers were to be placed in the wagon, even I had to get up. If that was part of leaving, it didn't make me very happy. Of course, my mom and dad had just about everything done and let me sleep to the very last minute. Gulping down my breakfast, I ran out to the wagon where my dad was putting in the last of our bedding. The early morning air was sharp against my face, taking away the last feelings of sleep. My dad told me that I should go on the bus with my mom and brother to help her, instead of riding on the wagon to help him.

"Bruno." I ran around the wagon and up on the porch where my mom was standing. Without saying another word, she took me by the hand and we went into the house. Inside, we just stood there. Sometimes I didn't understand adults, particularly my parents, but one thing I did understand. When I had that certain feeling, I had to keep my mouth shut, stand still and wait for whatever was to come. "Look at everything," she told me, "and remember." That wasn't hard. The house was almost empty. Our Romanian neighbors had been kind enough to let us use the furniture they had bought until we left. Everything was either gone or in our wagon. I didn't comprehend what my mom was telling me. Glancing up, I saw her looking where our furniture had been. It was then that I realized she was seeing, for one last time, everything as it had been. "This is the home of your birth," she said.

I saw the tears in her eyes. That was when I really knew we were going away and not coming back! This house, which I ran through a hundred times a day, was no longer ours. I had been so busy watching for soldiers, and figuring how to get out of carrying things to the wagon, that everything else had escaped me. Our village, the fields, everything would be gone. I felt tears come to my eyes. I didn't know why all of this was happening, but it was. Then my mom blew out the lamp and we walked through the front door and onto the porch. She had little Egon in her arms, all snuggled into a blanket. The morning cold seemed more penetrating and sent shivers racing across my arms and back. In the dim light, I could see my dad standing by the wagon. It was about the earliest I had ever been up.

"Did you lock the door?" he called to my mom, just as if we were going away for a few days.

She didn't answer. It was my dad's way of making her feel better. It was also a subtle comment on what was happening. As we reached the wagon, I saw a smile come across my dad's face; my mom smiled at him. This talking without saying words was something they would do a lot in the months to come.

After seeing the way my dad and mom were accepting things, I felt a lot better. From the porch, I could see and hear our neighbors walking toward the center of town, where the trucks and buses were waiting. The older women were dressed in long black dresses, wearing fringed headscarves. The younger women wore more colorful clothing; and they usually wore their hair in braids or rolled in a bun. In our village, for a woman to cut her hair was a serious matter, almost a sin. The boys and girls were dressed in their visiting clothes, not their Sunday best. Despite the importance of the occasion, we were still a practical people.

It was the time of our leaving.

# Land of Nowhere

The sun was just coming up that morning of October 8, 1940 when we left Friedenstal. My mom, little brother Egon and I were fortunate. We got to ride in one of the buses instead of the back of a truck.

"Be careful and come as quickly as you can," my mom said to my dad, reaching across me and through the open window to touch his hand.

My dad just smiled. I knew he would join us when he had finished everything he needed to do. Then, with those wrinkles around his eyes that I always saw when he was teasing, he said, "Be sure and get Bruno off the bus when you get there." That was all he had time to say. The big door of the bus slammed shut and we began to move. The last glimpse I had of him was when he turned away to go back home.

It was my first bus ride and I soon forgot my tears as I got to sit with the other boys. "Don't get in my way," Hugo Vossler yelled, above the noise of air rushing by our open window. He was pretending to be the driver, squirming about as we went sailing around curves and over bumps. I just glared at him. I couldn't see how he could be the driver, when I was. As the morning slipped by, we got tired of playing soldier and singing, so we watched the fields go by. I felt good sitting high and looking down on the wagons we passed. Whenever we passed through a village, which was often, a lot of the Romanian and Russian people stood along the streets, waving goodbye to us. Some were even crying. They felt bad about our leaving. They also knew their lives would be changed under Russian rule. When we got tired of looking and started scuffling and throwing things, our mothers made it plain we were not on a playground. Besides, it was time for lunch.

"Look at that!" Hugo said, hitting me to gain attention. It was late afternoon and we were entering the town of Galatz. I thought he was pointing to one of the big houses. "The river, dumbhead," he said, pointing. "That's where I'm going as soon as I can get away."

"You can find all sorts of things on the bank of a river," I told Hugo." Looking for hidden treasure along the river sounded good to me. We stretched our necks to catch glimpses of the shimmering water. Right then we made a solemn agreement to go to the river. When our bus finally stopped on the outskirts of Galatz, we were off in a flash. That is, until my mom called my name in such a way that it put an end to our plans. I noticed the other boys were also drifting back to their moms. In a few minutes we were gathered around a tall soldier in a black uniform. We boys stood by our moms, shuffling from one foot to the other as lengthy instructions were given.

"All families will stay together," the soldier ordered us in a commanding voice. "Meals will be served at eight, twelve and eighteen hundred hours, and no other times. You will sleep in assigned areas only, and be ready to leave when your men arrive." He looked at us as though we were soldiers. I liked that and stood up straight. "Come with me," he said sharply.

Doing an abrupt about-turn, the soldier marched off, leaving us to trail along behind. Soon he was far ahead, as though in a big hurry. When we reached him, he was standing in front of a long, one-story building. Beside it was a tent city, but instead of many small tents, these were more than 300 feet long. One of the buildings, as I was happy to discover, was our eating place. The soldier in charge of our group was giving orders to a short man wearing thick glasses. He talked. The man listened. We waited. After a long time, the soldier marched away and the shorter man came over to us. With the quick movements of a soldier, even though he wasn't in uniform, he took a black notebook from his inside pocket. "Witt, Walter, Wagner, Ross, Reule," he read names from his notebook in a loud voice. "Follow me."

No one said anything as we separated from the others and followed him. No one, that is, except Hugo. "Remember the river," he whispered, as I walked by.

"This is your sleeping area," the short man explained, as we walked to the far end of the big building filled with bunks. He was laughing to himself as though there was something funny. "I always start from the bottom of my list," he explained to us, peering over his thick lenses, looking even funnier than his little joke. "It always takes everyone by surprise." He laughed again and seemed to be friendly. "Supper will be one hour late," he said, still laughing. "Just for today." He opened his notebook to find a second group of names. "You will eat in the dining hall beside this building," he instructed us, and was gone.

The next morning, as soon as I could get away from the big hall where we had breakfast, I ran outside to find Hugo. He was waiting. There was a big scowl on his face. "Good thing you came," he said angrily. "I wasn't going to wait much longer."

"You weren't waiting that long," I told him, seeing the remains of some milk on his upper lip.

"Well," he said, as if he knew so much, "you want to see the Blue Danube don't you?" He spoke the name of the river as though we were in church.

Even though Hugo was a little bigger and a year older, I didn't think he knew as much as he pretended. "How do you know it's blue?" I asked, ready to argue.

"Everybody knows about the Blue Danube, dumbhead," he said, as if I was the only person in the world who didn't know.

"Not me," I said, glaring at him eye-to-eye. "I think it's muddy. It was muddy yesterday and it will be muddy today. It's the muddy Danube."

"Since when do you count as everybody or anybody?" he shouted at me with a disgusted look on his face. He started to walk away, but stopped. "If you want to fight about it, I won't go to the river."

"My mom won't let me go, either," I told him. "Blue, muddy, who cares? Let's go play."

My mom had not expected my dad to arrive until he finished his business in Friedenstal. I looked for him every hour. "He will get here when he gets here," she told me a hundred times, and each time with greater frustration. "Then your dad may change his mind and not come at all," she would say with a smile. "Now go and play."

Every day I met Hugo and we played and argued our way through our time of waiting. Our moms knew each other and all the other people so there wasn't much that we could get away with. Loyalty and communication among us was strong, something that would serve us well in the difficult times to come. Still, the time seemed long to me. Several times each day, I walked past the big houses at the edge of town and looked down the road, expecting to see my dad any minute. The long caravan with thousands of wagons streamed by in endless procession, but his wasn't among them. What I did see was Galatz, a big city with sidewalks overflowing with people. In our town of Friedenstal, with a little more than two thousand people, there were no sidewalks and the streets were seldom crowded, except in the evening when the cows came in from grazing. Everyone was busy working at home or in the fields. It seemed no one in Galatz worked. They were all in town.

I was too young to understand why I watched so intently for my dad. As long as he was not with us, I felt our sense of displacement. We were not complete. When he came, everything would be like it had always been. Finally, after I had looked for him a hundred times, he appeared when I wasn't looking. He just came driving up, as though he was right on time, instead of two days late. It was long after supper by the time my mom had inspected her prized dishes and furniture. She trusted my dad, but she also knew his ways. That was why she carefully checked to make sure everything was there. My dad hadn't traveled all the way alone. Uncle Emil Funk, my mom's half brother, had ridden part of the way with him. The six long days of waiting were finally over.

"Sleep fast, Bruno," my dad told me as we stretched out on our bunks. "The morning will come before you do." He smiled and gave me that pinch on the shoulder. It was sure good to have him with us again.

The sound of rain on the canvas roof and the growling pangs of hunger in my stomach awakened me the next morning. Still, I wasn't ready to get up. Never opening my eyes, I snuggled into the warm blankets, feeling safe and complete and pretended I was the driver of a big bus. It was loaded with children and I was taking them for a long drive in the country. They kept asking me a lot of questions about driving, but I could answer all their questions. In spite of the warm blankets and my happy dream, I kept thinking how nice it would be to have something to eat. Then I realized how quiet it was. Sitting up, I discovered nearly everyone, including my mom and dad, was gone. Jumping into my clothes, I hurried to the dining hall and slipped in by my dad, who was busy talking with the other men at the long table.

"Look at it this way," one of the men was saying. "Soon the German army will control all of Europe. What better place for us to be than in our own homeland?" He looked intently at my dad, trying to make him understand. "At least we don't have to worry about our people killing us in the middle of the night."

"That's right, Gotthilf," another man insisted. "The more countries the Germans conquer, the more difficult it will be for us to live in any land except our own." The men nodded in agreement. "Look how it was in Romania. A lot of those people resented the size of our farms, and having to work for us. If they felt that way in times of peace, it would be much worse in the time of war." Several men talked about the Russians and what it was like to live under communist rule in Romania for two months before the final agreement. No one said anything good about communism. In those two months, almost all the merchandise had vanished from the store. It was a plain indication of what it would mean to live under Russian domination. After awhile my mom brought me breakfast and I dreamily ate, looking about for Hugo, forgetting all the discussion going on around me.

"Are you sure we are being sent to Germany?"

My ears pricked up when I heard my dad's voice. His one question put a stop to all conversation and eating at the table. One man sat with his fork halfway to his mouth, looking in astonishment. Even I stopped eating and looked at him. What he said didn't make sense to me, but he was serious. I couldn't think what he meant. Of course we were going to Germany. That was what we had been told. Yet, I knew my dad. He talked a lot, but never just to be talking. If we weren't going to Germany, where were we going?

"Don't frighten us, Gotthilf," a man with a deep voice said angrily. "Of course we are going to Germany. That is what the German government has told us. They haven't lied before. Why should they now?"

The man sounded positive that my dad was wrong, but the silence after he had spoken left doubts. Inside myself, I got to thinking. It was the long ride from Friedenstal to Galatz that had done it. My dad, when he didn't have anyone to talk to, always got to thinking. He had ridden along, mulling over everything that had happened and spent his time putting together what could happen. Then, as he always did, he put it all together his way. For the first time, I hoped my dad was wrong. "If they take our horses and wagons," he said, his voice sounding even and hard, "you can be sure we are not going to any farmlands in Germany."

Again there was silence, as though the men were really concerned and thinking about what my dad had said. "Well," they haven't taken our horses and wagons," another man said. Then, more timidly, the same voice asked, "Where would they send us if not to Germany?"

The men all looked at my dad. He had started the whole thing so they waited for him to answer. "How would I know?" He shrugged his shoulders. "Governments seem to have a fondness for holding pens," he said referring to the resettlement camps. "Maybe that's where we will end up."

The men looked troubled. "Why would they do that?" the heavy voice asked. "We are farmers—good farmers. They need us to raise crops for the war effort." He sounded mad at my dad for saying such things.

My dad laughed, but it wasn't a nice laugh. "There are farmers in Germany just as good as we are." He looked at the men, his face grim. "We are farmers without land, without animals, without equipment and we don't have seed for planting." His voice was low and harsh. "What kind of farmers does that make us?" He was good at answering a question with a question. When he did that with me, I got all frustrated. I could see it was affecting the men the same way. Maybe my dad's way was right. The value of an answer is to make room for the next question.

"But they told us…" another man started to say, only to be interrupted by the heavy voice.

"If we are not farmers, then tell us what we are," the heavy voice demanded.

My dad looked around, taking his time. If we had been outside, I could picture him taking a whittled toothpick out of his mouth and spitting before he answered. When he felt someone rushing him, he just went twice as slow. "Have you seen the thousands of wagons on the roads?" he asked, knowing they had. "Hundreds of villages, not just our own, are being resettled all over Europe." His tone showed the distrust he held for the outcome of such wide shuffling of people. "That alone should tell you the kind of farmers we have become. We are not farmers at all. We have become a part of Hitler's army. We are being used as soldiers in this damn war and will be sent wherever needed." His voice was bitter. "As far as I know, we are not needed in Germany."

The next day, after all the wagons had been unloaded and the things reloaded onto a boat, the army took our horses and wagon. "They are needed for the war," a lieutenant told my dad, giving him a signed receipt.

"Where are we being sent?" he asked, looking at the small piece of paper, as though he didn't think much of the trade.

"Talk to the captain," the officer replied, without looking up from the table where he was writing. "I'm in charge of horses and wagons." Of course the captain was no place to be found.

"First my cows, now my horses," my dad said to my mom, as we walked along the outskirts of Galatz. "When they take the clothes off our backs, then we can take a bath and start out clean." He looked at my mom with a half grin on his face. She didn't say anything, but thoughts of losing her dishes made her look sad. It was like we were losing our farm all over again. The piece of paper in my dad's pocket, and the promise that everything would be returned to us, was worth nothing, compared to our horses and the many rides I had taken on them. Then, when I was feeling the worst, my dad gave a little chuckle. He put his arm around my shoulders and gave me that old pinch which hurt so much but felt good. "We'll make it," he said, and there was a smile on his face. "Maybe we haven't got everything we had, but hard work can accomplish a lot." He took my little brother out of my mom's arms and we began walking back toward the large building where we slept. "As long as we are together, everything will be fine."

But the next day, we were separated.

"All men ashore. All men ashore." A loud voice sounded across the big boat. The muddy Danube was flowing all around us, as a large number of the families from Friedenstal were crowded aboard. I was going to see a lot more of the blue river than I had anticipated. A few of our belongings were clustered about our feet. Most of our household things were on another boat waiting to sail. Again the voice called for all men to go ashore. "Last call," came the warning.

"I'll be on the next boat," my dad said, giving my mom a kiss and me a hug. "I don't know why they want us on separate boats, but some paper general is giving the orders." He looked like he was about to add something that wasn't nice.

"Now Gotthilf," my mom said, fearful that he would say something against the authorities and get into trouble. "We'll be all right."

"That's the way they are," he went right on, as if he hadn't heard her. "Efficiency first. People second, if at all. We stay behind and put our furniture on the boats while our wives and children sail off without us." He laughed. It wasn't a nice laugh—more like he was swearing without words. "Backwards," he said. "They do everything backwards." He looked at my mom with a lopsided grin. "The world is run by backward people." Again he laughed, his mustache curving around his lip in a real smile. "Want me to tell you where those backward people keep their heads?" he asked hopefully.

My mom kissed him again. "No," she said firmly. "We both know." She hurried him along, since most of the men had already left the boat. "We'll be waiting for you," she said, walking toward the gangplank, holding his arm. "And don't…" She didn't say any more, but just looked at him with tears in her eyes.

"All right, Olga," he said, as though he meant it. "I'll be careful," he smiled, "in all ways." Then he was gone, and in a few minutes the shore where he was standing was moving away from us. It took awhile before I realized that it wasn't my dad who was going away from us. We were going away from him. The muddy Danube would carry the boat and its passengers toward the destination of Zemun (Semlin) in the Croatian part of Yugoslavia, outside Belgrade (Beograd).

At first it was great being on the big boat. Hugo and I became very secretive and busy, looking everywhere for hideouts. It was exciting to know that there were places where no one could find us. What really made me happy though, beside our hideouts, was the fact that I could spit farther than Hugo. When no one was looking, we had crept out of our favorite hideout behind a lifeboat, and were standing at the back rail spitting into the river. The long drop to the churning water below was fun to watch. Then Hugo got the idea of getting some water in a cup and seeing who could spit it the farthest.

"You were standing closer to the rail," he yelled at me, his face all twisted, as I spit the last of the water and beat him again. He was taller and maybe a little stronger, but I could spit farther and that made me happy. "I don't want to play anymore," Hugo said. "I don't feel so good. Let's go back to our hideout."

I was going to say something about being a poor loser, but he looked sick, even to me. Making sure no one was following us, especially girls, we made our way between two of the lifeboats and spent the rest of the afternoon talking about being soldiers. Most of the time Hugo just lay there, rubbing his head and looking hot. After promising that we would keep our hideout a secret, we went looking for our moms, hoping that it was time to get something to eat.

The next morning, after standing in line with my mom and little Egon for breakfast, I ran topside, looking for Hugo. There were a lot of boys to play with—half our village was on the boat—but it didn't seem like I was playing unless Hugo was there to battle with. When no one was looking, I darted between the lifeboats and stretched out on the deck. For some reason, it felt good to lie down and feel the cool breeze across my face. I had liked the feel of the boat, but I didn't like it now. I felt funny in the head and kept seeing spots in front of my eyes. I expected Hugo to come running up and yell at me any minute. I waited, but he didn't come. Finally, after what seemed to be a long time, I got mad, so feeling dizzy or not, I went looking for him.

"Hugo is sick," Mrs. Vossler told me when I went below. She looked awfully serious like she had a headache or something. It's hard to tell whether adults are worried or sick because they look the same. Maybe it's the same thing. "He won't be able to play for a long time," she said, hurrying toward the back of the boat.

About that time, my mom came looking for me. That is always the way when I venture out of a hiding place and she finds me. Out of sight, she forgets all the things she wants me to do. As soon as she sees me, everything comes to her mind and I am caught. "Bruno," she called sharply. There was no place to hide. "Come here." Whenever my mom spoke to me like that, I knew I had either done something pretty bad or there was an important errand I had to run. Since there wasn't a need for running errands on the boat, I waited for the trouble. "Let me look at you," she said, paying no attention to the people standing about. Her hands felt cool on my face. I couldn't remember being so hot, and all of those funny little spots that I couldn't blink away kept dancing in front of my eyes. Then, right in front of everyone, she opened my shirt. "Just what I thought," she said. "You've got the measles, too." From the tone of her voice, I got the feeling that was the end of everything—no more roaming the top deck and finding the good hiding places and no more playing with Hugo. "You come with me," she said. Grabbing me by the hand, she marched me to a cabin with a big red sign on the door. Then, before I knew what to expect, she had knocked on the door and I was inside, while she was outside looking through the window at me.

"We will fix a bed for you over there," one of the officers of the boat said, taking me by the arm to make sure I went with him. That was when I saw Hugo. He was almost hidden in a pile of blankets. A woman was sitting beside him with a small bucket of water. She was bathing his face and talking to him. He didn't look very good, but I didn't get to say anything to him because the officer was in such a hurry to put me to bed. That didn't stop me from looking around. There were kids in piles of blankets, scattered all over the place. What made me feel funny was that some of them were girls.

"Girls," I said. Even sick, I couldn't stand them.

"Don't you mind that, young man," he said, while the woman who had been bathing Hugo's face quickly made a pallet of blankets for me. "They get sick, too. Now off with your clothes and into bed with you."

Trying to hide behind him and stripping to my underwear faster than I had ever done, I dove between the blankets.

"This is the quarantined area," the woman told me, rubbing my forehead with her cold hands. "You will have to stay here until we land."

Within minutes the bed was feeling so good and I was so tired that I didn't care how long I stayed there. I had even forgotten there were girls around me. There was this big pressure that was trying to come out through my eyes. But what made me feel so terrible was that nothing would stay in one place. Everything went swirling in big, slow-turning circles. No matter whether my eyes were open or shut, I felt as though I was going to fall off the blankets.

The next two days I stayed in the blankets. Whenever I opened my eyes, there was the woman bathing my face or wanting me to eat soup and there was my mom looking through the window at me. I'd rather take a licking than swallow one bite of that soup, but the cold water felt good on my face. "You will have to go to the hospital when the boat docks in Zemun," the nurse told me. "You are very sick." I felt hot tears come burning into my eyes. I wasn't going to any hospital without my mom, at least not without Hugo. "As soon as you are well," she said, washing my face for the hundredth time, "they will send you on to Liboch, where your dad and mom will be waiting for you."

That wasn't what I wanted. The trouble was that I didn't have the strength to do anything about it. The more I cried, the worse I felt. I held my arms flat against the deck so I wouldn't fall off the blankets. "Is Hugo going to the hospital with me?" I asked. The woman was suddenly a long way off—something like my dad when the boat had sailed away and we left him at Galatz. She just went farther and farther away and didn't answer. That was all I remembered. The next minute I opened my eyes and there I was in a white room.

"You have opened your eyes," said a heavy-set woman in a stiff, white uniform, fussing about my bed. She spoke in German, but it sounded strange to me. It was not like our people spoke. She looked at me with a serious face. "That is good."

"Where is my mom?" I asked, feeling afraid and starting to cry. I turned my head and quickly looked around the room. I didn't see anything that made me feel better.

"You will be all right now," the nurse said, and hurried away. For the first time I became aware of other kids in the room. In just a minute the nurse was back, followed by a tall man wearing a long, white coat.

"Awake are you?" the man said in a gruff voice, his teeth showing extra-white through his black beard. All I could do was cry. I had thought the nurse had gone after my mom. "I won't have any tears," he said sternly, pulling back the blankets and unbuttoning my nightgown. He examined my chest, then thumped it several times, listening through something stuck in his ears. I stopped crying, but only because I was more scared of him than the pain in my chest where he had hit me. The nurse put a thermometer in my mouth while the doctor rolled me over and examined my back. "You are a lucky young boy," he said. He took the thermometer and studied it intently. "Uh huh," he said profoundly. "Just as your fever has come, so it has gone." He motioned for the nurse to fix my gown. "Keep him quiet and in bed," he told her, although I had the feeling he was talking more to me than to her. "In a few days, if his temperature stays normal, he can be released." Then, with a swish of his long coat, he was gone.

The nurse, moving me around as I would a toy, tucked the blankets up to my chin.

"Where am I?" I asked.

She was a large woman, and her smile was just as big as she was. After she smiled, I liked her. She had blonde hair and was not any taller than my mom, but a whole lot wider and had a round, red face. She looked happy and that made me feel good. "You are in the hospital in Zemun, Yugoslavia," she said in her funny way of speaking German. "You have had a very high temperature and have been…" she paused searching for the right word, "sleeping. You've been sleeping for a long time."

Time didn't mean anything to me. Later I learned that I had been in a coma for several days. All I could think of was my mom. "Where's my mom?" I asked again.

She smiled and I found myself starting to smile in return. "Your mother went on to Liboch in Sudetenland," she told me cheerfully. "In just a few days," she wagged her finger at me, "if you are good and don't give me any trouble, you will be put on the train and join your family."

That was the best news I could hear. I knew my mom would be waiting for me. Several days after coming out of the "sleep," as the Yugoslavian nurse described it, a large group of us were placed on the train and sent to Liboch. It bothered me that my best friend was not with us. I hadn't seen him in the hospital and now he wasn't on the train. Either he wasn't as sick as I had been or he got well faster than I did. Then, like my dad, I got to thinking about all that had happened. Try as I might, I could only remember the first day on the boat. What else happened there really puzzled me! How could I possibly "sleep" when there was a chance to do all the things I really wanted to do? Miles of mountain scenery slipped by as I thought and thought. The closest I could come to understanding was to remember the times I had gotten into trouble with my mom and dad because I stayed at a friend's house longer than I was supposed to, or forgot some chore. That, I thought as the train clicked along, is the land of nowhere. Only this time, the very things I had wanted to do had gotten swallowed up in that place.

When the train from Zemun pulled into the busy station at Liboch, there were my mom, little Egon and my dad waiting for me. The sight of them and the feel of their arms around me were the best medicine I ever had. I didn't know where I had been, but it was the greatest thing in this world to know I was back.

# Camp Liboch

"Bruno," my mom shouted, as soon as I got off the train. How she ever saw me in the midst of all those running and screaming children was beyond me. But, that was my mom. She came running and locked her arms around me. "You are really home!"

She was as glad to see me as I was to see her. Then it was my dad's turn. He had a big grin on his face and his thin mustache curved around his upper lip just as I remembered. Forgotten was the hospital and being sick. All of that was like a bad dream. I was awake now. This was my family and we were together again. In one quick motion, my dad swung me high into the air, followed by a good, hard hug. I was happy all over and showed it.

"I'll sure be glad to see Hugo," I chattered to my dad and mom, as we walked toward the camp. I suddenly realized how long we had been apart. I started to tell them how I could spit farther than my best friend, but thought twice before telling my mom. My dad would understand and think I had done a good thing, but my mom had funny ideas about spitting. She didn't believe it was one of the most natural things in the world. But what I was feeling didn't have anything to do with spitting. Every time I mentioned Hugo's name, I noticed a strange look pass between them. I knew that of all my playmates, he wasn't my mom's favorite, but most of our troubles had been my making as much as his.

She squeezed my hand. "We're just glad that you are well and home with us," she said with a sad look on her face. Where all the happiness of meeting me at the train had gone, I didn't know. She pulled me close as we walked. "We didn't know anything about you until they told us the children from the hospital at Zemun would arrive in Liboch today." Tears came to her eyes. "Bruno,

45

you've been gone for weeks and we didn't know what had happened to you."

Getting off that train and seeing my family was one of the happiest days in my life. It put me back together again. Once I was with them and got all the empty places in me filled, I was ready to do other things. First, I wanted to see Hugo. It wouldn't be any fun exploring the camp unless he and I could do it together. "Can I go play with Hugo when we get to camp?" I asked, hoping that my mom wouldn't find a hundred reasons to say "no."

"You've been sick," she began, looking down at me, as if I didn't know. "You will have to rest." I walked along, my head getting lower and lower. She could add reasons quicker than I could ever hope to answer them. Still, things were not right. I had learned not only to hear what my mom said, but how she said it. Sometimes I could go ahead and do what I wanted, in spite of her objections, if the tone of her voice said it was O.K. This time there was something in her voice that I had never heard before. Despite that warning, I persisted like an old horsefly in summer. "Maybe Hugo can come over while I rest?" I was doing my best to turn her big no into a little yes.

"No." My mom stopped and looked down at me. I was puzzled. A lot of feelings began to build inside, but one thing I didn't do was to talk back, especially to my dad. I might hide out, forget or even skip some of my chores, but I never talked back. What my parents said was law even when it was no. I looked at her face and I suddenly realized something bad had happened to Hugo. "Your little friend died on the boat," she told me.

I looked at my mom and couldn't think anymore. All my feelings about Hugo and how I wanted to play with him grew like a mountain inside of me. I felt about to burst. Then came the tears. It was my sudden introduction to the fragileness of life and the permanence of death. Fifty-four children died on the boats or in the hospital during our trip to Sudetenland.

On the far edge of Liboch was a large, old school house that was no longer used. It had been converted into a dormitory for many mothers and children from the big boat. All of the desks had been removed from the classrooms and the walls were lined with raised wooden platforms about six feet wide so that people could sleep side by side. Another platform was also built down the center of each room, leaving a small aisle between the beds. There were about 35 or 40 people in each room with up to six families, depending on how many children they had. The older children slept in separate parts of the building. Since our possessions, taken from the wagons and put on the boat, had not reached us, storage was not a problem. Whoever planned the camps with families separated, the women and children tucked away at Liboch and the men settled into a camp several miles away, had never come across a man like my dad. Most Germans are good at taking orders, but not him. I remembered his words while we were still on the boat in Galatz: "I don't know why they want us separated, but some would-be general is bucking for promotion and using us as a stepping stone. You watch," he had said angrily. "Putting us on separate boats isn't the end of the matter." That was my dad's way. He could often spot trouble before it happened. The sad part was that even with such ability, he couldn't always stop it from taking place.

It was no surprise to me that my dad put an end to separated camps. After he had been in the men's camp for a couple of weeks, he stopped complaining. By his own authority he packed his belongings, told the other men they were fools to stay away from their families and caught the first train to Liboch. "Take care of my things," he told my mom upon arriving at the old school house. "I'm not going back." For him, it had been that simple. As for my mom, I am sure she was expecting him. She tried constantly to protect and change him; she worried about his stubborn ways and especially his open criticism of the government; but what my mom always tried to change in my dad is what made him great to me. That strength brought him home to us and allowed us to be together a little longer.

My mom was happy and quick to do as he told her. It wasn't hard. Placing his battered suitcase under our section of the long wall

47

bed, she considered him at home. During the following weeks, other men came to be with their families. Some of the women, perhaps a little more bold than their husbands, joined them. The various camps still existed, but because my dad had changed them, families were no longer separated.

Sudetenland was located on the slopes of the Sudety Mountains and it had been the border of Bohemia and Moravia in Czechoslovakia until the Munich Agreement of 1938 gave the region to Germany. In once sense, perhaps Hitler had told us the truth and this was now Germany. But a rocky camp in the cold mountains is a long way from the rich farmlands of Germany. As my dad had so accurately stated upon leaving Galatz: "We are no longer just farmers, but a unit in Hitler's army to be used in the conquest of Europe."

Snow and freezing winds came early to the rugged mountains surrounding the camp. As the snow grew deeper and heavy frost coated the windows, I spent more and more time in our little bed space or roaming the halls. During the Christmas season there was no school and that was no loss to me. One good thing: I liked having so many children to play with. Early in 1941 school started and that ended a lot of our playtime.

"I can't sit around here any longer," my dad said, in complete frustration, pacing rapidly about our little space in short steps. My mom was sitting on the bed sewing and I was halfway under the bed, having made that small space into one of my hideouts. She didn't say anything. There wasn't anything she could say. My dad wasn't expecting an answer. "It's not right for them to take away our living and give us nothing to do." She nodded her head in complete agreement. After lunch, without a word to anyone except my mom, he struck off across the surrounding hills, looking for work.

On those long, gray days when it seems to be evening all the time, I enjoyed the peace of my hideout. I had discovered, as children do, the power of imagination. The greatest playfield is not toys and places, but the mind. Tucked safely under the bed with my mom sewing above me, I could go anyplace and do anything. In my mind,

I was still dressed in a shiny uniform and marching in a faraway land when my dad came in, all excited.

"I've got a job," he told us with new pride in his voice. "It's just shoveling hay after it has made a little trip through the cow, but it gets me out of this place and back on the farm." His mustache curved into a smile. "I would rather shovel the real stuff than what those government officials…"

"You hush," my mom said, handing my little brother to him. She was all too aware of how my dad compared the workings of our government to life in the barnyard. He just laughed and took Egon into his arms. There was happiness in his laugh and that made all of us feel good.

From that time, my dad went to work each day. Once again he became his old self. That included talking about farming and his favorite subject—cows. A woman, whose husband was serving in the German army, operated the farm where he worked. My dad helped her until the ever-deepening snow and long distance made it impossible to reach the farm. Despite his love for farming, he finally had to quit. The next day he went into Liboch to look for a town job. Strong and eager for work, he was soon repairing tracks for the railroad. "At least I'm working," I heard him tell my mom one evening. He jiggled some coins in his pocket. "And we are saving some money." A grim smile came to his face as he looked around the crowded room. "God alone knows how long we will be in this place."

My mom could always find something that needed to be done and be happy doing it. With my dad working, she went about her duties, even singing some of the time. One of her jobs was to help with the cooking. Some of the older people had complained about the food. It was not like they were used to eating. As a result, several women of the camp obtained permission to help prepare the food. There was no complaint when my mom started helping in the kitchen. Gradually, our new way of life developed into a somewhat normal routine. My mom did cooking, sewing and washing. My dad went off to work each morning. I played with my friends during the day and watched and waited for my dad to come home each evening.

The biggest time in our day came after the evening meal. Following supper in the big hall, the men often sat around the tables talking while the women washed the dishes. All of us kids usually ran to play, but sometimes I stayed by my dad and listened. There was a big radio at one end of the hall. It crackled and popped, but by listening carefully, we could hear special speeches by Goebbels, the minister for enlightenment, and Hitler, the leader and chancellor of Germany. We also listened to the news. Most of the time, the men just talked. Their favorite subjects were problems in the camp, being resettled in Germany or the latest victories of the war. No one, except possibly my dad, realized how isolated we were from everything that was happening. Our only sources of information were German broadcasts and government controlled newspapers purchased in Liboch. From out of nowhere, someone always claimed to have the latest "official announcement" about our being relocated and all the other men sat nodding as though saying, "Yes sir. We will soon be leaving." No one, I was quick to notice, hurried to pack what few belongings they had. At least there wasn't much to pack. Despite the time we had spent in camp, all our possessions that had been so painfully selected and carefully placed in the wagon had yet to be delivered. All we could find out was that some boat on the Danube was running up and down that river looking for a place to dock. At least that was what my dad told me.

As the weeks of winter passed, the snow grew deeper and the hallways were cold and drafty. The hours of daylight became shorter. The war had affected our lives so drastically, yet seemed to be little more than headlines in the newspapers or a garbled voice over the radio. Then, the harsh reality of the war hit our camp.

During one of the evening prayer meetings that my mom urged me to attend, Mr. Wagner stood, indicating there was something important he had to say. "I want to tell you," he said in that low, hesitant way he had of talking, "that our Konrad received his draft notice this morning." There was sympathetic silence as Mr. Wagner looked at his small wife. We had great confidence in the German government. The fact that we had not been forgotten here in this camp reaffirmed that belief. They knew who we were, where we were; and, as I was to learn, how loyal we were. They were very efficient. "He is to leave next week." Mr. Wagner's voice choked and I saw tears on the cheeks of Konrad's mother, but there was also the look of pride on their wrinkled faces. That was all Mr. Wagner had to say. Konrad, tall and stooped like his dad, wasn't much of a talker, either, but had a slight smile on his face. Everyone, upon hearing the news, went to shake his hand. I did, too. I was pretty excited, imagining him in a fancy uniform, marching off to distant lands with a lot of other soldiers. It was a grand thing to be a soldier, I thought at the time.

A few evenings later two young men, who were impatient to wait for their draft notices and had volunteered, came to see my dad. "We want to be a part of the war before it is all over," they told him.

"You think the fighting will soon be over," he said in response to their enthusiasm, with a grim smile. "And all the glory of being a soldier and helping the Fatherland will pass you by."

The two men quickly agreed. They didn't know my dad. They didn't see in his face what I saw. And yet, according to the newspapers and radio broadcasts, they were right. There was every indication that the conquest of Europe was almost complete. We received the news that England had been brought to her knees by the Luftwaffe, commanded by Reichsmarschall Herman Goering. According to broadcasts the previous summer, Joseph Goebbels had proudly stated, the Adlerangriff (Attack of the Eagles), also known as the Battle of Britain with 2500 military aircraft, had destroyed the Royal Air Force. Immediate invasion of the English mainland, under the code name Seeloewe (Sea Lion), was supposedly underway.

The news actually sounded more victorious than that. With Britain soon to be occupied by German troops, Russia had been invaded. Operation Barbarossa was launched June 22, 1941. Using the blitzkrieg method of lightning air strikes coordinated with fast moving ground forces, the German army was rolling across large areas of that huge country. Inspired by reports of such quick victories, it was a common belief that the war would soon be over.

Despite my dad's attitude toward government controls, and particularly against war, he recalled what he had learned of army life and advised the young men as their parents had requested. "Sleep light," he told them. "You can do it even if you are exhausted. Train yourself to be alert at the slightest different sound. Never give in, no matter what happens. Things will change if you just hang on." It was obvious the young men were listening to every word. "There is no safe place," he paused to give special emphasis to his next few words, "and there is no one who is responsible for your life except you. It is nice to die for your Fatherland, but it is much nicer to live for it. Your safety and your chances of staying alive depend on how determined you are to come home." His voice suddenly became low, speaking for their ears alone. "Believe only what you see, almost nothing of what you hear and never believe a high official, no matter what he says." My dad's advice was a description of his own life, but such harsh words were dangerous. Overheard by a zealous informer, what he told them could be considered traitorous. "Obey your superiors." The look on his face said his words double. "That is absolutely essential to your survival. Death by the enemy may be avoided, but escape from the firing squad is not likely." He smiled and his words became more cheery. "You've got a lot of years ahead and the war won't last forever. Take care of yourselves and come home safely." He seemed to stop, then added something that I could tell he felt was important. "Volunteer when commanded, don't be first and don't be last. And always," he shook their hands, "keep a little thought about what you are going to do when you get home."

The next morning I watched as Konrad Wagner and the two young men kissed their parents goodbye and walked through the big gates toward the train station. That was what brought the war close to us—not Mr. Goebbels presenting accounts of great victories over the radio, but missing faces that had become a part of that distant army. Strange how we take things for granted until we no longer have them. Then as a reminder that life goes on, even while being stretched to the breaking point, a wedding took place at the camp. Along with news of great victories and several more young men being conscripted, my dad's cousin Gotthilf Stadel, and Lydia Entzminger were married. One afternoon, a few weeks later, as summer was about to spread across the mountains, Mr. Wagner brought the biggest news of all to my dad when he got home from work.

It's true this time," he said, excited and out of breath. "Sure enough. The Committee is being sent to Poland tomorrow to help select the land."

My dad didn't answer. Slowly he took off his jacket and laid it on the bed. We all watched closely to hear what he might say. He didn't say anything. Instead, he looked around the room like he was seeing things differently than he ever thought they could be. An almost invisible smile came to his lips and faded. The hard look on his face told me he knew something bad was going to happen. What he said made no sense to me. "So Hitler has sent us our draft notices at last."

There was much discussion after supper that night. The men were all excited, talking about how good it would be to leave camp and work the land again. A little later, an official wearing a brown uniform came into the dining hall. "You will soon be leaving our camp," he said. This made our "news" official. He was a big man who looked as though he wanted to be friendly, but didn't have any friends. "The Fatherland needs good farmers just as much as brave soldiers." He looked around at everyone with a broad smile. "Perhaps you are even more important, since who can go very far on an empty stomach?" He threw back his head and laughed, showing gold teeth, as though he had told a funny story. Everyone laughed with him. We were happy to know the long wait was over. The official held up his hand for silence. "There has been one change," he said, with a more serious look on his face. "Instead of going to Alsace-Lorraine as originally intended, it has been decided that you should be farmers in the conquered land of Poland."

There was silence when he confirmed that Poland was our destination. Strange how Mr. Wagner and many others in our camp knew where the committee was being sent even before it was officially announced. Secrets are hard for adults to keep. Hugo and I could keep a secret no matter how hard it seemed. Something else was not a secret—our disappointment of going to Poland rather than what we considered to be German land.

"It will be better this way," the official said, shaking hands with all the men and wishing them well. "Just a little time to get settled in your new homes and you will be happy again." He shook hands with my dad. "You can trust our government to do what is more than right for every one of you." Little did the big man realize, that of all the men in camp, he was talking to the one who least trusted the government, any government. "All your possessions from the boat will be delivered to you in Poland," he said to cheer us. "Everything will be just like it was," he smiled, "and better."

"Welcome to Hitler's army," my dad said to the men who had clustered around him after the official left. "We have just become front line soldiers instead of farmers."

# Stefanov

My dad pointed with a nod of his head. The four of us, along with other people from the camp, were in the process of boarding a long train in the Liboch station. He indicated the side of the car where our destination was printed. We had known for some time where we were going, but it still came as a blow that it was Poland. "Waldhorst," my dad said in that flat even voice he used when he didn't like what was taking place, but couldn't prevent it. I knew that Waldhorst was far away. I also knew that our lives would be different once we reached Poland. My mom gave my dad one of those helpless looks, showing she was near tears. That is something else I remember about my dad. He grumbled and fussed around, and it seemed my mom was always listening to what he had to say. But, when she was unhappy, he did everything possible to make her feel better. "It will be all right," my dad said with a smile. "We won't be in Waldhorst forever and any farm is better than a camp." He reached over and gave me that pinch to include me in what he was about to say. "Bruno and I will make a good farm out of whatever land they give us." I felt awfully important to know my dad was counting on my help.

Perhaps it was because we were together, we were happy and we weren't there to stay, but I remember Waldhorst with good memories. Waldhorst was a summer resort camp near Litzmannstadt, the German-occupied name for Lodz. We stayed in one of several little cabins. Ours had two bedrooms and a small kitchen. Since we had been given ration stamps and some German money, we went shopping for groceries. After that, my mom prepared meals the way we liked them. That made us even happier. It seemed that my dad went to the Resettlement Office every day to help work out the details of our transfer to a farm in Poland. He also found time to visit some of our friends already settled not too far away.

Two great things happened to us in Waldhorst: my little brother Egon started running and most of our possessions finally caught up with us. Both were a surprise. We had begun to doubt that we would ever see our things again. We had expected Egon to start walking, but instead, he skipped the walking stage and took off at a run every time he wanted to go someplace. It was fun watching him tottering along, about to fall with every step. It was even more fun watching Uncle Herbert Funk, my mom's half brother, teach him how to walk. Finally, with everything settled, we left to inspect our new farm.

"Are you Mr. Reule?" A short, stocky man dressed in the brown uniform of the Socialist Workers Party came up briskly to my dad as we got off the train in Kutno.

My dad gave the official a long, thoughtful look. I was well aware my dad didn't like uniforms. Sometimes I felt he didn't like the people in them any better. "I am," he answered, "and this is my family."

I watched as he took measure of the government representative. That is one advantage of being small. Everyone just looks over the top of you as if you aren't there. By looking up I could see a lot. Thoughts have a way of starting from the eyes, running down the face across the mouth, into the chin and finally spreading across the neck. The thoughts my dad was having were not the most pleasant.

"I'm Mr. Mantei," the stranger said in what could pass for a friendly greeting. He shook hands with my dad and mom, ignoring me. He didn't know how much my dad was counting on my help. Mr. Mantei took one of our suitcases, as if everything was more than perfect. "Just come with me," he called over his shoulder. "I'll help you pick up the rest of your belongings and have you folks in Stefanov in no time."

Exactly why Mr. Mantei had singled out my dad for personal attention wasn't hard to figure. Even I understood that. Although he had no love for uniforms, he walked like a soldier. When he spoke in that certain way, people listened. Mr. Mantei probably thought my dad was one of the leaders. What he didn't know was that my dad didn't lead anyone. If they wanted to tag along, he didn't stop them. Alone or with a crowd, he went the way he had chosen. Outside the station a long line of wagons waited to carry the families and their possessions to the various farms.

As invited, we rode with Mr. Mantei. "You will like the farm I have arranged for you," he said with heavy emphasis on what he had done for us. A few more statements like that and I figured my dad would get off and walk. Completely oblivious to the feelings my dad radiated, Mr. Mantei went on bragging about what he had done. "It's the best farmland in the whole district." He made a sweeping motion with his arm as if to include all of Poland. "I took four choice farms and made them into one large farm for you folks. It took a lot of hard work, but it's all ready now. Yes sir," he said in that "you-should-be-deeply-appreciative" voice, as though he had done everything on his own and not merely followed orders. "I've gone to great effort to make this the best farm you will ever have." All the time he was talking, he was nodding his head as though to emphasize what he had already said. On top of that, he gave my dad and mom a look that said again what he had said with words and the bobbing of his head.

One thing Mr. Mantei didn't do was to include me. He almost made me believe I wasn't there the way he looked and talked over the top of my head. As I was to understand later, Mr. Mantei was caught in the war just like we were. He wasn't anxious to be a Party member, nor did he want to be a soldier. It was that he was more afraid not to be. When officials told him to do something, he jumped to do it. In many ways, he was the opposite of my dad.

"After you folks are settled," he went on, talking in that positive voice, "you will want to set a fine example by becoming active in the Party." He flashed a smile of confidence. "I'm counting on you."

Gradually the sound of Mr. Mantei talking over the rattling of the wagon faded. I was too busy looking around to listen. Most of the fields looked as though they needed a lot of work, especially around the hedgerows. Weeds have a way of finding every corner. I should know. My dad had seen that I was well experienced in being a weed remover. Besides, the government representative spoke a different kind of German and I had a hard time understanding what he was saying. We were all German, but sometimes it didn't seem that way.

The memory of that wagon trip often comes back to me. Most of our possessions were in the back. The rest of them would be sent to us later. My mom, holding little Egon, was sitting on the second seat of the wagon. Mr. Mantei and my dad, with me squeezed in between, were on the front seat. It wasn't hard to tell that my dad was no more listening to Mr. Mantei than I was. He was looking across the fields. The land held a lot more interest for him than words with a stranger, that is, until Mr. Mantei once again began talking about the Party. "We must be strong and tightly joined together for the great work ahead," he said. "It will soon be a German world."

I felt my dad stiffen. He had been thinking of the land and being a farmer once again. Then all of those good feelings were jerked away. I felt his contentment vanish, much like the times when I was called to stop playing and do something I didn't want to do. Maybe that's what adult life is all about—a time when you stop playing and do all the things you don't like.

"It's a fine farm, Mr. Reule," Mr. Mantei said several times, as he showed us around. "Of course, it's a little run-down because Polish people just don't practice the better methods of German farming. But, a good farmer like you," his voice was full of confidence, "will have this land in fine shape in just one season. As for the buildings," he coughed and sort of choked, "a few boards here and there will work wonders."

I watched my dad's face as we walked through the old buildings. They were not only terrible; they were the worst I had ever seen still standing. My dad later described them as open-air buildings. The few pieces of equipment were not only old and rusty, but had parts missing and looked totally useless. It appeared that someone had gotten there before we did and helped himself to anything of value. It was the same story with the few animals standing in the filthy barn. I had never seen such skinny animals in all my life. My dad didn't say anything when he saw them. He just shook his head, as though for once, his great command of words had completely deserted him. Any thoughts of our well-kept farm and beautiful animals back in Romania must have been heavy in his mind.

Finally, we came to the house. It was not as Mr. Mantei had described. If possible, it was worse than the other buildings, or even the animals. I was scared to walk though the front door. The middle of the ceiling was sagging so badly it looked like it would come tumbling down any minute. There was no mistaking the look my mom gave my dad. We were in her domain now, not some barn or storage shed. Something had better be done about the house. That there would be, I was sure. I had seen his silent answer.

My dad looked from the sagging ceiling and damaged walls straight at Mr. Mantei. His sharp, flashing eyes never wavered. "We will make this livable for the rest of this year," he said slowly and evenly. "I can put up a center support and make the house strong enough to stand the snowfall." He paused. "But, that better be the end of it. In the spring we will have a new house."

Mr. Mantei got the message. "Yes sir Mr. Reule," he said all in one breath. "That's exactly what I was going to suggest myself. This house, with a few repairs, will be all right until spring. Then it's got to be a new one." He looked thoughtful and then enthusiastic as if he had come up with a real good answer. "I'll request one of those new prefabricated houses for you folks. They're the best. Yes sir, they're the best, and I'll do it first thing in the morning." He shook hands with my dad and started to leave. "The sooner I get the order in, the better chance I have of getting the house for you." He paused at the door. "I'll send you notice of the next meeting," he said with a big smile, as though it was something my dad wanted to know. "You will be happy in our local Party. We mostly have our meetings at Kutno, but occasionally some of us get together here at the school-

59

house. Sometimes we have a little more than just official business." He smiled at my dad. "Yes sir, you will be real happy living in Stefanov."

The winter of 1941-1942 in Poland was cold with great drifts of snow. We had experienced similar winters in Romania, but our home and outbuildings had been tight and warm. When the cold wind whistled and hummed its way through cracked and rattling windows, I learned firsthand what my dad meant by open-air buildings. Even in the barn, the animals stood hunched against the cold. My dad gave me solutions for both the snow and the cold. The snow, I shoveled; and for the cold, I needed to work a little harder.

I moved a lot of snow that winter, but not as much as my dad. It was something worth seeing when he took the shovel from my hands and sent me into the house to get warm. I would stand by the stove until I thawed out, then go over to the window and watch him make the snow fly in huge shovelfuls up and over the banks along paths to the outbuildings. After he had shoveled for a long time, I'd see him stop and lean on the shovel. Even from the window, I just knew his eyes had that far-off look; and he was seeing a bright summer day with fields of grain heading out, and our new house waiting when he came home. My dad was a dreamer, but he dreamed of the future. He knew how to let go of the past and make dreams come true.

We had just finished supper that winter evening when Mr. and Mrs. Wagner came to visit. We were sitting at the kitchen table. My mom hurried around and made them welcome. She also refilled the big platter of fried kuechla pastry my dad and I had about emptied. Then she gave them bowls of obst suppe, a fruit soup, all the time asking about their son Konrad. Even though they were eating and laughing and telling about their son who was serving on the Eastern Front, it wasn't hard to tell something was bothering them, especially Mr. Wagner.

It's not hard to know when adults are upset, even if they try to keep it a secret. Their eyes look at everything but see nothing. If it's a man, he gobbles his food like it was some unpleasant chore that had to be done. If it's a woman, she picks at her food like some old hen playing with a worm. Mr. Wagner ate his soup in quick bites, his eyes darting from one thing to the next, but always coming back to Mrs. Wagner, as though expecting her to do something. It was the same kind of exchanges I had often seen between my mom and dad, when they were trying to tell each other something without my knowledge while I was watching. The problem was, Mrs. Wagner wasn't paying attention to Mr. Wagner. She just went on talking and playing with her soup.

After a long time, Mr. Wagner became more and more open about his secret message. Finally my mom invited Mrs. Wagner into the bedroom to inspect a quilt that she was making. The position of women in our families was well defined. The man was the head of the family. In the privacy of the home, women could express their opinions, but in public, that is, in most of our meetings, the women waited for their men to speak. This did not mean, as I came to appreciate later, that the women had no knowledge or ability. It was that the women chose to be heard through their men. Mr. and Mrs. Wagner had come over because of some particular problem. In keeping with our ways, the women were expected to leave such matters to the men. When the women had left, Mr. Wagner glanced at me, expecting me to leave. I stayed.

We children also had definite rules. Our parents may have pampered and provided for us, but it was a serious fault not to show respect to our elders. We were to speak when spoken to and abide by the authority established in our homes and community. My dad noticed the look Mr. Wagner sent my way. Until then, he had not sensed that they had come for a particular reason. He may have been good at putting hard things together, but he often didn't see what was right in front of him. "Bruno," he said, in that tone of voice, making it plain I wasn't to question anything he told me, "better bring in another load of turf." My mom and dad had as many ways of saying my name, as there were things for me to do.

That was the fastest trip to the turf shed I ever made. Coming into the kitchen, I laid the square chunks of dried turf on the floor. I had already filled the box just as usual before it got dark. My dad saw me out of the corner of his eye, but didn't say anything. I took it as unspoken permission to stay as long as I wasn't noticed. Mr. Wagner was too busy talking to my dad to see me as I slipped onto a chair out of his line of sight, but certainly not out of my line of hearing. It pays not to be too big sometimes and quiet like our old cat slipping up on a mouse in the barn.

"What I'm telling you Gotthilf, is for your own good and the good of your family," I heard Mr. Wagner tell my dad. His fist was clenched, his face all red and his voice sounded like he was out of breath.

I watched my dad's face. The kitchen was so quiet I could hear the fire crackling softly in the stove. I saw that distant look come into his eyes. I knew he wasn't really in that shabby old house in Poland. He was somewhere out there—where fields need plowing, or in the barn where cows need milking. Already, I had begun to understand that side of him. Unless Mr. Wagner was talking of something my dad valued, he was wasting his time.

"I know what I am talking about," Mr. Wagner said pleadingly. He got out of breath whenever he was excited and spoke in little gasps. "I've seen it happen to others." He looked at my dad as though he was his best friend in the whole world. "Mr. Mantei is saying real bad things about anyone who is not a loyal member of the Party." He looked down at the table, avoiding my dad's eyes. "We all know he is talking about you." Perhaps it was the poor light in the kitchen, but I know I saw tears come to the old man's eyes as he considered what was sure to happen.

My dad sat listening, not even moving a hand, but the muscles in his jaw were real hard and made a ridge across his face. His eyes had lost that distant look and were blazing with feelings. When he spoke, there was no hesitation. "Damn it, Konrad," he said harshly, "I'm no socialist, and I'm not joining any Party." He laid a friendly hand on Mr. Wagner's arm to show his strong words were against what was happening and not against his old friend. "I'm just a farmer," he said, more gently with a smile, "not a politician." He squeezed Mr. Wagner's arm. "That's all I am or ever want to be."

"And a darn good one," Mr. Wagner said in strong agreement, which was the strongest words I had ever heard him say. The Wagners were staunch Lutherans and disappointed that there was no active church in our new German settlement in Poland. "Gotthilf." The way he spoke my dad's name showed he wasn't giving up. "You don't have to be active. Just sign your name and get the card, then Mr. Mantei will let you alone to farm and raise your family." The old man looked over my way without seeing me. His wrinkled face showed the effort it had taken to come and argue with my dad and how worried he was. "They're going to get you if you don't," he muttered in a low voice.

For a long time my dad didn't say anything. The kitchen took on that strange silence. Far away, I could hear the low voices of my mom and Mrs. Wagner. I sat wide eyed and watched and waited. "I spent three years as a border guard in the Romanian army," my dad said. "After that, I was called back for short terms." The look on his face showed his memories of service were not pleasant. "I saw what uniforms and guns do to men. Everything changes. They do what is not necessary and trample over what needs to be done. Wherever they go, they leave the land in worse shape than they found it. No matter what we are told by Hitler or anyone else, armies are all alike." He looked at Mr. Wagner to make sure he was being understood and would not have to say it again. "I don't feel a need to be in the Party." As he finished speaking those words, he looked over at me. I didn't understand all that was being talked about, but I understood that look. My dad was including me in what he had said, and that made me feel close to him.

That evening was the last time Mr. Wagner appealed to my dad about joining the Party. It was different for me. That evening marked a great change in my life. It was my coming of age. I stepped into the world of adult fears. Monsters hiding behind chairs, only to come out when the lights were off, were no longer real. Now I lived with fears as much in the daytime as at night. The war, the Party, my dad being taken away, all crowded out the monsters of my childhood and brought in those adult monsters that are so much worse. Every day I waited for the bad news. I was frightened by every official that visited our farm and always studied my mom's face when she opened mail from our box at the end of the lane. Mr. Wagner had been so sure that my dad would be drafted that I waited each day for it to happen.

As the days went by and nothing happened, I got more and more confused. Either it would happen or it wouldn't. My adult fears were still bound by youthful impatience, where all of life should take place in a day. I had yet to learn that adult fears are not so quickly resolved and often vanish only when a greater fear replaces the lesser. Then, along with my new fears, came feelings that were just as bad, or worse. Doubt! That twin monster to fear gripped me. I started wondering why my dad felt like he did. I knew a lot about him. I knew he was the bravest man in the world. But why didn't he want to be a soldier? I liked uniforms and marching. Thoughts of going to faraway places excited me. For the first time in my life, I was confused and began to doubt the person I loved most, next to my mom.

Try as I might, I couldn't stop the way I felt. Was my dad scared of being a soldier? He always talked of getting home before dark. Was he afraid to be far away and march from town to town? It never entered my thinking to ask him, and I was far from able to come up with answers, the way he did. I thought of asking my mom, but she was a woman and wouldn't understand. I was sure that was why women always moved to the other end of the room when men started talking about serious things, and why men always sat together at meetings or in church. Then, one afternoon several days later, I thought of someone who would tell me what I wanted to know. The first chance I got, I hiked across the fields to Mr. Wagner's farm. He was working in the horse barn and the familiar smell of horses came to me when I walked through the big doors and into the semi-darkness. "Mr. Wagner," I asked, after I had said hello, "is my dad afraid to be a soldier?"

Mr. Wagner stopped what he was doing and looked at me, his face making it plain I had said something pretty bad. "Bruno." I knew he was trying to be patient with me by the tone of his voice. "Don't ever question your daddy."

After my eyes adjusted to the darkened interior, I could see our old friend was sitting on the remains of a wooden chair, oiling and repairing a harness. He laid the leather straps across his lap, and despite my question, looked as though he was glad to see me. At the same time he was serious. His eyes didn't grin at me like a lot of adults do when they figure they're just talking to children. It made me feel good to know he was talking man to man.

"Your daddy is the bravest man I have ever known," Mr. Wagner said, slowly and carefully, so I couldn't misunderstand. "Now listen to me." He reached out and laid a hand on my shoulder, as though he needed to hold me while we talked. "It is not a question of your dad being afraid. I know him. He isn't afraid of any man on this earth." His eyes looked hard at me. "Your dad is his own man." Mr. Wagner's fingers tightened on my shoulder. "Do you understand?" My head sort of nodded because that was what he wanted, but my face still reflected my unhappiness and doubt. "This is what I mean," Mr. Wagner said, seeing my clouded face. "Your dad listens to what other people have to say, but he only does what he thinks he should." He still had his hand on my shoulder and was looking intently at my face. "Your dad isn't afraid of being a soldier, it's just that dressing in a uniform and marching around carrying a gun is not his way of thinking." Mr. Wagner shrugged his shoulders as though it was even beyond him. "That way of living makes him his own man." He dropped his hand and went back to oiling the harness. I knew he was through talking, but I had a lot more questions to ask.

"Mr. Wagner." He looked up. I could tell by his face we were still talking man to man. "Do you think my dad will be sent off to the war if he doesn't join the Party?" I had a hard time talking because it wasn't my way to speak right up to an adult. At least I had gotten the courage to ask the question that was making me stick closer to my dad than his own shadow and filling me so full of fear that I couldn't sleep at night.

Mr. Wagner's face tightened, but he never stopped rubbing the leather with oil to keep it soft. "Yes Bruno," he replied, without looking up. "I think your dad will be drafted because he won't join the Party." He looked at me and I could feel that he was a good friend not only with my dad, but also with me. Our eyes met and for just a minute, we were one with each other. "It's as simple as that," he said. "If a man is not willing to join the Party, he is considered to be against the government. The leaders can't afford to have a man like your dad around. They feel he sets a bad example for others." He gave a futile gesture with his hand. "Chances are, your dad being a former soldier and all, will be drafted anyway, so what difference does it make?" The old man shook his head sadly. He stopped rubbing the leather and looked through the open doors of the barn. "We are living in terrible times," he said softly, "and it is going to get worse." A grim smile came across his wrinkled face. "Only God knows what is going to come of all this."

I was sure that was what Mr. Wagner was going to say, I thought, walking slowly across the fields toward home. I had walked all that distance just to be told what I already knew. That's the way adults do things, and now I had done the same thing. What Mr. Wagner told me had made me even more proud of my dad. "We need men like your dad," he had said, walking me to the gate, just as he would any man that had come to see him. He pulled the latch and the big gate swung open. We stood for just a minute looking in the direction of my house. "There's not a chance in this world your dad or any one else will stop this awful war. But," he looked down at me with a smile and spoke with great conviction, "if more of us had the courage of your dad, there wouldn't be any armies to do the fighting." It was then that Mr. Wagner shook my hand. "Be like your dad, Bruno,"

he said, meaning when I grew older. "He's the best man I know."
Then as I started walking down the lane, he called to me. I turned.
He was still standing by the open gate, his voice sounding as though
he had almost forgotten something. "You be sure and come again,"
he said and waved. "You are always welcome."

After my talk with Mr. Wagner, I felt more accepting of what I
knew was to come. My fears didn't go away, they just stepped aside
so life could go on.

# Drafted

Spring had long been gone when our new house finally arrived. True to what he had said, Mr. Mantei had put through a rush order, but even my dad had expressed little concern about it coming as promised. He had been busy repairing equipment and getting the land ready for planting. That didn't stop him from having a few choice words about the speed of government officials, but he didn't complain with his usual fire. His interest was once again directed toward the land. The house was my mom's domain.

At first it was hard for me to believe that what I was seeing was to be our house. It came on two long, flatbed trucks accompanied by assemblers, or housemen as we called them. That wasn't what I had been expecting, yet, I didn't know what to expect, even after I was told. It just seemed impossible that our big house would come riding up in pieces on trucks. What didn't surprise me was that along with the house came Mr. Mantei.

"Yes sir, Mr. Reule," the Party representative told my dad with a laugh, that was more like "see what I've done for you," than that of a friend or neighbor. "In a little while, you will have the nicest place around here. Yes sir."

During the next few days I was all over the place, watching everything. It still seemed strange to think of our big house in Romania and to see our new home stacked in several big piles. The assemblers worked fast and everything seemed to go together quickly. Sometimes the expression on my dad's face showed surprise as though he had just learned something. Other times his clouded look indicated the work being done was not as he would have done it.

As our house neared completion, Mr. Mantei came again to inspect and talk to my dad about becoming active in the Party. "You're getting settled now," I heard him say, looking around. That was obvious. My dad and mom had worked hard. Everything looked so much better; it was hard to tell we had the same farm. "I got you that new house and now I tell you we need every loyal German." He didn't see the look on my dad's face as he mentioned our new house and the Party all in one breath. My dad had said a hundred times they weren't giving him anything, that our farm in Romania was worth ten times the Polish farm they were pushing off on us.

"It works both ways," Mr. Mantei continued. "We work for each other. The government gives you a new house and you support the government."

My dad listened in that special way he had of hearing bad news from somebody he didn't like. "I had a good farm in Romania," he replied with a sharp edge to his voice. Even Mr. Mantei couldn't miss what my dad was saying. "When this house gets built, I will have all I can do right here without spending my time at any meetings."

From that time on, I noticed Mr. Mantei wasn't as friendly as he had been. His "Yes sir," wasn't said with a big laugh like before and when he did say "Yes sir," without laughing, it was not very friendly. My dad didn't seem to notice, but I did. I had seen changes in adults before. I had learned that you don't listen to what adults say so much as how the words sound, and how their faces look when the words come out. After hearing what Mr. Mantei said and the way he said it, I got even more fearful. I watched my dad real close to see if he was worried. He didn't seem to be. He didn't stop and watch every time someone came down the road to see if they turned into our lane, like I did. Just looking at my dad, he seemed to be perfectly content. All of his problems seemed to be little ones that didn't take much thinking.

After the house was built, my mom was very pleased. She fixed a big dinner and had all of our many friends and relatives over for Sunday dinner. There was a lot of talk about how well the war was going and how soon it would be over. Again it was my dad who dared to suggest that the war seemed to be getting more complicated, not less, and that the end might be farther away than we thought. No one argued; and no one, not even Mr. Wagner, talked to him about joining the Party. It was apparent word had gotten around that he didn't appreciate any more invitations. Despite the fact he was the only non-member in the village, our friends were respectful of his wishes.

Where does life go when it never comes? It had happened in Romania and now it happened again. My mom and dad had talked to me about having another little brother or a baby sister. They couldn't make up their minds which it was to be. Since I already had a brother, I wanted a sister. But it never happened. When we went to the church in Kutno, the minister talked about angels and little ones who are eternally innocent. It's hard to love someone or something that you have never held in your arms or played with, but even I had feelings of not having something that I would have liked very much.

Our new house helped us feel more at home in Poland. The first floor was a combination kitchen and dining room along with two bedrooms. The large bedroom was upstairs. Harvest was also upon us and our life was once again, guided by the forces of nature. That is, all except me. It was time to start my second year of school. It seemed that summer had ended so fast, I hadn't had time to get ready or even think about it. The first Monday in September my mom got me ready while my dad started rebuilding the outbuildings. He had the assemblers build our new house in the middle of what had been the four smaller Polish farms. Then, taking all the usable lumber from the old farm buildings, he began construction of a combination stable for our horses, cows and pigs. Another building was to hold our hay and unthreshed wheat along with the equipment and there was to be a small building for the chickens. It was hard for me to head off to school when my dad was so busy and needed my help so much.

I could hear distant sounds of my dad working those early fall mornings as I began the two-kilometer walk. Our school had been a big, old house with two large rooms used for classes. About forty students attended each division and we had studies Monday through Saturday from eight until noon. Two of those days, classes continued until four o'clock. Discipline was very strict and any trouble at school meant even more trouble at home. Each morning we stood by our desks and gave the familiar greeting: "Heil Hitler" to start our day of studies. Then, on a word from our teacher, we sat down.

My teacher was Mr. Heer who had lived in Bessarabia, but was not from our village of Friedenstal. He liked to read and would often read to us about great historical happenings of Germany. He also loved to play soccer and often spent the noon hour teaching us the finer points of kicking and scoring. I had just settled into the routine of school when Mr. Heer was drafted. "You be good students and grow up to be loyal Germans," he told us before leaving. "The Fatherland will have great need for educated minds in the New World to come."

After Mr. Heer left, two women who were government officials became our teachers. They lived at the schoolhouse. Also living in the big house were eight air force men who watched for enemy aircraft from a tower built on the roof. There were many times when I saw the soldiers walking about the grounds and I sometimes looked up and waved at them in the tower. Besides the regular school work, all the students ten years or older had to be a part of Hitler Youth. That wasn't bad to my way of thinking. Unlike my dad, I was looking forward to joining. I wanted to wear the uniform and I especially liked the knife and holder fastened to the belt.

Through the spring and summer of '43, my dad continued to build while I went off to school. After framing what was to be the stable, he purchased a load of brown brick and hired a mason to make the stable tight and warm. "Animals need a warm home just like we do," he told me one Saturday afternoon while I was helping him. "Everything God has placed on this earth has certain needs and certain rights." That determined look when he was up against something difficult came to his face. "Individual rights, no matter who you are, make harmony and balance in this world." His lips came together to form that thin line indicating he really meant what he was saying. "When those rights are taken away, no matter who does it or for what reason, the purpose of life is destroyed." We were standing in our unfinished stable, but I got the feeling of being in church.

There was double meaning in his eyes. I should have understood, but I was only nine years old and so full of life that things often passed me by. Years later, I was to realize what a great man and farmer my dad had been. Standing in the unfinished stable that afternoon with the smell of cow strong in the air, he had planted one of life's most important seeds, that of respect for others, in me. I also learned another truth that day. My dad did have fears. They were not for himself, but for his family and the farm. He was fearful that I would not understand why he had to stand against joining the Party and risk losing the very rights he held so dear. There was also the fear of not having time to finish the work he had started.

There was something else that I should have realized. His time on the farm was short. He realized that and didn't waste time watching down the lane as I did or getting excited when the mail came. His kind of fear was for living -- not for running away. It made his eyes see all that needed to be done and feel the urgency of making best use of the time he had left.

"Bruno," my dad spoke sharply to me one Saturday afternoon. "Do it right." I was hurrying because it was almost suppertime and I was famished. The bricks I was stacking looked like they would fall over any minute. He came and helped me. "Make it straight and neat," he said, "and you feel neat and straight inside." In a few minutes he had the bricks squared. "There," he was satisfied with his work, "that looks the way it should." He gave me a smile of satisfaction. "Make what you are doing match the picture in your mind," he told me. "That's where the real strength of a man is to be found, in the pictures he carries in his mind." He put his arm around my shoulder as we walked toward the house and our waiting supper. "Have good pictures inside of you," he told me, "then make your world match what you see."

Two days later, the draft letter came. My mom had a baby girl in the spring that died shortly after birth, and my dad always blamed the midwife. Because my mom had become sick, his leaving had been delayed; but a few months later, he went into the army. After he left, much of the work stopped. In time, my mom picked up the work of farming; but frequently the good way my dad had of doing things, was left in the not so good hands of others.

"Bruno." The way my mom called my name told me she was happy. That made me happy. I had just come in from school, one of those long days, and grabbed a large piece of bread heaped with butter and jam. There was a big smile on her face, the first I had seen since my dad left. All the time he had been gone, she had been feeling sick, especially in the mornings. She was holding a letter in her hands. "We get to see your dad," she said, all excited. Because he had been a soldier in the Romanian army, my dad's training in Germany had lasted only a few weeks. He had written to tell us that he was being shipped to the Eastern Front and that his train was scheduled to pass through Kutno. It was really bad news that he was being sent to fight the Russians, but we were happy we would get to see him again. "I've got something special to tell him," she said with that mysterious smile which indicated I was too young to understand. What she didn't know was I knew and understood a lot more than she realized.

The day before my dad's train was due to pass through Kutno, we hitched horses to the wagon and drove the seven kilometers from Stefanov. We were excited and everything was fun. Even little Egon, who was three years old, knew something good was about to happen. Once again I had the feeling of Christmas when all the family comes together and your life is so full it can't hold any more. The seven-kilometer trip was something special for me. The anticipation of seeing my dad was so strong that it seemed he was already with us. I had a delicious taste for life. Singing and talking, we rode along, waving to people that we knew. Partway there, I got permission to get into the food basket. That was even more fun than singing. My mom had also brought a basket of food for my dad and one for some friends who lived at the edge of town near the rail station where we were going to stay. It was late afternoon when we arrived at their house. As soon as we got there, my mom had to lie down. I didn't know all there was to know about her illness, but I did know we were going to have a new baby in our family.

The next morning, we got up early, filled with expectations. Long before his train was due to arrive, we were at the station. It was a busy place with trains constantly coming and going. I felt my head swirling with so much going on. I didn't realize the war was uprooting people all over Europe. Huge armies were marching and people were trying to get out of the way. As for me, even an empty train on a side railing would have been of great interest.

The hours slowly passed. "Sometimes trains don't come when they should," my mom told me. Throughout the day, I tried to believe what she had said. The problem was that my stomach refused to cooperate and grew heavier and heavier. Every few hours a troop train loaded with soldiers and equipment pulled into the station and out again or just whistled on through. Uniformed men were jammed into every doorway and were leaning out the windows. Everybody waved, but we never did see my dad.

"You still waiting for a troop train from Germany?" The trainman, whom we had been asking all day about train schedules, walked toward us. He was a big, red-faced man and wore a cap with a badge. It made him look important. When he got close to my mom, he took off his cap and stood with it in his hand. He looked a lot friendlier that way.

"My husband has been in Germany for training," my mom told him. "He wrote that he would be coming through Kutno today."

I stood holding my little brother's hand and watching my mom's face. Even when deep inside I had felt my dad wasn't coming, she had kept that look of expectation in her eyes, as if any minute the train would come puffing in and there he would be. The big stationmaster looked down the empty tracks with a sad look on his face. "There are no more scheduled trains from Germany today," he said. "They must have been delayed." He smiled in an attempt to cheer us. "Maybe tomorrow."

Sometimes I have seen the light in our lamp go out and the wick still glow, but as I watched my mom's eyes, the light went out completely. The rest of her face never changed. Adults may control their faces, but seldom their eyes. I had not really given up hope until I saw the light in my mom's eyes go out.

We didn't wait the next day as the trainmaster had suggested. We walked back to the home of our friends and began the trip home. I did a lot of thinking as we rode along. Again I felt the full impact of forces that control our lives. I had seen it in Romania and I had seen it in Sudetenland. Now, worst of all, I had seen my dad sent off to war without so much as a goodbye from us. The adult world was so confusing; it got me all mixed up. It was a place where they talked of good things, but so often did the bad.

The more I thought, the more one answer came to me. When my dad and mom, my little brother Egon and I, were all together, we were more powerful than these forces. I felt my anger build until it pushed aside the overwhelming disappointment that had gripped me. My teeth locked together like an iron gate. I'd show them, I thought to myself. I knew what needed to be done. I'd take my dad's place and keep us all together until he came home. That was the only way to be stronger than the hidden forces that...

"Gotthilf!"

I jumped as my mom suddenly grabbed my arm and called my dad's name. My mom, her eyes wide and staring at me, looked as though she had seen a ghost. The reins were loose in her hands, the horses plodding along in a walk. She rubbed a hand across her lips, holding back what she was about to say. "I must have been dreaming," she said, slowly shaking her head. "For a minute I thought your dad was driving and you were on my lap like before." She looked at me, then back at the horses and lifted the reins taking up the slack. We continued home in silence.

# The Waiting

"Olga, you mustn't overdo." My Aunt Martha Ziebart's sharp voice cut across the room for the hundredth time. Of course, that didn't include me. Ever since she had come to look after my mom in her "last days," as Aunt Martha called it, she had insisted my mom do nothing and I do everything, or so it seemed. I guess I learned how much my mom did by hearing my aunt tell her not to. "When Gotthilf comes home," she told my mom, "I want you to be healthy and the little one alive and well." She blinked her eyes and looked at us as though my dad might walk through the door any minute. "After all," she was drying dishes and putting them away as she talked, "he made me promise: that I would look after you and that the baby would be born in the hospital."

That part I knew. When my little baby sister died at birth a year earlier, in the spring of 1943, my dad had always blamed the Polish midwife. He said when the woman had bathed our little one, the water was too hot which caused her to die. "The body is too red," he had told my mom. "The next time you will be in the hospital." That was that, and even though he wasn't there, my mom would do as he said.

I can give credit to my mom's half sister for at least one thing. She helped me understand the vast amount of work on a farm, even for women. We raised mostly potatoes, lots of sugar beets and rye, some wheat, and fields of poppy plants. The top of the poppy plant was harvested by hand with the upper cap being used to make morphine. Snow was still on the ground, but preparations had to be made for spring planting and all of our animals—the cows, pigs and chickens, needed constant attention. We had hired Polish neighbors to help, but someone had to be in charge and that was my mom.

"Olga." We were sitting in the kitchen several days later. I was eating and my aunt was looking at some official papers from the government. "It says here that all farmers must observe food restrictions like everyone else." She looked across the table at my mom and laughed. "There isn't a farmer who doesn't have a few chickens and a pig or two that even the inspectors don't know about."

I was listening, but didn't say anything and went on eating. My mom had received a lot of letters from the government. They came in blue envelopes and were often sent by Mr. Mantei who was in charge of official announcements. The letters usually listed some new requirement or restated an old one. These letters also reminded us that all farmers were soldiers and had to obey orders. Everybody received the same blue envelopes, but that didn't stop them from grinding a little extra flour and selling or trading a few chickens and a pig or two.

My aunt gave my mom that real confidential look and spoke in a low voice. "Gustav," he was my uncle, "said the inspectors are going to make us market every animal that reaches a certain weight. He says that meat is becoming scarce because the farmers are fattening them too long so they will get more money at the market."

What I didn't tell my aunt was that my dad had been the best hider and trader in our village. He always could fool the inspectors and knew families, especially from the city, that wanted butter, eggs or a case of smoked sausage. He seldom took money, but traded for equipment or items that the government made impossible to obtain, such as a rifle for himself and bicycles for everyone in our family. The trades were carried out by means of what we called suitcase food. Since so many people rode bicycles, the common way of carrying the eggs or meat was in a suitcase lashed on the back. For a lot of people, adding suitcase deliveries to food acquired legally, helped us eat well. "No one should be completely controlled by the government," I had heard my dad say one time.

My mom, looking as though she wasn't feeling good, gave a little sigh. "I try to do what I am told," she said. "Maybe that way this awful war will soon be over and Gotthilf can come home."

The kitchen was quiet except for the two women talking. Each afternoon, my aunt, heavy as she was, would bicycle to our home and spend the night. After supper, we often sat in the kitchen talking. Little Egon was usually sleeping; and it was a nice time, that is, until I was told to go to bed. My mom usually followed the many instructions sent by the government, but she never limited me on the food. When friends or our schoolteachers, or even the soldiers stationed at the schoolhouse, came to buy food, she always gave them more than they paid for. Except for that, which was more my mom's generous way rather than a desire to break laws, she never sold anything except on the legal market. From what my aunt and others said, I learned there was a lot of money to be made selling on the black market. That was not a part of our lives.

"Bruno." I tried not to hear, but who could escape my aunt when she called? It was just after supper. My regular chore of filling the stove fuel box was all done and I was busy playing. "Bruno." This time her voice was sharp and I knew it was time to hurry right in.

My mom was lying on the bed, talking to my aunt. I knew something was happening by the look on her face.

"You tell the hired man to bring the wagon and hurry." My aunt was excited. "We've got to get your mom to the hospital quick." I saw my mom looking in pain. "Bruno," my aunt's voice was extra sharp, "Do what I told you right now." She looked again at my mom. "This is not like the last time!"

I hurried. Two weeks earlier, the same thing had happened and they had rushed off to the hospital in Kutno. That had been a "false alarm" and two days later my mom had walked the seven kilometers back home. "Your little sister said she was coming and changed her mind," my aunt said. She had decided that the baby would be a little girl. "Can't blame her for not wanting to come into this world as it is now." Then she scolded my mom for walking home. "What if the baby had decided to come halfway between here and Kutno?" she shouted. "What would have happened then?"

"She didn't," my mom replied, and lay down on the bed and closed her eyes. I had never seen her so tired, but I didn't say anything. I knew the ways of my mom, and all the yelling in the world wasn't going to change her. Sometimes adults, who are supposed to know more than children, act as though they know less.

That night baby Charlotte was born. I knew she had been in my mother's belly; but how she got there and how she could get out, remained a mystery to me. The little belly button in the middle looked awfully small. But there was something I knew without a question at all. When my aunt came the next morning and told us we had a baby sister, I felt good all over. Our little sister was proof we were still a family. Those invisible forces that seem to follow us wherever we lived were not so powerful after all. We were stronger. The coming of baby Charlotte convinced me we had the strength to win.

"Well, get ready if you want to go see her," my aunt told me with a nice smile. She was letting me know that I could go to Kutno with her. She had begun to suspect that I was missing my mom terribly. That kind of understanding was something I had not expected. I never thought of my aunt as ever being young or knowing how I felt. Some adults were never children. They were born, then pulled, pushed and even kicked so fast into adulthood that they missed all the good times in-between.

We had a great time going into the hospital. It was the first time I had been there, and I was kind of scared by the big hall, and nurses in white hurrying from room to room, as though there was something really important going on. I just held my aunt's hand and we marched right past those nurses up to the window where we could see the babies. There, right in front of my eyes, was my baby sister. She was crying so loudly, I knew she was all right. It was great fun standing there, looking at her little hands and wrinkled face. I looked at her tiny feet, then glanced down at my aunt's big, heavy shoes. It was hard to think that someday those little feet would ever be that big. Then we went into my mom's room and she gave me a big hug and a kiss. That made it clear that she had missed me as much as I had missed her. I discovered how happy it makes you to miss someone so much and then be together again.

There were a lot of things I wanted to tell my mom, but my aunt's presence interfered. I wasn't about to say those things in front of my aunt. I stood at the end of the bed, first on one foot then the other, just looking at my mom and getting filled up with what I had been missing. That was when my dad's two sisters came walking in. They lived ten and twenty kilometers from us. As soon as I saw them, I sensed that all my happiness was about to break into a thousand unhappy pieces. I had spent all my life watching adults, and could tell by the signs that they were about to say something I didn't want to hear. Even my mom could tell something was wrong. Finally my Aunt Olga Schuett moved closer to the bed. I waited, knowing that she was about to say something terrible had happened.

"We've got some bad news," she told my mom. "It's Gotthilf. He has been badly wounded." It was then that both my aunts started crying.

I knew by my mom's expression that she didn't believe what they were telling her. It was worse than that, much worse. "Gotthilf is dead isn't he," she said.

They could only nod their heads. Then they walked over to the bed and Aunt Emma Welz took my mom's hand. The last thing my eyes would let me see was my mom pulling the blanket against her face. After that, I didn't look any more. All I could think of was my dad leaving for Germany, and then standing in the Kutno station, knowing he wasn't coming home. I don't remember anything about going back home.

It was one of those happy-sad days when my mom and baby Charlotte got to come home. We were all on the wagon. My aunt had let my little brother Egon and me ride with her to the hospital in Kutno. It was then that I discovered how life could be filled with laughter and tears, one after the other, and even at the same time, like sun shining through falling rain. We laughed at the funny faces my baby sister made and then at the self importance of my little brother when he was given the chance to hold baby Charlotte for the first time. Our laughter stopped when thoughts of my dad overwhelmed us.

In looking back, I realize I had learned one of the grim secrets of life during that short wagon trip – the relationship of loss and gain. When life takes something away, something is given in return. Sometimes one overshadows the other, but survival depends on this precarious balance of trade we call existence. Somewhere in the dynamics of this continual exchange is the raw substance of life. Whether or not you live is determined, not by what is destroyed, but by fulfilling the purpose of what is given. That's why baby Charlotte became so dear to us. She didn't take the place of what we had lost, but she helped us journey on with our lives.

One of the best gifts I ever received was my bicycle. It had a generator on the front wheel that powered the light on the handle bar. On the back was a rack where I could carry things and it served as a riding place for my little brother. I did a lot of bike riding that spring of 1944. Since Polish help was working our farm, and the two women teachers had suddenly vanished, I had a lot more time to play.

"Bruno." I had just ridden my bike alongside the picket fence around our house when I heard my mom call. "Help me get the wagon ready," she said, coming through the door. "We're going over to your Grandma Reule's."

It's hard finding a stopping place when you're having a lot of fun. But when my mom's voice sounded that way, the stopping place found me. I hurried and put the bike away.

"Your dad's cousin, Benjamin, is home on furlough," she said, as we drove toward my grandma's house. That was all she said, but I could tell by the low pitch to her voice there was a lot more. I looked across at my mom's face. My little brother was sitting between us and I was holding baby Charlotte. I saw that her lips were real tight and she was looking straight down the road, but not really seeing the horses or where she was driving. I got strong feelings that she was determined to do something she didn't want to do. I began to think about things. I knew Benjamin Stadel was about my dad's age and was with him when he was killed. Benjamin was the one who had written to my aunt, and that was how she knew to come to the hospital and tell my mom.

Even when I looked across the flat fields, I could still feel my mom's anger filling the air. Sometimes I'm pretty dumb. I don't hear what my ears are hearing or see what my eyes are seeing. It's like there was a third part of me that ignores the rest of me. "Are you going to ask him how my dad got killed?" I asked.

As soon as the question rolled out, I knew I had made a mistake. My mom gave me a look that made me wish I were back riding my bicycle. "I know how he got killed," she said, in quick, short words, her dark eyes flashing. "And I know the people who killed him."

I am always amazed at what adults know without being told. As for me, I always have to be told or learn the hard way. My amazement at what my mom knew brushed away caution. "How do you know?" I asked.

She gave me the very last look on her list of angry faces. That look caused me to hold baby Charlotte a lot closer and put an instant stop to the other questions bubbling in my head.

"I know because I know your dad," she said, tight-lipped. That was the end of our conversation, but it wasn't the end of my thinking.

After we arrived at Grandma Reule's, she got ready and rode with us to the Stadel home. Grandpa Reule didn't go. He was still upset over my dad's death and was becoming more bitter every day. The death of my dad's younger brother, Uncle Oskar earlier in the war had been a great loss to him. The death of a second son had been too much. Grandma was worried that he was losing his mind. She was also afraid he would be arrested for saying bad things about Hitler and the "damn" war.

At Mr. Stadel's place, we gathered in the big kitchen where my dad's cousin began telling us what had happened on the Eastern

Front. "Gotthilf was a good soldier, even though he didn't want to be," he said, looking first at my mom, then half smiling at me. We were sitting at the table, a pitcher of wine and some good cake in front of us. Mrs. Stadel had given me some milk. My mom wasn't eating or drinking. She was still angry about something. Mr. Stadel was a tall, thin man and dressed once again in his own clothes. In some ways, he was just like my dad. He didn't like wearing a uniform. "All of us were good soldiers," he said, without bragging. "We have to be to survive out there." His reference to the Russian Front brought a grim look to his face. "Men were killed around us every day and especially at night. Then, there was the cold. It was so cold out there." He opened and closed his fingers as if they, too, remembered the sharp freezing winds and endless miles of frozen snow. "It was so cold even our guns wouldn't fire."

"The guns don't fire?" Mr. Wagner had also come over to learn what had happened to my dad. He leaned close and looked intently at Benjamin, as though he had heard something beyond belief. "I thought our guns were the best in the world." His face showed great astonishment.

"They are the best," Benjamin replied, "the best guns any soldier has ever had. That's the trouble. It doesn't take precision to kill, just guns that fire." His face had that barren look of eyes that had seen life brutally taken away. "The tolerance of our guns is so close that the terrible cold freezes them like it does us. When the enemy attacks, half our guns won't fire." Benjamin looked down at the table; and he paid one of the greatest soldier-to-soldier compliments. "It takes a brave man to face the enemy, knowing that the very minute when his life is depending on his rifle, the damn thing won't fire or it blows up in his face." He stopped talking. I studied him out of the corner of my eyes not really understanding what he was saying, but feeling the terrible sadness of his words. He was looking down and seemed to have trouble swallowing. When he did speak again, his voice was husky as if he had a cold. "We left a lot of good men in the snow." He paused. "Some of them, like Gotthilf, were my best friends." With hands that were trembling, he reached for the pitcher of wine. "Some were not dead when we had to leave them." He poured some wine and set the pitcher down with a thud. "They are now."

Mr. Wagner had not tasted his wine, but sat with his eyes glued on Benjamin. There came a hostile look to his face as he asked harshly, "How can that be? The radio tells us every day about our great victories. Why are you telling us all these bad things?"

"Victories!" Benjamin slapped the table so hard and suddenly that I jumped. "We are retreating," he shouted at Mr. Wagner. "We are losing the war! It's the Russian winter." He hit the table again, but this time with his fist. "It is not over, but we are beaten." His lips came together in a thin line of futility as he drew the back of his hand across his face in a fateful gesture. "I'm going back to die," he said dully. "I know that. That's all there is out there, death and more death until all of us are dead."

Mr. Wagner didn't say anything. His breath came in short, little gasps, and I knew he was thinking of his son Konrad. His letters from the Western Front had been filled with news of endless, glorious victories. After hearing what Mr. Stadel had said, I wondered if Konrad's letters were like the news on the radio—just lies. Every day there had been reports of thousands of the enemy killed and captured. Sometimes they announced maneuvers that involved moving back, but they were never called defeat or even retreat. The incredible part was that we believed Germany could not be defeated. That was impossible, and never considered by our people. The unbelievable fact to us was that Russia and England could continue to fight the war with only women, children, and old men, since all their trained soldiers had been killed or captured. That was what Dr. Goebbels, his commanding voice backed by stirring band music, told us daily. Mr. Stadel's words and the desperate look on his face made me feel twisted inside. It was even harder on Mr. Wagner. He began to have one of his asthma attacks. For the first time, I understood something far beyond my years. The Great War that adults discussed was not the same war our soldiers like Benjamin and Konrad were fighting. For the first time I had different thoughts about uniforms and soldiers marching off to distant cities.

"What happened to Gotthilf?" my mom asked, her voice indicating she had heard all that had been said, but her real interest was in learning about my dad.

Benjamin looked across the table at my mom, with an even sadder expression on his face. "Gotthilf wasn't killed on the front line," he said slowly. "We had been," he paused, and I could tell his memory of what had happened was painful and the words came hard, "out there for about three months. Then we got pulled back and fresh troops were sent in." He looked at me and I will always remember what I saw in his eyes. "We were on a sleigh coming back from the front," Benjamin continued, "when we stopped for a little break." He looked off in the distance as if once again seeing what had happened. "It was late afternoon or evening, except when it gets dark, it all looks the same out there. After we had stopped, one of the men walked away from the sleigh. That was not good. He could get lost or be an easy target." Benjamin looked at the floor. "Maybe he wanted to shoot himself."

"Shoot himself!" Mr. Wagner broke in. "A German soldier shoot himself?"

Benjamin just shook his head and didn't answer. He looked at my mom. "When we got ready to go, Gotthilf went looking for him. That was when the guerillas attacked us. There was heavy shooting and we all took cover in the snow or in back of the sleigh. I don't know how long we were under attack. Time is different when you are trying to save your life and take another person's. I think Gotthilf was hit first. He had walked right in the direction where the guerillas were hiding. The soldier who had walked away from the sleigh was with Gotthilf. He was not hit. He told me that Gotthilf's last words were: 'God, don't let me suffer too long.'" Benjamin gave a little sigh. "He didn't. By the time the guerillas were gone and I got to him, he was dead."

We were all silent. Mr. Wagner was so upset by what Benjamin was saying, that all he could do was breathe in short, little gasps because of his asthma. Grandma Reule was wiping the tears from her eyes. But my mom was a complete mystery to me. She didn't disbelieve Benjamin, but her expression revealed that he hadn't even come close to what she suspected concerning the death of my dad.

"We buried Gotthilf and two others in the snow," Benjamin said. He shrugged his shoulders in a gesture of futility. "There was nothing else we could do."

"You mean the Russians are actually behind our lines?" Mr. Wagner asked, his disbelief so strong that his voice came out as a squeak.

Benjamin gave a fateful sigh. "The Russians are everywhere," he said, with a wide swing of his arm. "They kill as many of our men behind the lines as in actual battle."

Mr. Wagner sadly shook his head. He had come to believe what Benjamin had told us, but it was obvious his memories of soldiering had left him only remembrances of gallant men fighting equally gallant men on fields of honor. Such dishonorable fighting, as guerillas attacking behind lines, was unbecoming to real soldiers. "It's terrible," he said, "simply terrible."

"Then you didn't see Gotthilf get killed," my mom said sharply, her dark eyes flashing. I had the feeling my mom was thinking something entirely different.

"No," Benjamin said slowly. "I didn't actually see him get shot." He looked away from my mom's face and into his wineglass, moving uneasily in his chair. "One of the guerillas must have shot him." He shrugged. "That's all I know, except I helped to bury him in the snow."

My mom didn't say any more. She had that look about her face that reached down to her shoulders. I had seen it twice before and it was something I really dreaded. It started at the top of her hair, flowed across her face and twisted itself into the peculiar hunch of her shoulders. I had seen that look when we first arrived in Poland, and my mom saw the old house we had been given for a home; the second time was when my dad went off with Mr. Mantei and came home drunk. That never happened again. She saw to that. Each time she seemed to become twice her normal size. The bigger the problem, the bigger she got. This time she seemed the biggest of all. Maybe that was because this was our biggest problem.

From my mom, I learned to hear what people didn't say, before I made up my mind about what they did say. Seeing my mom so angry over my dad's death and certain there was more to be told, I looked at Mr. Stadel and waited. The kitchen became quiet. Benjamin sat there looking at the table. After what seemed a very long time, he just shook his head without looking at any of us. It was no use. Either he didn't know any more to tell, or there was some terrible reason for being silent.

My mom wondered why he didn't bring home some personal item of my dad's, such as a billfold. Whatever the secret might have been, if there was one, could not have been any worse than what my mom was thinking. Deep down, she had never expected my dad to come home from the war. Of course, she had hoped and prayed that he would. But she knew beyond anyone else how stubborn he was, how he refused to join the Party in the very face of being drafted, how he hated army life marching around in uniform and taking orders to do things he didn't want to do, and how quick he was to do things his way. All of that gave my mom plenty of reason to believe the most terrible thought of all—that my dad had been shot by one of his own officers for being himself. The very best thought she had was that he had gotten tired of the killing business and deserted.

There was no need for any more questions. It had all been said in words and silence. My dad was dead and it didn't really matter how he died. What killed him, what kills all soldiers, is that disease of mankind called war, a disease that gives people the opportunity to do such terrible things to one another. That night, looking at Mr. Stadel and listening to more than his words, I felt the horror he had been through. In the dim light of that strangely-quiet kitchen, where for a minute each was thinking about what had been said, I watched Mrs. Stadel refill the wine pitcher and found myself being filled with the cares of the adult world.

"The war is going badly, very badly," Benjamin finally said, holding his glass but not drinking. He looked at my mom. There was a look of acceptance on his face. His words were spoken softly, almost as though what he was saying was unimportant. It was more like he was talking about the weather or just adult talk that fills in the threat of silence. It was the grim look on my mom's face and Mr. Wagner's that made me realize the grave importance of what Mr. Stadel was saying. "We were falling back on all fronts when I left," he said, lifting the glass to his lips.

"You mean retreating!" Mr. Wagner mumbled, his leathery face looking even more wrinkled. The disbelief had vanished. "Just yesterday," he said absently, "the radio…" His voice drifted off. He looked at his thick, heavy hands clasped together on top of the table. What Benjamin had said, and the way he looked, was too much even for Mr. Wagner's loyalty. It was very obvious that despite the exciting band music and the strong, vibrant voice over the wireless, what we were seeing and hearing in the Stadel kitchen, was the real war. Then it came to me. It was all clear. The proud words describing great victories and the capture of thousands of enemy soldiers was a part of adult make-believe. The radio was as much a weapon as the guns. Those words weren't lies like I might tell. They were dreams, old dreams, just before the dawn. It was like going to bed hungry and dreaming of all the good food you ever wanted to eat, only to awaken with the bitter taste of an empty belly in your mouth. That dream was ending and the brutal awakening for those of us who had never dreamed the dream was about to take place. That was what Mr. Stadel was telling us.

"There are so many of them," Mr. Stadel said, referring to the Russians. "We kill and kill and they keep coming. They come from all directions, the front, the sides, from the back, during the day and all times of night." He lifted his arm, but let it fall back to the table in a gesture of hopelessness. "We will hold them as long as we can." His voice trembled as he spoke.

I looked over at Mr. Wagner. He didn't say any words, but his face said a great deal as he looked at Mrs. Wagner. She was a little woman, even smaller than my mom, with quick, bird-like movements. For the first time since I had known her, she was sitting still. What they had heard and seen had made them look much older. They both seemed very tired of living. "We haven't received a letter from our Konrad for a long time," Mr. Wagner said, looking at my mom. "Have we really lost the war?" he asked of Benjamin, in a slow, heavy voice.

Benjamin seemed lost in thought. "It's all over except the running," he answered. Again there was silence. "The Russians will be coming this way and it won't be long." He sat up straight and squared his shoulders as though once again a soldier. "Be ready to move out as soon as you are told." His words carried a deadly warning. "That will be the worst time for you," he said, "after our soldiers have retreated and you are left by yourselves!"

# Russians

"Bruno. Bruno." Stasczak called excitedly. "The planes. They come." Just as we had so dreadfully feared, two Russians planes suddenly swooped low across the sky, machine guns blazing.

Even though Stasczak spoke in Polish, my mom instantly understood. The roar of planes and the strange whistling sounds of bullets quickly filled the air. People began running and screaming. Remembering the advice of the previous night, we had already planned what we would do. Stasczak was riding in front with me. We were to stop the wagon, then jump and run for the ditch and take what shelter we could find. I was to take Little Egon with me. My mom, taking baby Charlotte with her, was to jump off her side and run to the ditch on the other side. That way, if one got hurt, the others could help. The plan was not complicated, but speed was essential.

Quickly locking the brake and wrapping the reins in one quick motion, I jumped to the ground yelling at my little brother to come on. From the very start, I had dreaded this minute. In my mind, I imagined it many times and each time with terrible results. Now that the planes had come, I was too busy running for that ditch to think of anything. Fear has a way of blanking out the mind and giving fleetness to the feet. Then, something painful happened to make me realize that the best-laid plans seldom turn out that way.

"Bruno." My little brother's voice was lost in the roar of the planes, but not to me. "Help me."

I turned and looked back. Stasczak had gotten off, all right, and was low in the ditch. My mom, hugging baby Charlotte close to her, was almost in the ditch. Although I had heard Egon's desperate cry, I couldn't see him. "Egon," I yelled, "come on." Then I caught a glimpse of his head beyond the front part of the seat. He was desperately trying to pull himself back into the wagon. Maybe he was too excited; maybe the horses had bolted. Somehow he had lost his balance and toppled near the front edge directly in the way of a wheel. To make things worse, the horses, terrified by the planes and dreadful excitement, reared and started to break away. I ran toward the wagon, but it wasn't any use. I couldn't move that fast. Besides, how could I stand against the force of two powerful horses? The whole world for us was coming apart. People were screaming and running in all directions. The planes were on us as our wagon dashed away from my outstretched hands. I could see my little brother's legs dangling in the air as he struggled to hold on. His sharp screams kept calling for me to help.

"Run Bruno, run," my mom screamed, coming out of the ditch.

I ran, as fast as I could, but there wasn't a chance. At that moment a miracle of God took place. That was what saved my little brother and gave me something good to remember all of my life. Not all people are mean; and miracles do happen when someone risks his life to help someone else. Maybe that is the only time they ever happen. A man—perhaps he was German, maybe Polish, I don't know—saw what was happening and ran toward us. He was a big man and looked strong. I saw him stop directly in front of the charging horses. Then, at the last second, he jumped to one side and grabbed the nearest horse around the neck. In an instant, he was halfway on the horse, grabbed the reins and fell back to earth, pulling with such strength as to force the horses' heads high in the air. They would either stop or have their necks broken and the bits cut through their jaws. After dragging the man a short way, they came to a prancing stop.

My little brother's screams changed to sobs, and he dropped to the ground and raced back to my mom. Throwing his arms around her neck, he hugged her with all his strength. I ran to the man. He was standing there smiling, but didn't say a word as he handed me the reins. I took the leather straps and looked back to make sure everything was all right. Little Egon was clinging to my mom as though he would never let go. When I turned around, the man was gone. I never saw him again.

During the short time all of this happened, the planes were gone. What they had done to us was bad. Some of our people had been killed, many had been wounded and everyone was frightened. Strange as it was, the most terrified were the horses. Those that were dead could be cut out of harness, but the injured animals were thrashing and screaming just like people, only much louder. We had started out as a village, but discovered how quickly trouble can turn things into survival of individuals.

"We're not getting off the wagon any more, no matter what happens," my mom said, when we finally got rolling after the long delay. It was good that she had made up her mind about staying on the wagon because two days later that decision saved our lives.

"It is no good," Stasczak said to me in Polish. "The Russians will come again in planes or in tanks." He shook his head in dismay. "I will do better by myself." He handed me the reins and jumped from the wagon. "Goodbye," he said, and headed off across the fields.

The rest of that day, I drove looking more at the sky than at the road. The planes could come so quickly and the heavy, gray clouds provided good cover. All we had as a warning was the sound of their motors and that wasn't much. Every sudden noise put a lump of fear in my throat so big I couldn't swallow. Like Stasczak, all I wanted to do was jump from the wagon and run. My little brother kept asking if the planes would come back and we sat closer and closer together. The day was long and our way was slow.

"Can we ride with you?" It was late afternoon that day. I looked down to see a young man and woman about the same age walking beside us. The man was looking past me and toward my mom. "I can help drive and take care of the horses," he said. He motioned toward the young woman. "We've been walking a long time and she's pretty tired."

My mom didn't hesitate. The two of them didn't have anything except the clothes on their back. "Stop the wagon," she told me.

I was glad to have them. Stasczak had been a big help in driving and taking care of the horses. I always liked driving, but this was different. The ice and constant need to listen and watch for planes made me eager to have help. I could tell by the look on my mom's face that she was pleased to have another man with us. As it so happened, the stranger was good with horses. When the road was real bad, and other wagons were slipping into the ditch, he would jump out and either lead the horses, talking to them all the time, or push on the side of the wagon to hold it on a steady course. With his help, we managed to keep going.

As early winter darkness came, the people in the wagons ahead of us began turning into any place that would offer shelter. It seemed that most of the farmhouses were deserted. By that time, I was more tired than I had ever been; and despite my dad's big fur coat, I was numb with cold. Even then, I didn't want to stop. As more wagons left the road, we began to make a little better time. Thoughts of planes and cover of darkness made me anxious to keep going.

"The horses are getting tired," the stranger told me, but loud enough for my mom to hear. That was all he said.

It wasn't hard to see that our animals were nearing exhaustion. They had to have food and rest. Passing a large farmhouse, I turned in, following several other wagons. Quickly, we had unharnessed the horses and fed them from our supplies. When the stranger and I went into the house, my mom had already made our beds on the floor and was laying out some food.

"There is no chance for us to reach Germany traveling this slowly," the stranger said to my mom as we sat on the blankets, eating bread and sausage. I felt my eyes grow bigger as the familiar lump of fear clutched my throat. He had said exactly what I had been so fearfully thinking, but struggling not to believe. The stranger looked steadfastly at my mom. "We've got to go faster." He spoke slowly with great emphasis, trying his best to make her understand the urgency for speed. "The Russians, at best, are just a few days behind us." He pounded one fist into the other. "When they catch us, it's going to be bad." The man lowered his voice and spoke so softly I could hardly hear him. "Especially for her." He nodded toward the young woman who was holding baby Charlotte. "We're not going to make it," he said again, all choked with desperation. "The wagons are just too slow on these winter roads and the Russians are coming in tanks."

I could tell by the look on my mom's face that she was thinking real hard. "What do you think we should do?" she asked.

The stranger, apparently too nervous to stay sitting, stood up. Holding an old cap in both hands, he never took his eyes off my mom's face. "You take one of your horses and we'll take the other one," he pleaded. "That's our only hope. Without the wagon being blocked every time someone goes into the ditch or a horse falls, we stand a chance of outrunning the Russians."

My mom didn't answer right away. She looked at baby Charlotte, sound asleep in the girl's arms, then over at my little brother and finally at me. It was a hard decision to make. "No," she told him in that way which ended the idea. "We have to stay with the wagon."

The young man's face showed his deep disappointment. He looked at the woman and gave a little shrug of his shoulders. Maybe she was his wife, maybe just a friend. I didn't know, but felt badly as they walked away. They were doing what they needed to do and my mom did what she thought best for all of us. The young man was of military age, and if caught by the Russians, would probably be shot. From what my dad's cousin, Benjamin Stadel, had told us, the Russians were taking no prisoners. Women found a different kind of trouble that was as bad, if not worse. I glanced at my mom. I could tell that she really wanted to help. But, the chances of baby Charlotte, even my little brother surviving a wild horseback ride across the winter land of Poland were not good. While our wagon was slow, it was our only shelter and home. More than that, it was our only connection with all we had ever known.

"Bruno." I awakened to find my mom shaking my shoulder. For a minute I was all mixed up. I had finally gotten warm and the bed felt so good. It was still dark and seemed as though I had just gone to sleep. "Come on, Bruno. Wake up." She wouldn't let me settle back into the warm blankets. "We've got to get ready."

I rolled over and looked around. We were the first to awaken, but other people, as if waiting for a signal, began stirring. Someone lit a kerosene lamp and little children began whimpering as their mothers got them dressed. I finished pulling on my boots and didn't say anything. I had liked Stasczak, and he had been a big help. At the same time, he was Polish. Fleeing across his native land with Germans while being pursued by Russians must have given him many fearful and contradictory thoughts. If, as most of us were thinking, the Russians were to catch us, it might go double bad for him. So, I understood his leaving. Deep down, I felt that he had done the right thing separating from us and staying in his own country. That left just four of us and perhaps that was also best. At least, it was just my family.

I remembered the young couple from the previous day. They must have walked beside our horses as they left. How simple for them to have stolen our animals and left us stranded. That must have taken indescribable courage. When everything was so wrong, those two young people did what was so right.

"Have you two boys got your money?" My mom, holding baby Charlotte close to keep her warm and with my little brother tightly sitting against her in the wagon, looked sternly at us. I had been driving since dawn and my stomach was growling. She sounded so serious that I forgot about being hungry. I quickly reached into the right pocket of my dad's big coat and pulled out my roll of money. It was more than I had seen in my whole life.

"We're not rich," my mom had told Egon and me two days before, when we left our farm, "but I have been saving every reichsmark that I could." Then she took all the money she had and divided it three ways. "Now," she said, "if we should get separated, this money will help us get back together." She had watched us as we tucked the money into our safest pockets. Then, to make sure that we understood exactly what she was saying, she had knelt down and looked us right in the eyes. "The Russians don't like rich people. You remember that. If they should catch us, throw the money away before they see it."

Being told to throw all that money away sure made me unhappy. But, thoughts of what the Russians might do to any German with a large sum of money in his pocket left me no choice. Asked for his money, my little brother began to search, but couldn't find it. Pretty soon his hands were flying from one pocket to the other.

"How can you throw it away if you can't find it?" my mom asked harshly. "The Russians will find it quick enough if they catch you," she said.

Mention of the dreaded Russians caused my little brother to start sobbing, and if possible, looking even harder. The heavy clothing tightly bundled about him didn't help. Finally, under his coat in an inside pocket, he found his roll of money. "I got it," he said sniffling.

"Now put it where you can find it," my mom told him, a little softer. Then she took her handkerchief, wiped away his tears and pulled him close. "It will be all right." She put an arm around his shoulders. "We must be prepared for whatever comes."

We drove all the long, cold hours of daylight. The caravan stretched along the road like a dirty white thread being slowly pulled through a tattered cloth. We constantly watched and listened for planes, but even the fierce danger of another air attack could not overcome the dull hours of plodding mile after mile. Late that afternoon, we passed through a deserted German village. Some Polish people had moved in, but were unsure of themselves since they could not believe that the once invincible German army was really defeated. For the time being, they didn't know what to, but remained friendly to us. There never had been good relations between the Russians and the Poles, so their future was about as dark as our own.

As we had done the night before, we stopped at a deserted house when it was too dark to go on. After helping my mom make our bed on the floor and eating some supper, I began looking around. The house had several rooms, as well as an upstairs. Three or four families had stopped along with us and were in the process of getting settled. Seeing them busy making beds and fixing food caused me to feel good. I even felt an attraction for the old house and just knew there were places to be explored and treasure to be found. I looked down at my little brother. He was all curled up in the blankets to get warm and was almost asleep. My mom was busy talking to some of the women. So, at the right minute, I vanished off the blanket and through the open door that led upstairs. The old steps creaked and groaned beneath my feet. Even though some of the lamplight made its way up the stairs, it was still darker than I wanted. But, I was determined. Groping step by step, I reached the top and stood, looking down what seemed to be a long hall. There was a small window straight ahead. By the cold wind coming down the hall, the glass must have been broken. At least it let in all the moonlight it could. From what I could see, there was a door on each side. Walking softly to the one on the right, I stood for a long minute, making sure there wasn't anyone in that room. The only sound was my own breathing. That was so loud anyone on the other side would have heard me. Finally, courage up, I opened the door and stepped inside. Immediately a strange rustling across the floor brought sudden terror, causing me to become as rigid as a door. That something grabbed at my legs and held on! I gripped the knob hard and forced myself to look down. A large piece of crumpled paper had been caught in the draft when I opened the door, and it wrapped itself around my legs. I swallowed the lump in my throat and kicked it aside. Except for a three-legged chair with no back and that paper ghost, the room was empty. There had to be more than this, I thought, and went across the hall.

Often I have wondered about my feelings and how they give me messages. I hadn't been in this house before and yet I knew there was something upstairs that I would like. The message was so strong I would have gone up there even if that old newspaper had been a real ghost. Sure enough, as soon as I opened the other door, I knew it was there. My heart pounding, I saw the dim outline of what appeared to be a chest of drawers. The excitement of what I was going to find bubbled so much inside of me that I was in another world. As if I knew what I was doing, I pulled open a drawer and there was a small box. I had found my special treasure!

Returning to the better light of the hall, I opened the box. Then I really caught my breath. There they were, row upon row of shiny, black swastika pins. They were really something. Since the people who had lived there were gone, never to return, I felt as though I could take them without it being stealing. First, though, I put a lot of them across the front of my cap and on my coat. Sticking the box in my pocket, I went downstairs to bed feeling extra good. I didn't get a chance to show my mom my wonderful treasure before I went to sleep.

We had been in the caravan since dawn and it had just become light enough to see where we were going.

"Bruno! What have you done?" My mom's sharp voice of disapproval carried the same edge as her spanking voice. That took all the fun out of things and ruined your whole day. "Do you want to get us all shot by the Russians?" she shouted at me in that same voice. She reached over and began jerking the swastikas off my cap and coat and threw them into the snow. "Where did you get those things?"

I tried to explain, but like grown ups, they ask questions and don't want any answers. Their own thoughts stop them from listening. I took off my cap and threw away the last of the pins. She saw the tears in my eyes and that was an answer she could understand.

"If the Russians catch us and see those things, they'll kill us for sure." Her face was grim, but her voice was soft. She straightened my cap and touched my face. Then we both smiled as I brought the box of swastikas out of my pocket, showed her, and threw it into the snow.

I hadn't thought about the crosses as a symbol of the Nazi Party. To me, they were just fun and something mysterious to have. Here again was something about adults I didn't understand. They seldom look on anything for what it is, but for what they have made it. I liked the swastikas because they were shiny and there was something special about all those arms that went round and round. Right then, while I was throwing my treasure into the snow, I made a promise to myself. I would never become like adults.

A short time after getting rid of the swastikas, the road we were travelling cut through a small woodland. We had been on the same road for three days. During the early morning, we had heard gunfire, sometimes far away; sometimes it seemed to be just in back of us. More and more we felt the Russians were close. It is that woodland I will always remember. As we drove beneath the trees, a roar of heavy machines swelled from behind us. All at once the people began shouting, "Pull over. Get over. Stop the wagons." Everyone was excited and began yelling to each other.

I drove to the edge of the road and stopped. Climbing to the side of the wagon, I looked back. It was then that I saw Russian tanks coming down the road with soldiers sitting atop. Seeing that really made me scared. Jumping back into the wagon, I looked at my mom. Her face was white, and her lips were pressed into a real thin line. The enemy had caught us!

The tanks were even bigger and more frightening as they thundered by our wagon. When several had gone by, they suddenly stopped. The presence of such big machines made the horses uneasy. I kept a firm grip on the reins, watching everything at the same time. Each tank held between fifteen and twenty soldiers carrying rifles. I watched, open-eyed, as they jumped to the ground, their guns held ready to fire. It was at that minute that many of our people became panic-stricken. We had been frightened by thoughts of the Russians catching us. Now they had. They were coming toward us with guns. It was more than a lot of the people could take. Jumping from their wagons, many began running across a little strip of snow toward the trees. I looked at my mom. Everything was happening so fast that I didn't know what to do. It seemed everybody was screaming and running. I was as scared as they were, but I remembered my mom telling us two days earlier, "No matter what happens after this, we stay on the wagon."

Before my mom could tell me anything, some of the soldiers dashed around our wagon and began shooting the women and children running for the woods. Their screams of fear instantly changed into cries of terror and moans of pain as they fell, bleeding, into the snow. It was over almost as soon as it began. All the people who had tried to run away were on the ground. Those who were not seriously wounded made their way back to the wagons. My mom, sometime during the shooting, had reached across and was holding my arm. She was making sure that I didn't get off the wagon. She didn't need to worry. I was too scared to move. Besides, there was nothing that I could do. Although, there was something she could do—pray. Her prayer, one that I had heard before, sounded so clear, in that strange silence, when the rifle fire stopped.

# Journey Back

Not all of the soldiers had shot at the people attempting to run away. Some walked between the tanks and wagons, carefully looking us over. One of the soldiers came toward us. Earlier, even before the tanks came, we had thrown our money into the snow. Seeing that soldier coming sure made me glad my mom had made me get rid of all those swastikas. The soldier began talking to us in Russian. We didn't understand. He was a young kid, not much older than I was. He looked us over very carefully, then walked around to the back of our wagon. When he saw our little bit of furniture, the boxes and that we were just three kids and a woman, he turned toward the wagon directly in front of us.

I watched him walk away. There was something about him, maybe the pistol strapped about his waist, maybe the soldierly way he walked, that made me think he was a lot older than his birthdays. Pistol in hand, he lifted the canvas on the wagon and looked in. From where I was seated, I could see over his shoulder and see what he saw. I felt that old lump of fear choke me again. Rifles and hand-guns, enough to equip a small army, were in the wagon. My mom saw them also. We had been as scared as we could get, or so I had thought. But, when we saw the guns, we just got more scared. There is no limit to fear, I tearfully discovered. I heard her gasp as we sat frozen to the seat, waiting for something dreadful to happen.

While the young soldier was looking at the guns, the two old men who had been driving the wagon sauntered toward our horses. They moved slowly and yet I got the distinct feeling they were trying to make it appear they were with us. The young soldier knew better. He turned and strode briskly toward them, speaking harshly in Russian. Reaching the two men, he holstered his gun; and using both hands, jerked open their heavy civilian overcoats. They were both wearing uniforms!

No longer able to hold my breath, I gulped in air as I recognized what they were wearing. The two old men were not a part of the regular army, but members of Hitler's last fading miracle known as the Volkssturm. The Fuehrer had the "inspired" idea, as his kingdom, built to last a thousand years, was crumbling before twenty years had elapsed, that when the Russians came, the German people—all that were left—would rise up against the hated enemy in a great self-sacrificing storm, a people's storm. Actually, it was a desperate plan poorly conceived and without a chance of succeeding. The old, very young and crippled, armed with cast-off guns, could not stop the onslaught of Russian tanks and trained soldiers.

I looked at the two old men. They seemed so helpless before the Russian soldier. Why they hadn't gotten rid of the guns and uniforms I'll never know. There had been time. By the increasing sounds of gunfire, we had known the Russians were close. Perhaps the two old soldiers were under orders and their acceptance of discipline was too strong. Perhaps, like adults often do, they had just talked about what would be best to do and did nothing. Now it was too late!

The Russian soldier, when he saw the uniforms, said, "Volkssturm," followed by several German swear words aimed at the two old men. He, at least, knew one side of the German language. Then, without hesitation, he drew his pistol and shot one of them. The old man did an awkward, backward jump and fell arms outstretched, into the snow. He must have died instantly.

The other man held out his hands, as if to protect himself. He began to plead. "Don't shoot me. Don't shoot me." Seeing the gun being aimed at him and the look on the Russian soldier's face, his plea changed to a prayer. "God in heaven…"

That was all I heard as the soldier shot the old man in the chest. He didn't fall. He just stood there, a stunned look on his face. The young soldier fired again. This time he crumpled into the snow and didn't move. His eyes were still open and seemed to be looking up at me. The Russian, perhaps seeing something that I didn't, went over and put his gun to the man's head and fired a third time.

The young soldier didn't even look up as we sat terrified on the wagon. He bent down and went through the pockets of the dead men. Taking their billfolds, he quickly looked through them. Apparently reichsmarks were no good to him and he didn't find anything else of value so he threw them into our wagon. There was something, though, that he did want—the dead men's boots. Lifting each leg, he jerked off their high leather boots and tucked them under his arm. Without paying any further attention to them or to us, he disappeared in the direction of the tanks.

After the young soldier was gone, I couldn't stop looking at the two old men. The one, his face turned toward our wagon, still had his eyes open. Did people always die with their eyes open? Were they really dead? For an instant, I thought they moved and that I could see them breathing. My eyes raced from one fallen form to the other. The more I watched, the more I was convinced they were alive. Something forced me to look at their feet. It was then that I accepted the fact that they were dead. The soldier had pushed up each pant leg to take the boots, but he had left their socks. It was their unmoving feet dressed in those ragged gray socks that took away all doubt.

I looked over at my mom as I felt tears start to flow. I was still scared, but it was something else that made me cry. It wasn't even the death of the two old men. It was over in an instant, but the memory would last forever.

My mom was looking at the Russian soldiers as they milled around the wagons ahead of us. "There is nothing we can do," she said looking at me. "We will stay where we are." Then I heard her praying.

We sat for a long time. Every so often we heard cries of the wounded. Several bodies lay unmoving at the edge of the woods. "Turn your wagons around and go back where you came from," a Russian officer striding briskly along side our wagon, shouted at us in German. After he had given orders for us to return to our farms,

103

he climbed onto one of the tanks. In a few minutes, with a tremendous roar, the Russian column moved ahead. Doing as we had been told, our captured caravan began the journey back. Turning the wagon, I found it hard to leave the two old men in the snow. Even the faint hope that we could outrun the Russians had been a strong force within us. All of that was over. Perhaps, in a tragic way, it was fitting that our part in the Great War should end with the foolish actions of the two old men and their helpless murder. That seemed to be in keeping with what war is and what it produces.

The road back was just as cold, just as slippery, but lonelier. At least in the going, we had the feeling of a group of people traveling together. Now it was much different. Our lives had been taken over. In a way, that had been our lot since leaving Romania. But when you can mingle even the smallest of hope for the future with the hardest of times in the present, life can still have that upward look. Now our only way seemed to be down. A big part of that downward way was the terrible fear constantly gripping us—that of not knowing when something was going to happen next, only that it would be bad. We sat huddled on the wagon, watching Russian soldiers flow by us in armored cars, riding horses and even walking. The sky was heavy with a solid blanket of gray. Flakes of snow whirled through the air and struck against our faces. Despite all that had happened, I clung to the one belief—that if we could just stay together, we would make it. My mind jumped from thought to thought, but always came back to the basic feeling that separation would be the end of us. Maybe that way of thinking was so strong because I had heard my dad tell my mom, "As long as we are together, everything will be all right."

The strength that we drew from each other gave support to what I was thinking. The dreadfulness of what surrounded us on that road, if we had not had each other, was so awful we would have been consumed. Dead bodies, twisted and grotesque, lay alongside the road and in the ditch. Dead horses with bloated bellies and legs sticking into the air seemed almost as bad. I knew that everyone in those slow moving wagons felt as I did. How easy it is to forget that people are really the same. They get cold, they hurt, and they die just like it has always been. At the same time, there are those times when survival means that you do what has to be done. Some of the dead were from our caravan. To drive away and leave them behind was more than we could bear; yet it had to be. The ground was frozen and there was no time or way for a service of any kind. It was necessary for us to discard our dead much as life discards the body when it can no longer serve. Just when I thought I couldn't stand it any longer, I felt my mom's arm reach around my shoulder and hold me tight. Our horses were pulling the wagon, but it was my mom who was holding us together.

After hours of slow travel, we ate some bread and sausage. We had been so concerned about what was happening around us, that there had been no thought of hunger. Food tasted good once I forced some into my mouth. It suddenly occurred to me that no Russians had passed our wagon for some time. I watched more keenly, wondering what the change might bring. There had been uneasy feelings within me when I realized they were no longer flowing by us. Their absence meant we were at the mercy of the Polish people who had understandably hated the years of German occupation. I didn't know which was worse.

As the long afternoon became the cold, gray of evening, I saw a Russian cavalry unit coming toward us. I looked at my mom. She had seen them. I didn't know what to feel at the sight of more Russians.

Sight of the cavalry made me remember wild talk about Russian horse soldiers riding among people, especially women and children, cutting off their heads with quick slashes of sharp, curved swords. Russians tanks and soldiers, Polish people and now Russian Cavalry—it all presented a lesson that the greater danger is the one nearest.

As the Russian cavalry got closer, despite our fears, I was mindful of the terrible condition of their horses. The once proud animals were lean with sunken flanks and walked with heads hanging down. Both of our horses, even though they had been badly used for four days, were in far better shape. Apparently one of the Russians thought the same thing. He rode over to where I had stopped our wagon and began talking to us in Russian. At least he wasn't shouting or swinging a sword. He was just sitting on his horse, one of the poorest I had ever seen, and talking even friendly to us. He talked several minutes, and then a look of frustration came to his face. I was answering him in Polish. He didn't understand me any better than I understood him. For a very good reason, I didn't speak German.

Without saying any more, the soldier quickly dismounted. In a few minutes he had our best horse out of harness and under his saddle. As we sat helplessly watching, relieved that he was only taking our horse, he buckled his worthless mount into our harness. Swinging into the saddle with the flair of an experienced horseman, he gave us a snappy salute and rode off.

After he had gone, I jumped to the ground and examined the horse. It had been so badly used that the poor animal was ready to drop. I lifted the front leg. The shoe was so thin and bent that it was impossible to twist in the metal studs needed for walking on ice. For a long minute, I stood looking down the road at the vanishing Russians. I was not conscious of anything else as a flood of thoughts and feelings broke loose inside of me. I felt no hatred toward the soldier who had taken our horse. In fact, he had been rather nice to us. Sure, he had taken our horse, but he hadn't mistreated us. And, he had taken the time and effort to put his old horse in our harness. Maybe I was so scared and so many bad things had happened, that I could no longer determine what was right or wrong. When you expect the very worst, anything else seems kind of good.

It was nearly dark when I got back in the wagon. As soon as I started the horses, I knew it would be impossible to keep going. The old horse could barely walk and promptly fell down. I got out and with a lot of effort prodded it into getting up. There was nobody to help. By this time all the other wagons had left the road and we were by ourselves. It was either go or freeze, and we weren't doing much of the going. That was when we saw the first of the Polizia. Polizia were Polish men who had made themselves into policemen by fastening white bands around the upper part of their right arms. Three of them suddenly appeared in the road, blocking our way. Two were carrying heavy clubs and a third was holding a large manure fork.

"Hey, you Germans. Stop that wagon," one of them yelled at us. His voice was harsh with profanities.

Stopping the wagon wasn't hard since the horses would rather stop than go anyway. I reined in and told my mom what the man had said. From the frightened look on her face, she already knew.

"Get down you——Germans," the same man said. "All of you."

I told my mom what we had been told to do, without repeating the swear words. Somehow, those ugly words sound the same in all languages. After we got down, the man carrying the manure fork came to where we were standing and looked us over real close. When he had finished glaring at my mom, holding baby Charlotte, and at my little brother, he stood for a long minute staring at me. Then he did something that was really frightening. He moved his big fork so it was just a few inches from my face. That was all I saw when I looked up at him. Some feelings can never be put into words. The feelings bursting inside my chest when that Polish man stared at me through those ugly prongs were feelings of pure terror.

The man muttered something in Polish that I was too scared to hear, and got on our wagon with the other two men. They drove off and left us standing in the snow. Through the gathering darkness, I watched our wagon leave. I was scared and I didn't know what we were going to do, but I had one bitter thought of happiness. I was happy that the Russian had taken our best horse. The Polizia can just have that old horse, I thought to myself, and I hope it falls down!

"Come on Bruno," my mom said. "We'll freeze to death if we just stand here."

Holding my little brother's hand, with my mom carrying baby Charlotte, the three of us began walking the dark road. During all that had happened, Egon hadn't cried or said a word, even though he knew the Polish language, at least as well as I. "Bruno," Egon said, after we had walked quite a way. "Did you hear what that man with the fork said to you?"

"No," I told him. "I was too scared."

"Do you want to know?" he asked. "I can tell you what he said."

Egon was almost five years old. By something in his voice, something more than what I had heard before, he seemed older. "Sure," I told him. At the same time, I wasn't overly anxious to think about those dreadful minutes. "What did the man say?"

Egon gripped my hand a little tighter. "He said that if you had been a little bigger, he would have run that fork right through you."

That news really shocked me. I didn't say anything for a long time. "They're gone now," I finally said. We lowered our heads against the cold wind and walked in silence. That's what made the Russian soldier, who took our horse, seem rather nice. He had done what he felt he had to do and was kind about it. The three Polish men did what they wanted and were mean about it. So often life does not consist of isolated events, but grows in meaning by what comes after. In many ways, what happens never stops happening.

After we had trudged through the snow for what seemed to be hours, I looked down at my little brother. The road was filled with ruts cut by passing wagons that were now frozen into slippery ridges. Every so often one of us would slip and fall. I was very proud of Egon. I knew he was scared and frozen stiff, but he walked right along, taking steps almost as big as I did. The night wind whistled down the darkened road; and the later that it got, the colder it became.

"We've got to find shelter," my mom said. By this time, the thought of just lying down in the road and going to sleep didn't seem bad. "Watch for a light," my mom told us. She was thinking what I had been thinking for some time. We didn't stand any chance on the road, but what kind of people would we find at one of the houses? Baby Charlotte hadn't been changed in a long time. Every so often the condition she was in flashed through my mind. I had helped my mom by sometimes changing her diaper, so I knew all about that. I also knew that her clothing was frozen on the outside and must be starting to freeze inside. We were really looking for a light as our last hope. Then my mom grabbed my arm. "Over there," she shouted all excited. "There's a light."

I had to look twice, but sure enough there was a little glimmer of light off to the side. We began running and stumbling toward the house. I felt the cold shake me as we ran, much like a dog might shake a rat. Reaching the porch, I went up and knocked on the door. After a little while, I heard some shuffling and scraping inside. Then the door slowly opened and a Polish man, looking big and shadowy in the yellow lamplight, stood looking down at me. "Will you help us?" I asked. My words had that funny ridge because of the cold that had put such a shaking ache in my throat and back.

There was what seemed like a long wait. The man didn't say anything. My mom, holding baby Charlotte wrapped in a sling around her neck in front of her and holding my little brother's hand, stood off the porch behind me. I was sure that he saw only me standing there. "What do you want?" he asked rubbing his chin. While his Polish voice was rough, it did not sound unkind.

"We've got to go back to Stefanov," I told him, through my teeth, which were chattering so badly, I could hardly talk. "We need something to eat and a place to sleep."

A woman came and peeked over his shoulder at me. "Oh, he's just a boy," she said. They must have been good people since I heard her tell the man, "He could stay in the cowbarn."

By this time, the tall man had seen my mom. He stood there as though he was thinking real hard. At least he didn't shut the door on us. "All right," he said, agreeing with the woman. The tone of his voice made it his decision. "There's the two boys, a baby and their mother."

The woman rose on her toes and peered through the darkness at us. "Are you hungry?" she asked nicely. The sight of Charlotte caused the woman to forget about boundaries that so often separate people. She immediately set about to help us.

We were treated well. They gave us some food, milk for the baby and allowed us to sleep with the cows. The straw was clean and the shed was warm. We had been people of the farm all of our lives so the feeling of soft straw and the warm scent of cows were like being home. After we got ourselves settled in the barn, helped by the friendly glow of a kerosene lantern the Polish man had hung on the wall for us, my mom began changing baby Charlotte's diaper. She spread the wet clothes out to dry. That was when I discovered where she had hidden her wedding ring.

"Here Bruno, hold this," she told me.

I couldn't see what it was, as it was so small. She carefully placed something in my hand. It was cold and wet. That something was her wedding ring that she had hidden in the diaper. I hadn't even noticed it was missing from her finger. We had been told many times to get rid of all our money and especially any gold watches or rings before the Russians caught us. The thought of hiding her ring in a dirty diaper struck me as funny and I began to laugh. Even my mom grinned and laughed with me. My little brother couldn't figure what was so funny, but he wasn't going to be left out. He started laughing too. I just knew that my mom was the smartest person in the whole world. And so that day, which had been so tragic for us, ended in a happy way. We went to sleep on warm straw with our stomachs full of potatoes and very thankful for what we had.

The next morning the Polish people gave us some more potatoes and small pieces of dark bread. In the early morning cold, we returned to the road and began walking. "Just stay right beside me," my mom ordered Egon and me. It had been terrible when we saw people killed or lying dead alongside the road from the safety of our wagon. Now we walked beside them, trying not to look, but we always did. Death is much more acceptable from a distance; but something inside always makes us get closer. The grotesque, mutilated bodies of men, women and children scattered along the ditches were Germans who had been killed by Russian and Polish people. The Russians were moving across Poland, striking wherever they found resistance, but worse than the Russians were the Poles. They were taking revenge. Some of the terrible sights were in a small village. One man was tied to a pole with a large manure fork sticking in his belly. He had been dead for some time. We kept walking, trying to look Polish, trying not to look German, and trying to be anything but ourselves, or where we were, or what we were doing.

For three long days we walked, covering the same distance traveled in our wagon. We were blessed. No one bothered us; and each night we were taken in. Maybe it was the way my mom chose the houses. She had special feelings about that sort of thing. Then it could have been the sad way we looked and having baby Charlotte. Maybe those people were also tired of killing. That wears out too.

It was a terribly mixed-up time with people going in all directions. We Germans, mostly women and children, were under orders to return to our homes. The Poles, many of the men with bands around their arms claiming to be Polizia, were grasping every opportunity to regain what they considered to be theirs, along with a good measure of revenge. The Russian soldiers, victorious, were riding across the land, eager to crush any force that dared to oppose them. It was a time when knowing who you were was highly questionable; and whether you would live to see tomorrow, was the most questionable of all.

# The Homecoming

"Look Bruno." Egon tugged at my arm and pointed to a large farmhouse we both recognized. "We're almost home." His face was shining and he was happy at the thought of being back. I started to say something, but stopped. No need to take away his happiness any sooner than necessary. From what we had been seeing, there was every possibility our homecoming might not be all that he was expecting.

In keeping with what I feared, the bad things did not wait until we got to our farm. For the last few miles, we had begun to see some of the Polish people we had known. Many times on our way back, my little brother and I had talked to people in the Polish language. We spoke so naturally that strangers probably took us for natives. As we got closer to home, people knew we were Germans and that got us into trouble.

"Hey you. Where're you going?" We were less than half a mile from our farmhouse when we met Jozef. He was much different than the Polish boy I had known ever since we moved to Stefanov. He came up close to me and stared into my eyes with a mean look on his face. "You," he said sticking out his lower lip as if I had done something to make him mad. "I asked where are you going?"

I could feel the knots twisting in my stomach. He was a big boy. "We have to go back to our farm," I said, and tried to walk around him. He moved over and stopped me.

"Back to your farm," he said with a sneer. "You don't have a farm any more." He glared at my mom. "You don't have anything." The boy spit the words at us like we had gotten what we deserved.

I didn't say anything. There wasn't anything to say. He was right. We didn't have any rights in Poland under Russian domination. We had learned that the hard way. His harsh words merely helped us to accept what was to come. I looked at my mom. She was exhausted. We had taken turns carrying baby Charlotte, but she had done most of it. Little Egon was so tired he could hardly stay on his feet, but he hadn't complained, nor had he cried very much. Again I tried to go on. One way to avoid trouble or prevent it from growing is to keep your mouth shut and walk off, especially when the trouble is bigger than you are.

Jozef wasn't about to let us go. He moved in front of me again. "That's a pretty nice coat," he said, looking at my dad's big winter coat I was wearing. It had fur on the inside and was extra warm. He suddenly grabbed the front of it and jerked me close. "I think it would fit me better than you," he said into my face. He pulled back the collar and rubbed the soft fur. "Take it off and give it to me."

I felt like running. He was big, but I knew that if it were only the two of us, I could outrun him. He must have read what was on my mind because he held on to my coat, the look on his face daring me to make a move. I glanced at my mom. Even though she couldn't understand what he was saying, his actions made it obvious what he wanted. Slowly, I unbuttoned my coat and gave it to him. The cold wind whipped through my light clothing, but for the moment I was too angry to notice.

Jozef put my coat on over his thin jacket. Even then, he wasn't through with me. "Now your boots," he said.

"You can't wear my boots," I told him. "They're too small for you." I started to say, for his big feet, but didn't want to cause any more trouble than I was having. Before being drafted, my dad had taken me to the boot maker and had the boots made just to fit my feet. They were something special to me, but not as much as my dad's coat.

Jozef grabbed my arm. "You want something bad to happen to you?" he asked.

I wondered what he thought was happening to me. He drew back his fist. There wasn't much choice, so I sat down in the snow and took off my boots. At least he didn't take my socks. He stuck my boots under his arm. Now you can go," he said as if doing us a favor. We walked on. "Stay out of my way," he called after us, "or it will go bad for you."

The last distance to our farm was long. Without my dad's coat, and with no shoes, I felt every sharp edge of the winter wind. We walked as fast as we could. Then, a short step from being frozen stiff, we turned down the short road to our house.

"Come on Bruno," little Egon said as he saw our house. "Let's run."

Nothing looked so good as the sight of our home. Off we went trying to run, too tired and cold and hungry even to stand, and yet there we were running and stumbling toward the house. Some things fade and even disappear beneath the press and changes of life. Certain things, often unconsciously, grow brighter and brighter. The sight of our new house and warm barn that dad had built were just like I remembered. My eyes seemed to feed upon them, as though I had a special hunger. I felt their welcome, but also knew that we had been gone a long time. Actually, we had been gone six days, but our journey started when we left Romania. In all of my life, I never had such mixed feelings as when we half-ran and half-stumbled down that short road leading to our home. I no longer knew who we were. We didn't have anything; we didn't belong anywhere; and we were frightened of everyone. As I was discovering, it is impossible to know yourself when today is so different from yesterday, and you just know that tomorrow is going to be worse.

Reaching the house, I hurried up on the porch and knocked on the door. I couldn't help but think of the thousands of times I had gone bursting in. Now, I stood and waited. My mom and baby Charlotte came up on the porch behind us. The door opened and our old neighbor, Mr. Sobczak stood looking down at me. He looked the same. That was reassuring. In that instant as we stood looking at each other, the crazy thought came to me how often my mom had told me to wash after coming from their house. They were not exactly clean and now we were about to ask if we could live with them. "We're back," was all I could think to say. The words tumbled through my chattering teeth so quivering I couldn't understand myself.

Mr. Sobczak smiled. Even if he couldn't understand my chattering words, he could see the dreadful condition we were in. "Come in. Come in," he said and ushered us into the warm house. "We have moved in, but you are welcome to stay with us." It was only fair that they should be living in our house. Some of our land had been theirs before German occupation officials issued it to us.

We staggered into what might have been Mr. and Mrs. Sobczak's old house, the way it was cluttered. Their living style was the same, but I was sure thankful they were still the same friendly, outgoing people who didn't use much soap, but had a great love for people.

"Can we have some warm water?" my mom asked Mrs. Sobczak as soon as we came through the door. Without waiting, she laid Charlotte on the table and began peeling off her blanket and clothes. There was a hurried intentness about her that scared me. I had seen the snow on the baby's blanket and knew an icy crust had formed on her clothes inside the blanket. I hadn't realized that water, her own and from the outside, had frozen all the way to her small body. Our poor little one had become wrapped in ice. She was only a step away from dying. "Not that warm," my mom told Mrs. Sobczak, as she brought a large pan of steaming water.

I watched and shook as the cold deep inside of me shivered its way to the surface. The two women hurried about the table, mixing warm water with cold until it was more on the cool side. When it was just right, my mom began bathing Charlotte. She looked bad. Egon hadn't said a word, but stood with big eyes not missing a thing that was happening. After what seemed the longest time, and after several changes of water, baby Charlotte began crying. It was then my mom took a big cloth and began gently rubbing her. From the look on my mom's face, I knew how close we had come. That look told me everything was all right.

We lived in the house with Mr. and Mrs. Sobczak and their six children, Marianna, Henryka, Jozef, Stanislaw, Zdzislawa and Jadwiga for about a week before something bad happened. During that time, they had been good to us. They gave us some of the food we had left behind, and we got one of the bedrooms all to ourselves. For the first few days we mostly slept, trying to get rid of that awful cold which soaked up all the warmth we could get. After getting warm, we still had no desire to go outside, for fear of being caught up in what was happening. During those days I talked with Mr. and Mrs. Sobczak and played a few games with their children. That was when I made a big mistake, one that I have always remembered, regretting my stupidity.

"You know where my mom hides her wedding ring?" I asked Marianna one afternoon as we sat talking. I should have been warned by the way Marianna instantly turned her head and looked at me. I was too young, too proud of my mom, to read the warning signals suddenly written into the girl's face.

"No," she replied moving a little closer to me as though we were the best of friends. "Where does she hide it?"

I smiled at her and looked smart. "In baby Charlotte's diaper," I told her. "She has hidden it there all the time." The girl laughed with me at what a funny, but good idea it was and we went on talking.

Later, when I went into our bedroom, my mom took me by surprise. "Bruno," she asked sharply, "did you tell Maria where I've been hiding my wedding ring?"

I looked at my mom, feeling a giant sinking sensation in my stomach. A look of shame came to my face. I didn't know what to say. In fact, words wouldn't even form in my mouth. I slowly nodded. From the expression on my mom's face, I knew what had happened.

"Well, my ring is gone," she said, not in a voice to blame me, but very unhappy about what had happened. "Marianna came in and demanded that I give it to her or she would make trouble." That was all my mom said, but the loss was big, since her ring was the last thing she had which my dad had given her. I felt tears come. Me and my big mouth, I thought. Mom's silence didn't help. Harsh words or even a spanking would have been better. I found a corner to sit in and just let my terrible feelings spank my big mouth. How simple it would have been to have gotten a spanking and paid for what I had done.

"Listen," my mom said to me one afternoon about two weeks after we had arrived at the farm. We were in our bedroom. I looked at her in sudden alarm. The tone of her voice meant trouble, big trouble. She was sitting on the edge of the bed looking alert, as though something strange was happening. "Horses!" she said. I didn't hear a thing, but I knew she had. I jumped to the window. Sure enough, a troop of Russian cavalry had ridden into the farmyard. My mom and I watched through the window as the Russian officer dismounted, then ordered his men to dismount. We held our breath as the officer walked briskly toward the front door.

There was no mistaking the sharp knock that echoed through the house. My mom and I went into the front room as Mr. Sobczak opened the door. The officer, broad shouldered and commanding in appearance, stepped inside and quickly glanced around. "I am sorry to inconvenience you," he said. To my surprise, he spoke excellent German. I glanced at my mom. A slight smile came to her lips as she heard the German words. "It is necessary that I should quarter my men at your farm." He looked us over and addressed his words to my mom. "I will need a room here in the house while my soldiers will find sleeping quarters in the barn." Relaxing for a minute, he removed his cap, showing heavy, black hair. He stood at ease with cap and gloves in hand, his eyes looking all around the room, but coming back to look at my mom.

Mr. Sobczak didn't understand German, so I told him what the officer had said. We moved out of the way so he could see the house. It was obvious that he was talking to my mom and took her to be the one in charge. "I'll take that bedroom," he said pointing to the one across from ours. "And don't worry," he said, more to her than any one else, "none of my men will bother any of you."

During the next two weeks, I learned many things. First, some Russian words. The officer was very friendly and often talked with us in fluent German. He always seemed eager to answer my questions about the Russian language and about horses. He talked of everything except the war. It seemed that when he put on his cap and marched out the door, he was every inch a soldier and war was his business. When he rode at the head of his men, he made a commanding figure. But, when he came in at night, took off his cap and unbuttoned his tunic, he was done with war. He would stand in our doorway and talk of children and holidays, describing the great Russian festivals. True to what he had said, neither my mom nor the Sobczak girls were in any danger from either the officer or his men. It was as though we were wearing an unseen badge of authority. Later we, especially my mom, were to learn the terror of long, dark nights with no one to protect us.

Something else I learned without intending to do so. It was as though something inside of me was looking for answers when the rest of me didn't know enough to ask questions. My little brother and I began going outside to play after the Russians came. It was there, watching the soldiers that I became aware of the hidden force known as chain of command. It is that force, I came to understand, that creates position and boundaries, and although invisible, are more real than fences in a field. It is the controller of lives.

I also learned, during the Russian officer's brief stay, that he and his men were people. The many cruel and frightening things I had heard about Russian soldiers made them appear to be terrible demons. And yet, here was a Russian speaking to us in excellent German and protecting our lives. Fear had persuaded me to hate a people I didn't know; experience was teaching me that blind hate is a destructive force used as a weapon by warmongers.

"Auf wiedersehen." The tall Russian officer, his uniform buttoned tight, his cap square on his head and looking every way the soldier, stopped for just an instant in the doorway of our room. Outside, his men were mounted and ready to ride. As he said goodbye, he looked at my mom with a look that even I could understand and appreciate. In the midst of overwhelming fear and isolation, and the most destroying force of all, that of not knowing what was going to happen the next minute, this unknown Russian officer had created an atmosphere of respect and dignity. His eyes left my mom's face and he looked down at me. "Be brave," he said and was gone.

As the sound of horses faded, the farm seemed empty and open to danger. I realized, in the silence, how alone we were. During the past two weeks, I had gotten to know the Russian officer far beyond his name. He had smiled a lot and made jokes with my little brother and me. Outside, he didn't smile or joke. He walked among his men, inspecting them, giving quick, sharp orders that were instantly obeyed. There were times he didn't even wear a gun. That surprised me. Then, remembering my dad, I understood. Soldiers who have guns and do shooting in wartime do not have power over those guns. They are just like the guns. They wait to be used. Thoughts of my dad once again came rushing into my mind. Standing in that empty farm-yard, I missed him terribly. Even though I no longer had his big coat, it came closer to fitting that day than ever before. I saw more clearly why he never wanted to be a soldier in Hitler's army or any other army. He wasn't like a gun waiting to be used. He was a man, his own man, as Mr. Wagner had told me. He was responsible for what he did and wasn't about to surrender his life to those invisible forces that write letters, give distant orders and send others to do their killing. Maybe, when everything was considered, my mom was right about the way my dad's life on this earth had ended. He was killed by his own people.

We stayed close to the house after the Russians soldiers left. We had seen what happened to many German people. From the news that reached us, matters were getting worse, not better. It was not, I am sure, that the Russians were better people or kinder than the Poles. It was that the Russians were conquerors and they could do what they wanted. It seems that complete control creates a certain toleration, while the Poles, freed from one enemy and now caught in the force of another, felt the need for brutal revenge. In all of life, you are either looking up or looking down. It takes a lot of inner strength not to be controlled by what you are seeing.

"The wagon is here, Mrs. Reule." Mr. Sobczak stood in the doorway of our room. He spoke to my mom in a soft voice as though he was sorry about what was happening. It was early in the morning and I was still sleepy, but some Polish men had come for us. For several days we had been hearing that all German families were being placed in a war camp a few miles from the farm. We were not surprised. Already I had learned that life doesn't stand still. Our staying with the Sobczaks had all the obvious marks of one of those things you do, but not for long. In a way our leaving wasn't so bad. We no longer owned our farm and we weren't invited guests. It is difficult to be in your own home, but it isn't yours: to eat your own food, but it is given to you by someone else; and the most difficult of all, to know that something is going to happen, but you don't know what or when.

"Bruno." My mom's voice cut across my sleepy thoughts. "You thank Mr. and Mrs. Sobczak for taking us in."

As best I could, I expressed our thanks in Polish. They had been good neighbors in good times and they had been good friends in bad times. Mr. Sobczak shook my hand. There was a sad smile on his face. He didn't have to say anything. He had done all that he could for us and that speaks a lot louder than words.

Carrying our few belongings, including a little food the Sobczaks had carefully packed, and wearing an old coat along with a pair of worn-out shoes I had found, I got in the prison wagon with my family. There weren't any guards to speak of, just some Polizia. If they had guns, I didn't see them. Two or three German families were sitting in the wagon, looking grim and forsaken. There were three children about my age, but we just looked at each other. The wagon didn't have a canvas top, and the cold wind made us huddle together, much as I had seen chickens do on a cold night. We just faded into each other like snowflakes once they hit the ground. It is hard to be a person when everything, including the weather, is bigger than you are.

No one said anything as we rode along. The snow covered road was marked by frozen wagon tracks, causing us to sway as a single body when the wheels slipped from rut to rut. The fields where my dad had plowed and planted were cold white, untouched except by the whipping wind. It was as though he had never been there and I had never run down that road to meet him. The sight of growing things and the sound of laughter were gone.

When our wagon finally reached the camp, we were all numb with cold. It was not a war camp with guards and a high barbed wire fence. It was just an old farmhouse that had been designated as a holding place for about eight German families. By this time, March of 1945, all Germans who had not escaped or been killed in the attempt were being confined in such places. There were no younger men, just cripples and old men along with women and children. The Poles collected us like so many infested animals and put us in designated areas. That is where we stayed without a thought about escape. The best guards, as I sadly came to know, are not men with guns, but lack of food. There is no reason to escape because there is no place to run, and the very best reason of all, no hope.

The third night in camp, a terrible pounding on the door suddenly awakened everyone. "Thud, thud, thud." The big house shuddered in the darkness with vibrations of great force. "Open up," a man shouted, over and over, in slurred German.

One of the old men went to the door. Through the darkness, I caught a glimpse of his shuffling figure as he walked past the doorway of our crowded room. I didn't know what the outsiders wanted. By the twisting fear inside of me, I knew it was something bad. I looked around, trying to see the best I could. My mom was sitting on our bunk, staring toward the door. I couldn't see her face, but I could feel her fear. All four of us slept on the same wooden bunk with straw for a mattress and a ragged blanket over us.

As the old man opened the door, I saw a flash of light sweep across the room. Then I heard the same slurred voice, only this time speaking Russian. The old man didn't say anything. From talking with him earlier, I knew he spoke Russian. The rough voice sounded harsh and demanding. Maybe the old man was too scared, and then, maybe, he was wise enough to know there was nothing he could do to stop what was about to happen.

Pushing their way in, three Russian soldiers came clomping into our room. I heard my mom gasp as they flashed their lights on us. It was as if she already knew what they wanted. When the light shone across my mom, I saw that she was holding Charlotte tight against her breast. Then the bright light hit me in the eyes and I couldn't see for a minute. I heard the Russians seeming to argue among themselves. When I could see again, they were forcing three young girls to go with them. Two of the girls were about eighteen and twenty. They were daughters of the old man who had gone to the door. The other one was the oldest daughter of Mr. and Mrs. Mantei. She was about fifteen. No one moved to help them. Harsh circumstances teach quickly what can be done and what had best be let alone.

From the scuffling noise and crying of the girls, I could tell they had been taken into the kitchen. Then I heard sharp screams and rough Russian words that sounded like curses. After what seemed a long time, the girls came creeping back to their bunks. They lay sobbing as the soldiers staggered out the front door. The big house was silent after that, but I knew everyone was awake and darkness hid our fears and helplessness.

# Night Visitors

"It's those Polish people," the old man, who had opened the door for the soldiers, sadly told my mom the next morning.

I was playing with my little brother, but was listening carefully. The old man had been a soldier in the First World War or the "big one" as he called it. What had been done to his two daughters had made him even more stumbling and old. He was talking to my mom in a soft whisper, the way adults do when they speak of certain subjects in front of children. They forget our hearing is much better than theirs is, especially when we want to hear. "The Polish people know we have young girls over here, so they just tell the Russian soldiers to come over." The old man seemed about to weep. "That's what they do and will go right on doing."

"It's dreadful," my mom said, in that same soft, adult voice. I pretended to be busy playing. I wasn't exactly dumb about what had happened in the kitchen. I had grown up on the farm and had learned about breeding stock to produce a good herd. The only thing that bothered me was why the Russian soldiers would walk all the way to our camp on a cold night for something that wasn't very important. But, I was sure curious and did I ever listen!

The old man was quiet for a minute. His ancient, but kind face reflected the deep anguish he was feeling. "We've got to hide the girls," he said. "Once the other soldiers know..." he paused and glanced at me to make sure I was busy playing and not listening. "After what happened last night, we will have a steady stream of those swine until the girls are either killed or kill themselves." He looked very sad. "I've heard of it happening."

My mom made a little clucking sound as she nodded her head to agree. "Where would we hide them in here?" she said, looking around. "The soldiers could find them in no time."

The old man was quick to agree. "Not in here," he said. "Somewhere out there." He motioned outside. "Anywhere but in here." He pressed his lips together and nodded his head, as though agreeing with himself. "I'm sure the Russian soldiers come here without permission. If they come a night or two and don't find any girls, they might stay in town or go somewhere else."

My mom didn't answer. From the look on her face, I knew she was thinking some disturbing thoughts. "If they don't find the younger ones, they'll take the older ones." Her voice seemed accusing.

The old man's eyes snapped to her face, his bushy eyebrows puckered together over his nose, as though he had not thought of what she ventured to guess. "They might do that." He gave a little shake of his head, as if to indicate he didn't know what to do and would drop the whole idea if my mom wanted.

"The girls will need some warm clothes," she said. That was all I heard as the two of them went off to see what could be done.

That night we lay in the darkened house and waited. It was not hard to picture each family stretched out on their bunk, staring into the dark and wondering what was going to happen. The hours passed and then, the next thing I knew, it was light. The Russian soldiers had not come. I looked across the narrow distance between the bunks and saw the girls who had been taken the night before. They were sound asleep. Shortly after dark, they had left and had returned just before the dawn. How welcome was the morning light. I lay there and wondered if darkness changes people or if they hide what they are during the day.

That night, they came again.

"The girls are gone," I heard the old man tell the soldiers in Russian as he had promised.

He was pushed aside as they forced their way into the house. Once again I saw the shadowy light of their lanterns and was frightened. This time there were four soldiers, wasting no time because everyone knew why they had come and they knew where to go. Their heavy steps shook the house as they came into our room. Walking to the bunks where the girls had been sleeping, they flashed their lights about. The girls were gone. One of the soldiers demanded something of the old man, but he didn't answer. Knocking him aside, they began to search, but in a few minutes they came stomping back into our room. One of them put his lantern close to my mom's face. From the way the soldiers clustered around our bunk, it was obvious they intended to take her into the kitchen. I was scared, but got ready to jump them when they touched her.

"Bruno," my mom said low and harsh, "you stay with the children." One of the Russian soldiers, the closest to our bunk, suddenly reached out and grabbed her. This time she wasn't holding baby Charlotte. "Bruno," she said again. The way she spoke my name was one of the many times she was to place herself between us and danger, even the certain threat of death. I watched with tears in my eyes and dreadful feelings of helplessness as they forced her to go with them.

From the sounds of scuffling and muffled screams, they must have taken some of the other women as well. After a long time of painful waiting, my mom came quietly back to bed. She was alone. The soldiers had gotten what they came for and were gone. I couldn't see my mom's face, it was too dark, but I knew she wasn't crying. She suffered and I cried. Perhaps that's what love is. Something so big and overwhelming that it just bursts inside of you when something happens to the one you love.

Two nights later, the soldiers came again. All of the girls and younger women were hiding away from the camp. Not being able to find what they wanted, the soldiers forced Mrs. Mantei into the kitchen and knocked out her teeth that were capped with gold. Her terrible cries of pain caused us to shrink into our beds. After that night, all of the women went into hiding.

Life, after the three painful visits of the Russian soldiers, was not the same in our camp. It got better. The soldiers never came back. Despite the terror they had created, they had accomplished one thing. When such dreadful things happen to people who care, they come closer together.

Then, as the cold, winter winds gave way to spring breezes and warm days, the Polish farmers began working the surrounding fields. It was good. And even though everyone in the camp, except for small children, was forced to work in the fields, it was still good. In some ways, those who work the land still own it. In that respect, we still owned our farm.

"Don't you know me, Bruno?" It was about two months after we had started working in the fields when this small Polish man came to our camp. I thought I had seen him before, but events of the last year had taught me to know very little and see even less. "I knew your daddy," he said, and seemed very friendly.

I looked at him more closely. His German was understandable, but had a Polish ring to it. Then I remembered seeing him with my dad. During the early years of the war, he had worked as a gardener on a large estate near our farm. All Germans had been forbidden to have business dealings with the Poles, but my dad had never let that stop him. He wasn't about to abide by any rule imposed by distant forces, that made no sense to him, and stood in the way of something he wanted. The man's name was Mr. Paranowski. He and my dad had done a lot of trading, mainly farm goods for flower plants. My dad liked cows; and next to cows, he liked flowers, especially roses.

"Would you like to come and work for me?" the Polish farmer asked. "I have a cow that needs to be taken each morning to graze and returned each night."

I was eager to accept. By now the Russians were in complete control of Poland and Mr. Paranowski had left the large estate. Germans operated it, but under Russian control it had become a government owned farm. Mr. Paranowski was farming a small piece of that land. Although the fighting continued in distant places, life under Russian occupation was settling down in our area. Still, there was danger of a single cow in some isolated place being stolen. Also, grass was not plentiful. The cow would have to be moved several times during the day and I figured I could do that well.

The Polish farmer, not a lot taller than I, looked thoughtful for a minute as though he was thinking about something important. "You work for me all day and I will pay you a whole bottle of milk." He looked at my mom, my little brother and baby Charlotte. "The milk will help you a whole lot."

That was the way I spent the warm summer of 1945, herding one cow and coming home with a bottle of milk. I also learned that Mr. Paranowski was mayor, and therefore a very important man, at least to our little village. Although, almost all of the people in our camp were working, everything was in reverse. Before the war, the Polish people had worked for the Germans. Now, we worked for them. It seems that everything in this world is always turning, and for us, it had turned backwards.

"The war is over. The war is over."

I had just returned from watching Mr. Paranowski's cow. Walking through the front door of the camp, carrying my bottle of milk, I heard the old man shouting that the war was over. He was talking to everyone, and no one, at the same time. He was too excited to be really talking, just letting out all the feelings that were bursting inside of him. Each person learning the news hurried off to tell another. By the time I got to our room, everyone was talking. No one was listening.

The war was over! I had a flood of angry feelings and ugly thoughts as the news slowly got between my ears. The stupid war that had killed my dad, almost killed baby Charlotte, raped my mother, taken away our home and scattered us across the hostile land of Poland, it was over! How could it be over? That wasn't possible. How could a war that destroyed so much quietly disappear as if it were only a little quarrel between children? The war is not over, I thought to myself; it will just hide under another name.

"Bruno." The old man of our camp who spoke Russian spotted me. He quickly came over to me. "The war is over," he whispered to me with a big smile on his face.

I looked at him and for the first time since hearing the news, felt a little of his happiness. We had known for a long time that most of the shooting and killing, even the Great War that was described over the wireless, were over and done. The Russian soldiers had stopped coming into our camp looking for girls; the Polish man who was in charge of our camp had stopped kicking and beating us. Everyone, with the possible exception of myself, was radiating the grand feeling that the war was over.

"Hitler's dead," the old man said. Despite the happiness he felt by knowing the war was over, a sad look came to his face as he talked of the Fatherland being defeated. He had been a soldier in the First World War and never accepted defeat. It seemed to me that old soldiers never stop fighting old wars. Against all reason and against all that actually happened, they change defeat or victory into something noble and fine. Perhaps that is the greatest lie of all. "We will be shipped back to Germany," he said and looked happier than I had ever seen him. "It won't be long now." He looked around at the long bunks and crowded house, as though we were already on our way. "No sir," he said with such strong convictions that I almost believed him. "In a little while we will be out of all this."

The Germans had surrendered on both Eastern and Western Fronts in early May, but it was not until July that the "Big Three," Churchill, Stalin and Truman worked out the complicated terms, at the Potsdam summit

For me, the summer of 1945 became a search for green grass, shade and the continual care of one cow. I got to know a lot about that cow. In some ways, she was exactly like some of the people I had known. She did exactly what she wanted, when she wanted and where she wanted. She had a voice that could be heard for miles and a smell that wasn't too bad except on hot days. I learned to keep one eye on her tail, that she could flick so quickly even the lies couldn't escape, and jump so as not to get splattered. I had also learned the hard way to stay out of reach of her back legs. I was amazed to discover that she could go off both places at the same time, and that she took great delight in eating her food twice. It was a good summer, those hot days of my eleventh year. Once I learned the ways and wisdom of a cow, we became friends.

A few weeks after I began watching Mr. Paranowski's cow, his son and daughter came home. That was another sign the war was over. Anna and David, along with young men and women all across Poland, had been taken from their homes and placed in work camps near big factories in Germany. Coming home was not always a happy time for them. "It is terrible around here," Anna told me one sunny day as we sat in the shade a few feet from the cow that was busy chewing her cud. "There is no work and our farm is too small. We can live here for awhile, but what will we do in the future?"

It's the same for everybody, I thought, as Anna talked. The war changes everything and at the same time accomplishes nothing. Yet, I liked talking to Anna who was about eighteen, and David who was about twenty. I think they liked talking to me because they could speak German.

"It was exciting living near Berlin," David told me. "Sometimes we got permission to attend the theater or even a concert." He shook his head as a sign of his unhappiness. "What is there to do around here? I can't even find a job I like."

That evening I went home with more than my daily bottle of milk. My head was filled with thoughts. Everyone that was in one place wanted to be in some other place. I wondered if anyone was where he wanted to be.

"We'll be going just any day now," the old man told me after supper of that same day. He was as anxious as the young people to be someplace else. Maybe it was because I had a job that made me content; and then, maybe, the easygoing nature of my four-legged friend had rubbed off on me.

What was true was that the harvest, which had been abundant, was over. The fields lay empty where there had been so much activity. The flying winds, no longer the hot breath of summer, placed more chilliness in the air than dust and chaff. As winter once again encircled our camp, rumors that we were about to leave for Germany rode in on every breeze. The old man talked to me as though reaching Germany would be the grandest thing ever to happen. I just listened. In some ways, he reminded me of Mr. Wagner before he became so bitter. "It will be good," the old man told me over and over. "The happy days will be ours again." Then he laughed and talked about the Germany he had known as a boy. "Every Sunday," he said, "we would go to church. Afterwards, we would have a big dinner." To make sure I appreciated how delicious those Sunday dinners were, he rubbed his stomach in circular motion and smacked his lips. "Then, after dinner, we would walk. All of us." He threw out his arms to indicate how big his family was. "All the afternoon we would walk through the forest. We would meet our friends and we would sing. Oh, how we would sing."

As the old man talked, he nodded his head up and down and sighed, as though his memories gave him a special kind of happiness even better than the big dinners. I knew they were better than the half-spoiled potatoes we had been living on day after day. "It will be that way again," he said with great conviction. "By the time we get back to Germany everything will be settled. You'll see. All of this war business will be over. Once again we will eat good food and walk through the forest on a Sunday afternoon. And we will sing. Ah yes. We will sing." The old man stopped talking and I knew he was no longer with me, but somewhere in a forest where happy, well-fed people were walking and singing on a Sunday afternoon.

I listened with respect to the old man, but I couldn't believe him. He was old and he spoke of what had been as if it would be again. I liked his memories. They were happy. I liked his dreams. They were filled with hope. I, too, wanted to have a big dinner with my family, even go to church, and walk and sing. I wanted that very much. It was just that what the old man said was unreal. I didn't have any "brighter tomorrow" feelings on which such hopes are built. I hadn't realized until then how far it is between belief and disbelief.

As the old man talked of returning to Germany, David and Anna's words came back. "The German cities, especially Berlin, are destroyed," they had said. "The American, Russian and British bombers were constantly dropping bombs. The Americans were the worst. They killed thousands upon thousands of civilians, as the country people fled into the cities to escape enemy soldiers. It will be years before the rubble can be cleared away and new buildings built." After talking with David and Anna, I was convinced that the conditions of war, mainly defeat, would not be over even in a lifetime. I never told the old man. It just seemed strange to me that someone who had been born in the midst of war, served as a soldier in the first Great War and lived through the second Great War could speak so positively of peace. I had lived only on the frayed edge of the Second World War, but found it impossible to share the old man's happy dreams.

In November the great announcement was made. Three Russian officials came to our camp. "All you Germans are to gather in Kutno," the tall, stern Russian officer said to us, as we gathered in the large room where we took our meals. I was standing with my mom. Again I had feelings of resentment. Who gave them or anybody else the right to send us here or send us there? The war was over. I found myself having the strong feelings of wanting to go where I wanted to go, not where they wanted to send me. Of course my problem was that I didn't know where I wanted to go, or how I would get there, even if I did know. I glanced out the window. The fields surrounding our camp were freezing beneath the winter winds and drifts of snow often whipped against the rolling hills. I no longer looked after my four-footed friend, but stayed more and more inside. I had not looked forward to being cooped up all winter in the old house that had become our home, but I liked that better than being packed off to who-knows-where by the Russians.

The Russian officer continued to stand at attention as he spoke. The two lesser officers stood at attention by the back wall. "From Kutno," he spoke in a deep, military voice of command, "you will be taken by train to Germany."

All the people burst into applause at the mention of being settled in Germany. As soon as the Russian officers left, I heard the high pitch voice of the old man. His shrill laughter showed how happy he was. Excited, in spite of feelings of resentment, I moved away from my mom and to the window. Through the window I saw the Russian soldiers stop on the porch to light cigarettes. They were talking and laughing. The sight of them clustered, like they knew something they weren't telling, made even more of an impression on me than their laughter.

So we were finally going to Germany! The words of the Russian officer kept ringing in my ears. At the same time, I couldn't forget the three of them standing on the porch, laughing. Still, I was happy. I was happy for the old man; I was happy for my mom; I was happy for everyone because they were so happy. My happiness had come to me much like a song that drifted in from the people around me like a welcome guest. Beneath my happiness of joyous excitement lurked a gift from my dad, a realistic attitude of wait and see. I had learned from him, and by actual experience, not to trust the unseen forces behind official documents and pronouncements. They always tell you almost the truth. Strange how almost the truth is the greater lie and sounds the most convincing.

"Bruno," my mom hurried me along. "You bring those two sacks." She was standing there holding baby Charlotte in one arm; under the other arm was a sack that contained our clothes, ragged but clean and patched. Little Egon was holding my mom's sleeve as if he was afraid she was about to go off and leave him. "The wagons are waiting," she said impatiently. I guess my reluctance to do the Russian's bidding was showing. We both took one last look around the room where we had lived almost a year. Looking back was our way of saying goodbye to what had been.

I picked up the sacks and tried to carry them. One held about twenty pounds of potatoes and the other one held two loaves of round bread. Ever since the harvest had been completed, rumors of our leaving had grown with each day. Again my mom had made preparations for our trip. She had managed to obtain enough flour to bake two large loaves of bread in the outside oven. I had brought the wood for the fire and watched her use the long-handled paddle to remove the bread. She had also traded to get the potatoes that I was trying to get under my arm. The old room looked different now that we were leaving. The long bunks, bare of straw, seemed forlorn as though they had feelings and would miss us. With strange thoughts twisting inside of me, I stopped at the front door and watched the people hurrying to get on the wagons. For an instant, it seemed unreal. It was something I had done before, and this was just a dream. The scary thought came, where would I be if I were to wake? Catching sight of an impatient jerk of my mom's head, I forgot everything else and ran toward the wagons. At least everyone was happy.

The crowded wagon trip to Kutno didn't seem long, in spite of the cold wind. Perhaps the happy excitement of beginning our trip to Germany kept us warm. Near mid-afternoon, the wagons stopped in front of a large building in Kutno. That, as I quickly discovered, was to be our living quarters until the train arrived. Hundreds of people from our Romanian district of Bessarabia were already waiting there, with other wagons coming constantly. It was a grand reunion. "Going to Germany. Going to Germany." That was on the lips of everyone.

"I've got a brother living just out of Frankfurt," I heard one man say. "That's where we'll be going until we can get settled," he said, with a big smile.

"My cousin lives near there," a woman replied, and they talked excitedly of good times ahead in Germany.

My mom joined in the happy talk and I, between running here and there to play, listened. "We'll be staying with my sister in Germany," she told some women. It seemed so good to hope that somewhere there was a place where we were wanted. There are a lot of ways to talk about what is most important in this world. For me, it is simple. All of life has but one coin to spend. One side of that coin is being wanted. The other side is not being wanted. That's the difference.

Every so often another group of people would join us in the big building. There would be squeals of delight and a lot of hugging, as those people who thought others to be dead, met once again. It must have felt strange to see friends, given up as dead, get off the wagon and walk over as big as life. Something like the resurrection our pastor in Friedenstal had talked about on Easter Sunday. I just watched. The one I wanted to see really was dead.

As the second day went by, some people started asking questions: "Were we being sent to Germany? Was it really going to happen?" Hopes were still strong, but doubt had begun to creep in. The keen edge of happiness was gone. On the third day, officials came to the big building. "Be ready to leave tomorrow," they told us. "The train will be here in the morning."

It was as simple as that. A few words and dreams come true. The most excited was the old man. "See Bruno," he told me the next morning, as we walked from the big building to the rail station. "We are going to Germany."

Sometime before, I had heard rumors that instead of Germany, we were being sent to some other place in Poland, maybe even Russia. The old man didn't remember hearing that, even though he had been told several times. I enjoyed being with the old man. When he was happy, it was all the way. It was easy to be happy with him because he had so much to share. Part way to the rail station, I left the old man and walked beside my mom. She was carrying baby Charlotte and walking with several other women. Little Egon was walking along behind her. Then, when we entered the station, I saw the old man again. He was leaning against the gate, his head held in his hands. His two daughters were trying to comfort him. "We're not going to Germany," he wailed over and over. "We're not going to Germany."

The train was waiting for us as we had been told, but the destination sign on the sides of the cattle cars where we were to ride read Brest-Litovsk. That one printed word made clear everything that the old man had been able to believe. At last, he too believed. Brest-

Litovsk (later named Brest) was a Polish border town, the last stop before Russia. There is only one place in that big country where unwanted people are sent—Siberia. Even though I was young, I knew that. I helped the old man get into one of the cattle cars. Our long and tragic trip to Siberia had begun.

"We'll escape!" The old man leaned over and whispered in my ear, as the train gave a jolt and began moving. "First chance we get, we'll jump and make a run for it."

I looked at the old man. He wasn't any bigger than I was. The wrinkles were heavy in his face. Where could we escape? I thought. The only place we had was on that train. It was winter and even though they said the war was over, I had the definite feeling it was just beginning for us.

# Train East

We were crowded into about thirty smelly cattle cars with rough, bare floors, pulled by a single steam engine. One car was reserved for the guards and another, as I bitterly discovered, was filled with food. No one, not even the old man, offered any resistance when we were ordered to climb onto the train. At least the guards allowed us to ride where we wanted. About twenty-five people were in our car and near that number in each of the other cars. There were a few old men. There were more old women. Almost 900 people boarded those cattle cars on that first day of December in 1945. Our family had lost most of our household possessions in January when our wagon was stolen. Now all we had was two pillows, two thin blankets, a cooking pot, a blue enamel pail and a knife; each one of us had a bowl and a spoon. There was little clothing other than what we were wearing.

"I want you to understand about our food," my mom told my little brother and me shortly after the train left the station. The mention of food immediately got our attention. We were getting hungry. "I'm giving you just a little food twice a day." She handed Egon and me two small pieces of potato. "That means we will always be hungry, but we will always have something for the next time."

I took the potato and promptly popped it into my mouth. Hardly bothering to chew, it seemed my stomach reached up and grabbed it. That little bit of food left me even hungrier than before. As I was to learn in the days ahead, eating that way was a big mistake. Food, when I was that hungry, must be treasured for even more than it is. I learned to hold it in my hand until I had fully convinced myself I really had some food. That takes time. The overwhelming power of an empty belly creates illusions that are hard to overcome. The fact that for a few seconds my eyes saw some food or the fact that my hand placed a bite or two in my mouth – neither of these was enough. Food must be treasured, studied, even talked to. Then, after I had convinced my screaming belly food was really there, I forced myself to nibble. The more times I could put my front teeth through a piece of potato before it was gone, the better.

I learned another lesson in the difficult task of making a little food seem to be more. After I had taken a small bite, I would send the food to every corner of my mouth. Hunger, as I came to know, did not lurk in just my empty stomach. It invaded every inch of me; and especially, it came to dwell in my mouth. After I had experienced hunger, which takes time because you can't get hungry in just a day or a week, the mere thought of food would cause my mouth to water, my hands to tremble, my eyes to go blank and a strange, fanatical concentration upon some good thing to eat. Food was constantly in my dreams. Hunger, I found, is a living nightmare where food in great abundance comes to you in sleep and you awaken to an empty world.

That was what I learned in our trip across Poland and Russia in a train made to haul cattle. I learned to chew slowly as though I had a whole plate of food and was just trying to decide what to take next. Even more than how to eat, I learned the one big lesson that all that have been hungry know so well. It takes very little food to stay alive. A couple of mouthfuls a day will do it, but what I went through in the process would not be called living.

"Bruno, Bruno." My little brother grabbed my arm and whispered in my ear, loud enough to be heard three families away. "Those people over there got some sausage."

I didn't say anything. We had a little potato to chew on. That was because our mom guarded the last few wrinkled potatoes with her life. What could I say to Egon? Some of the people in our wagon were eating better than the others. Some had brought large quantities of bread and sausage. Only a few had saved like my mom. It all depended on how much money, gold or clothing they had. Each time the train stopped, Polish people swarmed around the open doors wanting to trade potatoes, carrots, dark bread and even white bread for anything of value. High on the list were gold rings or watches. Our trouble had been my big mouth. The last gold we had was my mom's wedding ring and it had been stolen because of me. I tried to make up for that. Every time the train stopped, I was off like a flash with my bucket, looking for food. I seemed to have a knack for stealing; and the better I got, the more my stomach enjoyed it.

During the days it took us to reach the Polish-Russian border, our lives painfully adjusted to the terrible conditions forced upon us. Inside the cattle car, it was either dark because of having the big doors and windows closed, or freezing cold when we had any of them open. Generally we compromised by opening the doors slightly during the day and keeping them closed at night. As we got closer to the Russian border, there was more than enough cold air swirling about our heads, whether the door was open or closed. Once in a while at night, I opened the wooden flap of a window for just a little while and looked out on the frozen fields of white. Sometimes the moon was so bright and the stars so clear that it gave me the feeling of being a part of them.

None of the guards ever came to check on us. Some of the people in our car, especially the old man, continued to talk of escaping.

"Where would we go?" my mom asked him one afternoon, as the train traveled along miles of frozen fields. "It's a long way from here to Germany and no one to help us." I figured that she was thinking of the bad time that we had after our wagon was stolen. That memory would kill any desire to try escaping. I saw my mom reach over and touch the old man's arm to show how much she admired his courage. "It would take weeks for us to get anyplace," she said as gently as she could. "The winter is getting worse every day. Our only hope is to stay on the train." Discouraged by my mom and the miles of snow covered fields, the old man stopped talking about escape. Maybe that was not good. He was weak and had a coughing spell every time he got a blast of cold air. This happened often.

Thoughts of escape had given him reason to fight all the problems he was having.

Our basic concerns aboard the train were food, water and surviving the cold. We managed to overcome all three, in one way or another. As long as the train was crossing Poland, we did all right for food. The ground was only frozen on the surface, and potato fields were often planted beside the railroad tracks. Whenever the train stopped to take on water and coal or to wait for another train to clear, everyone was out of the cars and digging in the fields. As for water, the trainmen were good to us. They gave us a little hot water from the engine. That hot water was beautiful to have, even though it was almost cold by the time I got it back to my mom.

Our two pillows and two blankets didn't provide much padding against the constant jarring of iron wheels over uneven tracks. When sitting, my poorly padded bottom seemed to have pointed bones in all places. It got so bad I envied some of the women. Lying down was even worse except for one thing. The almost musical, but monotonous click...click...click of the rails caused a strange kind of sleep. There were no stoves or toilets. We ate half-frozen potatoes and drank ice water. The old man liked to eat snow.

"It feels good to my throat," he told me one afternoon, as I brought him some from alongside the tracks. "You're a good boy Bruno," he told me, and ate snow much as I might eat some special dessert. To me snow always seemed empty in my mouth. It looked so good, but produced nothing except a cold feeling that I sure didn't need.

As for toilets, we did our best to wait until the train stopped. That was a terrible guessing game. As soon as the wheels locked, it was everybody off, squatting wherever we could find places. Coming from a farm and knowing the value of manure as fertilizer, I figured we were paying the farmers for the potatoes that we stole. Some of those fields were going to have the best crops ever. Although perfectly natural, it was quite a sight to see hundreds of people jumping from the train and running to relieve themselves from what little food they had eaten. The women, anxious over their small children, adopted various methods to care for them. Strange as it may have been, in spite of the lack of buildings, trees or even brush, it was a private affair. As I learned, privacy is of the mind, not of walls.

After four days of endless clicks, stopping for wood, water and long waits, for no apparent reason, our train pulled into Brest-Litovsk. This time the guards came to us. "Off the train," they ordered. They looked a lot better than we did. I was quite sure the food car was empty by now. The guards herded us about half a mile to a large building, similar to the one where we had been in Kutno. The walk was a painful experience for the older people. Their legs had gotten stiff, and their backs were so sore that they could hardly hobble along. Reaching the building, we were told to wait. No one explained that the railroad gauge in Russia was a different size than in Poland, or how long it would be before a Russian train came for us.

"The longer we wait," the old man whispered to me the second day of our stay in Brest-Litovsk, "the more chance we have of being shipped to Germany." He smiled and sort of shook his head as if he knew some secret reason for that to be true. "I know," he said and moved off, mumbling to himself.

I watched him walk away, his thin shoulders all humped over. He was just a little bit of a man a long way from home. Yet, I marveled at his perpetual hope and ability to hold onto his dream despite what was happening to us. Our home had been in Romania near the Black Sea and that no longer existed for any of us.

That afternoon, as if further delay might make the old man's hopes come true, Russian guards came for us. "Get your things and leave the building," they strutted among us shouting. "You are to march to the railroad station."

The Russian train was just like the one we had ridden across Poland, except for one big difference; there was a stove in the middle of each car. The sight of that stove sure encouraged us. The big building had been cold and I hadn't been warm for so long I couldn't remember when. Now that winter was settling in for real, I couldn't bear the thought of returning to a freezing train. That's why the stove was such a welcome sight. "And where do we get the turf to burn?" my mom snapped, as I pointed to the stove with great joy. That ended my happy feelings about the stove. Then, after thinking it over, I just made up my mind to steal something to burn, as well as something to eat. If we were put in a position to starve and freeze, then there must be a higher authority somewhere that gives us permission to overcome the problem. There were birch trees near the railroad tracks and in the freezing cold the branches broke easily. Even though the wood was green, it burned well; and the small amount of heat helped warm us a little.

As our train crossed the endless white land of Russia, more and more stops were outside the villages. It was obvious the authorities did not want contact between us Germans and the Russian people. One afternoon, as I sat talking to the old man, I asked him why our crossing Russia was such a secret.

"Maybe for our own protection," he said, between fits of coughing. "A lot of Russians were killed in the war. They don't forget so soon."

He may have been right. The war had created hatred between large numbers of people. Some of the most brutal killings had taken place after peace had been declared. Right and wrong, revenge and justice were all mixed up. The result was a train filled with sick, starving and freezing old men, women and children, crossing the snowy hills of Russia, completely cut off from the rest of the world.

"Bruno." My mom said excitedly. "Look at the grass." At first I didn't know what she was talking about. The train was coming to a slow stop just on the edge of a Russian town. The big, open door to our car was right by a steep bank. She pointed to the tall grass not yet covered by snow. "If you can get some of that grass," my mom said, "we will have something to sleep on."

Not waiting for the train to completely stop, I jumped down, crossed a second pair of tracks and began gathering the brown, winter grass. I kept one eye on the train, which I had learned to do from the first time off, always listening for that awful jerking sound of it starting to move, and I ran back and forth carrying arms of the brown grass.

"Hurry Bruno," my mom called to me. "The train is about to leave."

Despite her warning, I made several trips, running as fast as my legs would carry me. The tall grass was tough and cut into my hands as I frantically pulled it. My mom wanted it and that was enough for me. Then, as I was jumping the tracks and running for the train, I saw something that slowed me down. Two of the guards were walking toward town carrying a large sack that looked heavy. Even I could tell what they were doing. They were taking food from the supply car to sell on the black market. I didn't have the courage to tell my mom. She had been telling us that before long the guards would give us some food. I just kept running back and forth with the grass and watched the guards disappear with food that should have been in our stomachs. What I saw matched what we had known of the authorities for some time. If I hadn't been so hungry, what they were doing might have been funny.

A few days later, because of the cold and the lack of food, the old people began to die. "We've got to have some medicine." My mom's face indicated what was going to happen if we didn't do something. She was talking to my cousin Annemarie Ziebart, who was eighteen years old. The two of them were attempting to help Annemarie's other aunt, Berta Ziebart. The old woman just lay on the floor, so weak that her head rolled back and forth with every sway of the train. We had tried to make her a softer bed using the dried grass and one of our pillows. There was nothing that they could do but let her die.

"They have some medicine in the food car," the old man told us. "I saw them give some white pills to the people in the car next to us." He looked at Berta and shook his head. "Go get the medicine before it's too late."

The next stop of the train, as the old man had suggested, Annemarie ran to the food car. "I got the medicine," she said climbing back into our car. She opened her hand and showed us two small, white pills. "It is good that they at least give us medicine."

I watched as my mom helped Annemarie give Berta the pills. I felt responsible that the old woman was dying. When we were told about being sent to Germany, I ran to their home and told them the news, asking them to come with us. If it hadn't been for me, they wouldn't have been on the train. I felt better when almost at once Berta seemed better. Her breathing became easier and she looked a lot more peaceful. A few hours later, she was dead.

Without really having thought about it, I had expected death to be much more. On our earlier escape there had been the loud noise of the soldier's gun and the old men fell in the snow. Berta had died and there was nothing. Deep down, I had expected angels to sing or the sky to light up. How that would take place in a crowded train had not occurred to me. But nothing, absolutely nothing, happened. The old woman just seemed to have gone to sleep with her eyes half open. The adults sat around talking in low voices as though they were afraid they might wake her.

"Berta is better off," my mom said.

Annamarie had tears in her eyes. "It was the medicine," she said bitterly. "That's what killed her." She put her head into her hands and sobbed. The thought that she might have helped kill her aunt overwhelmed her. Perhaps those little white pills had actually been to kill, not to heal.

The old man came over to be with us. He looked at Berta for a long time, then laid a friendly hand on Annemarie's shoulder. "I will help you bury her when the train stops." Annemarie nodded. I could tell by her face that she felt better by his offer of help. When the train stopped, the old man, Annemarie and my mom buried Berta beneath the snow. Ever since we had entered Russia, the snow had gotten deeper. Now, with the ground frozen solid, only snow and ice could be used for graves. "It will be softer than the ground," I heard the old man say to the women.

Something happened to all of us when Berta Ziebart died. Maybe it was already there, waiting, but we were different. For many, it was the time of giving up. After that, there were burials in the snow every day. Several died in our car. No one, I noticed, talked of going after any medicine and there were few, if any tears. We had come to accept dying much as we had come to accept the lack of food. That was what was happening to us. We had become accepting.

As our train clicked across the frozen, white land of Russia, dull days, without meaning, filled our lives. We were having a losing affair with life. Frequently, I jumped from the train to help spread snow over an old man or woman or even a small child. It never dawned on me that the old ones would eat less so the young in their families might have a little more. Then, there wasn't that much food. None of those thoughts came to me until the night the old man died.

"I like the snow," he told me for the hundredth time. "It feels good to my throat." His cough had gotten worse and he had become weak. The last day he lay on the floor, his head rolling with the sway of the train. Sometimes I went over and sat by him. That day he had seemed better and asked me to bring him some snow. "Straight from heaven," he said, after the train had stopped and I brought him the snow. "Pure, Bruno." He held a little in his hand as though that old snow was something special. "Just like we are when we come to this earth."

That night, while I slept, the old man died. The next morning, when we found him, I wished I had been there when he went away. He had always shared such beautiful dreams with me. We buried him beneath the snow he loved and I hoped his dreams had come true.

"Always keep one ear and one eye out for the train," my mom had told me many times. "If the train goes off and leaves you..." her expression said the rest. I feared that one night in the cold, where no houses could be seen, I would be left behind. In spite of what she had told me, I forgot. Somehow the train had started moving and I wasn't even aware of it.

"Bruno." My mom's voice, frightened and shrill, startled me. I looked up to see her leaning out the door of the moving train, frantically waving at me. "Run," she screamed. "Run."

A little while before, we had been huddled on the floor of the car with our shoes off, trying to get our feet warm. My small blue water bucket was empty and I planned to get water at the next stop. As soon as the wheels stopped, I grabbed the bucket and jumped into my mom's shoes to save time. Hurrying up to the engine, I got the hot water and was carefully walking back to our car. I was so intent on not spilling the water that I didn't realize the train was moving. That was when my mom's scream caused me to look up just in time to see the door to our car go by. Forgetting about spilling the precious water, I began running as fast as I could, back toward the open door where my mom stood screaming. What I had not realized was that the train had stopped on a small incline. That was why it could start so quietly and pick up speed so rapidly. The snow and my mom's oversized shoes didn't help.

"Faster Bruno," my mom screamed, getting farther from my outstretched hands, although I was running as fast as I could. One by one, the cars began to pass me by. Already, I was three or four back from where she was standing.

"Boy, give me your hand," I heard a man shout from behind me.

I looked at a car passing by. A man had braced himself against the side and was reaching out for me. Grabbing for him, I felt his hand lock around my wrist as I flew off the ground and into the open car. Many hands made sure I didn't roll back into the snow. I lay on the floor of the car, holding onto my empty bucket and sobbing. It felt so good to be on the train. All I could think of was my mom and how much I wanted to be with her. Only later did I think about the man who had saved my life and how much it was like my little brother being saved on the run-away wagon. Good things do happen.

During our four-day ride through Poland, the only food we had was what we brought with us. Now, about every two days we got some food from the Russian guards. Those days without food became very long. Almost all the food the people brought with them was gone. We still had a potato or two, but that was because my mom was always saving for tomorrow. When the train stopped and we were told to line up for our food, it became more and more difficult for the older people. They became increasingly weaker. What they gave us was a small pail of potato and cabbage soup. A few more days of such treatment and there wouldn't be much need for the food or even the train. It might have been hard for the soldiers to explain why they were guarding a train of dead people. I learned that it doesn't take much food to stay alive; what I was still learning was the painful lesson that some people don't care what happens to others. Occasionally, I would see some of the soldiers strolling about or talking to the trainmen, but they didn't speak to us. Our isolation was so great that even our guards, a few cars away, were in another world.

By this time, we had been crossing the deep winter-land of Russia for two or three weeks. It is not easy to keep track of time when everything stays the same and it is so cold. I didn't know what day it was, nor did I care. Looking forward to something and remembering how good yesterday was are what makes memories. Without memories and hope, there is no time.

"This is our last potato," my mom said, cutting it into small pieces so we each could have more than one. It lasts longer that way. She looked at me and I knew she was thinking of all the times I had jumped off the train and frantically searched for food, but now it was hopeless. As they had done from first entering Russia, the engineer stopped the train outside of villages. The snow was too deep for me to search the fields, and the houses too far away. There was absolutely no food to be found.

I have heard it said by those who have never been hungry that hunger sharpens your wits. It doesn't. Hunger takes all you are and what you never thought you could be and focuses on one thing: food. You think food; you dream food; you talk food; you imagine food. Your total being is attempting to reach out for something to eat. It was that total commitment to food that saved our lives. I learned to see what was going on about me in complete relationship to food. There is so much that happens and so little that we see until there is a reason. Eating that last little piece of potato gave me the greatest of reasons. It was either get some food or die. I was determined that we would live.

# Christmas Eve

"Pull hard," Helmut said to me, through clenched teeth. I grabbed a snow-covered edge of the big train door with freezing fingers and pulled with all my strength.

Now that the last of our potatoes was gone and the thin soup made by the guards was handed out about every two days, I had to find us food. During the night, I had been thinking about a bigger boy in one of the other cars. He must have been fifteen or sixteen, which was unusual, because most boys that age were in the army. For some time I had made up my mind that wherever he went, I was going too, since he was the best thief on the whole train. As soon as it got light, I waited for the train to make a stop. When that happened, I was at the door and watched for him to jump to the ground. As quick as a flash, I was after him. This time I had my shoes on and was ready to run just as fast as he could.

Set to chase him, I was surprised to see the boy walking slowly through the snow alongside the train. I came up beside him. "What's your name?" he asked, as I stayed with him. His face wasn't friendly, but I was sure he sensed he'd have to kill me before I'd go away.

"Bruno," I told him. "What's yours?"

"Helmut," he answered. "And stop looking around," he said harshly. "I know where to go."

I looked at him, then down the tracks. All I could see were three or four railroad cars sitting on a siding. Despite his warning, I glanced back. Some of the soldiers were smoking and walking alongside the food car, just like they always did. They weren't paying any attention to us, but I knew they wouldn't hesitate to shoot if they saw us stealing. Walking to the far end of the sidecars, Helmut made one fast glance back at the guards and darted to the opposite side. I was right

on his heels. "Find something to pry with," he said, frantically looking around as though he knew there was lots of food inside. I didn't
see how he could know, but I sure did what he told me.

Seeing a small timber sticking out of the snow, I grabbed it. The
wood broke so suddenly I almost fell. "Here," I called proudly to
Helmut. "I've got something."

"Well, don't tell the guards," he said, jerking it out of my hands
and starting to pry one end of the big sliding door. "Don't just stand
there," he said between clenched teeth. "Grab hold and pull hard." I
forced my freezing fingers under the edge of the big door and pulled.
Suddenly, giving a loud popping sound, so loud that any guard listening would have heard, the car door broke loose and swung out
about six inches. That was far enough for Helmut to look in. "Flour,"
he said. "Just like I thought. A whole car loaded with flour." He was
excited. "Find another stick," he told me, holding the door open
with the timber. "A sharp pointed one."

Fighting snow almost to my knees and higher in some places, I
thrashed around looking for a stick. Plunging through a ditch that
ran parallel to the tracks, I broke a dead branch from a scrubby looking tree. "Poke a hole in the bottom sack," Helmut told me. His
voice came in gasps as he held the door open. Jabbing as hard as I
could with the stick, I forgot about the guards or the train starting
and leaving us behind. That flour was the most important thing in
my life. Then, despite my fingers being stiff and numb from the
cold, I managed to tear the sack and rich, brown flour came tumbling through the opening onto the snow. "Here," Helmut said and
indicated I was to take a sack out of his jacket pocket. "Fill it up and
hurry." Filling his sack with flour, I grabbed the empty sack I always
carried and quickly filled it. Then, like two frightened animals, we
dropped everything except our precious flour and scampered for the
train.

That flour saved our lives. I was proud to hand it to my mom.
Day by day, mile after mile into Russia, I had become the food pro-
vider for our family. In the process, I discovered that becoming a

man is not a result of passing time. Manhood comes out of learning from what happens to you during that passing time.

My mom took the flour and in her usual way put us on rations—about three spoons in the morning and three in the late afternoon. That flour provided something for us to eat for almost two weeks. It was a meal of necessity. A mouthful of flour and a drink of lukewarm water from the steam engine were the way we ate, day after day, licking our fingers clean, we were so thankful.

As the Russian cold became more severe and the snow so much deeper, no one in our car went outside to answer nature's call when the train stopped. By this time we were so accustomed to the sights and sounds of body functions that they created no embarrassment. Then, the dreadful lack of food made those calls less and less frequent. When they did come, old containers collected along the way, served as our toilets. The smells from those old cans were pretty bad, but at least they served the illusion of making our car seem warmer.

There was yet another problem with these toilet facilities. When the train stopped, one of my chores, and for others, was that of emptying the can. Sometimes, I didn't get it done. Then, as we were taken deeper and deeper into Russia, the train made fewer stops. The cold became so bitter that we sat in a mindless huddle in order to survive. Still, certain needs went on. Due to that necessity, and especially one smelly experience, I learned how to empty the can while the train was speeding down the tracks. The first time, I pushed the door open and threw the contents into the open air. That was a big mistake. The speed of the train was not that fast, but the strong, winter wind created a smelly disaster. My own waste was bad enough, but somebody else's coming back and hitting me in the face was a terrible experience I will never forget.

As the month of December slowly went by, the outside of our car and all the other cars became highly decorated with frozen waste. The wind was so strong and cold that everything thrown through the door was swept back against the train and frozen there. One of my happiest finds along the way had been a small can that I could use for a dipper. The risk was also much less if no one was throwing from the car ahead.

Increasingly, the hopelessness of our journey became a life-taking force. People die from other causes than just the lack of food. When the train stopped, we carried their bodies to the side of the tracks, brushed the snow aside and covered them, as though they were asleep beneath a blanket of white. I helped. My mom helped. Then we got back on the train and waited for it to go. Where else could we go? What else could we do? Life fades into darkness unless you have the light of hope, no matter how dim, glowing within. The light for many on our train was going out. The darkness of death was coming for them on a faster train than we were riding.

We began to talk less as we rode along. There wasn't anything to say that we had not said and there was no energy with which to repeat it. Yet, when that train stopped, I forced myself to jump into the snow and desperately search for food and something to burn in our stove. Food was almost non-existent. I did much better finding wood. Once we stopped beside an empty passenger train. Some of us slipped into the coaches and demolished the seats and whatever else we could carry away to burn. The guards were too busy staying warm in their own car to notice us. As the weeks went by, I waited for that incessant clicking of the wheels to stop. Deep within me was the thin hope that somewhere ahead was a place where it was warm and there was enough to eat.

Aside from my hasty searches for food and wood, I dwelt in a land even more barren than the frozen plains of Russia. I watched endless days of snow pass by. I felt people gather close against me in the swaying train, but was removed from them. I dreamed of food and being warm, but my dreams had lost all touch with reality; I identified myself with the winter wind and barren fields. I was not in the flow of existence, but waited as the winter land waits for spring.

"Do you know what tonight is?" One of the women was talking to my mom in the evening darkness of our car. The gray daylight seemed short and the long darkness of night seemed to last forever.

It was Egon's turn to have the pillow, so I was trying to sleep on what grass I could keep under me. Grass might seem soft when you stretch out on it under some shady tree on a hot, summer day, but on that bumpy train it was the worst bed I ever had. Since I had slept most of the day, the long hours of night lay ahead like some kind of black forever.

"No," I heard my mom answer. By her tone of voice, I could tell she was feeling as terrible as I was. She didn't know what day it was and didn't have the strength to care. Whether it was Monday or Wednesday, no one really knew; and it didn't make any difference anyway.

"Tonight is Christmas Eve," the woman said. "I know. I've been counting the days."

"It's Christmas Eve," I heard some one else say.

"Can't be," one of the other women said. "We've been on this train too long." Two or three others agreed with her. It seemed like it could be. The few weeks we had been on the train had reached far beyond any time we had known.

"It's Christmas Eve," the woman said again, and was so convincing that even I began to feel a little stirring of excitement. Then I felt the train smack up against my bottom as it went over some rough tracks and thought, what do we have to celebrate? Christmas is for warm homes, where there is lots of good food and presents to open. It's not for people like us who haven't got anything and don't even know where they are going. I lay back on what grass was left and felt worse than before the woman had told us. It didn't seem fair. I felt a lump in my throat. On this old train where we were cold, starved, sick and our guards hated us, how could it be Christmas? I closed my eyes and gritted my teeth. There wasn't Christmas any more in the whole world. And even if there were, I wouldn't let it be.

Until that night in the vast snow-covered eternity, I had felt Christmas, I had seen it, I had enjoyed it, but I had never really understood it. And that is when the true Spirit of Christmas came to me. The spirit of being so close to others that you love them more

152

than you can possibly love; the spirit of giving more than you have to give and receiving more than you have any right to accept. That is the eternal miracle of Christmas as I discovered it in the darkness of a freezing cattle car. It is not warm homes and good food or even presents. It is the blessing of love.

Then, someone started to sing a Christmas carol. Before long, we were all singing and having a wonderful time. After some songs, one of the men told of Christmas at our church in Friedenstal. His words were so real that I felt we were really there. Others told of Christmas meals or special presents they had received years before. There was so much to talk about and everyone was happy. It truly was Christmas Eve.

*"Silent night, Holy night,*
*All is calm, All is bright…"*

As the people sang one of our favorite carols, I left my grass bed and went over to the small, board window. I wanted to look out on the world and see if it was different. I was different. Opening the window, I saw miles and miles of snow reflecting the bright rays of a large, yellow moon moving across a cloudless sky. In the distance I saw bare birch trees silently dotting the snow. And then, for an instant, I thought I saw a light. Perhaps it was a home where a family was gathered around a warm fire and the lamp was for them. Perhaps it was a star low on the horizon. All I know is that I saw a light and I felt warmed by it. As the people sang about the baby Jesus in a manger, I closed the window and went back to sing with them. We didn't know if it was really Christmas Eve, but to us, it was. I knew that not only was it Christmas, it was the most unforgettable Christmas I would ever know. It was the time I had received my greatest gift. Through the miracle of Christmas, I had come back to being myself.

After the singing, I lay on the floor. More than feelings of happiness had come to me. I was at peace and filled with love for life. For the first time since we had left Poland, I slept the night without being afraid.

"The train, Bruno, it is stopping!" It was several days later on January 1, 1946. The afternoon light was so dim in our car that I could barely see my mother's face. "What is happening?" she asked, all excited. I couldn't think why my mom was upset about the train coming to a stop. It often stopped for no apparent reason. Then in a few minutes or hours, whenever someone decided, it would start up again. The sudden sound of harsh voices made me realize that again my mom was aware of something long before I was.

"Get out. All of you get out."

I ran to the door with several other people. The guards were marching alongside the train, yelling in poor German for everyone to get their things together and get off. We quickly made a bundle of all we had. It didn't take long. Gritting my teeth against the cutting wind, I jumped into the snow and helped my little brother down. Then I helped my mom, holding baby Charlotte. The cold was so bad I felt my nostrils stick together as though someone had poured them full of sticky horse glue.

"Hurry it up. Hurry it up." The guards were prodding the people who were hesitating to jump into the snow and yelling at them. I looked around, but couldn't see anything except snow. Instantly, I was fearful that we were going to be left in the snow to freeze or that they were going to shoot us.

"Line up and come this way," the guards shouted. Once in line, they marched us about 300 feet. Then I saw the barracks. The reason I had not seen them was because only the roofs stuck above the ground. They were the first underground buildings I had ever seen. Leading us down the wooden steps, the guards showed us where we were to live. Each barrack was about 200 feet long and 30 feet wide. Wooden platform beds stretched in long rows along the walls. Windows were in the top portion of both ends, with a big stove in the center. Overhead were electric bulbs that cast a shadowy light. It seemed awfully nice compared to the train, and so much warmer. Besides, it wasn't constantly moving and clicking.

There was one thing though, more than anything else, which I didn't understand. Some Russian women were in our barrack, sweeping and cleaning, but I didn't understand why. Why would they want to help us? Maybe the understanding, or the lack of it, was mine. I had gotten so I could understand and even accept something bad. It was the good that gave me trouble. Then, after time spent in Siberia where survival is hard, good people did some good things and I came to a new understanding of the relationship of those opposing forces of life.

"It's frostbite," one of the Russian women told my mom in broken German, as she looked at Egon's fingers. The short walk from the train to the underground barracks had been so cold that the tips of his fingers had turned a strange white. The pain had started when we began to warm up by the big stove. It was then that Egon broke into tears. "Take some snow and rub his fingers until the white disappears," the same Russian woman said.

"Get some snow," my mom told me.

I ran outside and brought in a handful. Using the snow much like soap, the Russian woman gently rubbed my little brother's fingers. "The snow will melt from the warmth of my hands," she told us, "and then the little boy's fingers won't hurt so much."

Egon had stopped crying. By the expression on his face, I knew his fingers still hurt, but there was something special about the attention he was getting, and that made everything all right. He was too little to realize his frozen fingers would bother him the rest of his life.

Winter in Siberia is a sight to behold, and to feel. The sky on a clear winter day is as blue as any place in the world. The sun is a great ball of fire, moving all too rapidly across the low horizon. For a little while, if there is no wind, the bright sun makes it seem almost warm. Everything changes once darkness rises from the frozen ground, even if the day is a gray, wind-swept prairie of existence. As it so happened, we had come at the worst time for snow and freezing winds, the month of January. It is then that Siberia truly becomes a land of prisoners. In spite of those extreme conditions, we were never cold in our underground home. The big stove was constantly going; and there were so many people in our barracks, we stayed warm, even hot.

The problem was not the cold. It was the thieving rats. When it grew quiet and most of the lights were turned off so we could sleep, they came out of a hundred little holes. They were after food and could find it no matter where we hid it. "Bruno." I awakened to find my mom shaking my arm. "The rats," she said. "They're taking our food." I grabbed the stick that I kept by my side and began swinging. My mom kept what little food we had under her pillow. Since we all slept on the one long bunk, the rats ran over us to get at the food. They were running this way and that. I helped them along. At least for the moment, I had scattered them, but they would be back.

"Did you see the towers?" Mr. Kunz and I were sitting on the side of his bunk, talking. He was one of the few old men who had managed to stay alive. He could speak pretty fair Russian so I spent a lot of time with him, trying to learn that language. I wanted to know the words for various foods, since that was all I could think about. I would be thinking of something else and then thoughts of food would rush into my mind quicker than the rats running across the floor. I thought of food before I went to sleep and woke up thinking the same thing. Nothing was more important than food. "Did you see the towers?" Mr. Kunz asked again, his voice indicating there was something important about them.

"Yes sir," I answered, forcing images of food from the center of my thoughts. "I saw them."

"Did you see how tall they are?" Again, I answered that I had. He looked at me with a peculiar glint in his eyes. "We're in a prisoner-of-war camp," he said, as if he had figured out some secret move of the Russians. "That's where we are. They got us prisoners." I didn't say anything. It wasn't exactly hard to figure what the old man was saying. Even I knew that. But Mr. Kunz wasn't through with his thinking. He looked at me with a real secretive look on his whiskered face. "You know why we're prisoners?"

For a minute I forgot about food. Mr. Kunz had been good to me. He had taken a lot of time to teach me Russian. I had learned to say potato, bread, milk, I'm hungry and other important words. A lot of possible answers came to my mind, none of them polite, when he asked if I knew why we were prisoners. My dad might be dead, but his way of thinking and his spirit still lived in me. Out of respect for the old man, I kept my answers to myself. I looked at Mr. Kunz and waited. Most of the time he was right, but every so often he got a funny look in his eyes and went around muttering under his breath. With everyone so hungry and sick, a little strangeness seemed to make him more normal. This was the first time Mr. Kunz had talked to me when he was not his usual self. He leaned close. "The war's not over," he said, his low voice chilling me all the way through. "The Russians are losing the war and need their soldiers back that have been captured by our boys. They brought us way out here and put us in this camp for a reason. Any day now they're going to ship us to Germany so they can get their soldiers back." He glanced around to make sure no one was listening. "They're going to trade us for their captured soldiers."

I looked around the huge underground barrack. The long hall was crowded with starving children, exhausted women and a few old men. Who would want us? There was only one thing more pathetic than Mr. Kunz's unbelievable statement. That was the light in his eyes. Yet, I think I knew the source of his belief. In the past we had heard lies over the wireless and in newspapers about German victories. It was easy for an old soldier to continue believing. That belief was easier to hold onto than to accept defeat. Many adults of this world, as I had discovered and would discover again and again, often make lies more believable than the truth. I looked at Mr. Kunz and smiled. He had leaned back against the wall with his hands folded across his stomach. A look of contentment was on his face, as if all the troubles we were having would soon be over. I didn't know what else to do so I got up and went to where my mom was sitting. I was still hungry, but felt that Mr. Kunz's hope was a kind of food for him. His eyes were closed and he looked happy as I left.

As it had been on the train, so it was in Siberia. No one, even the guards, was looking after us. We were by ourselves. There was no distribution of food or medicine. It was as though we were locked out of the world. We had nothing any one wanted and certainly no one wanted us. For three days, we waited and wondered what was to become of us. By that time, all of our food was gone and no one else had any. Then, on the fourth day, the soup wagon came and everyone got a small bowl of soup. From that time on, everyday just before noon, the wagon came and we got a little bowl of soup that was mostly cabbage with some potato. Strange as it may seem, the soup made our hunger worse. It was like being in the cold and coming in by a small fire, but remaining perpetually in that shaking condition of starting to warm up. Outside, the wind froze everything in sight and the snow was too deep to measure. Inside, we were warm, but starving and many were so weak that life was rapidly draining out of them.

"Bruno." My mom spoke softly as she gripped my arm. "Do you see that boy?" It was late afternoon. I had gone outside, but only for a minute. The wind was howling across the rooftops, filling the air with snow. My mom was sitting on our bunk when I came in. I turned my head and looked at the boy who had just walked by. His coat and cap were covered with snow. There was no mistaking what my mom was thinking. He had a sack of food clutched in one hand. "I watched him leave this morning," she whispered to me. "He's been gone all day. Now, he's back with food." She looked at me in her peculiar way of making certain I understood. "The next time he leaves, you have to go with him."

She was right. There was no doubt about that. At the same time, I was scared. The boy was bigger and it didn't take much to know he didn't want company. There were also the freezing wind and deep snow. I had studied the white fields around the barracks two and three times a day. Mainly, those surveys came on quick trips to the privy. There was every opportunity to lose sight of the rooftops, once you walked away. Within a short time of wandering around, I would be just another frozen lump in the snow. It would be spring before someone found me; and by that time, I would have starved to death! Despite such crazy thoughts rushing through my head, I never had the thought of not going.

For the next several mornings, I went to great effort to watch every move the boy made. Then one morning I was awake early and sure enough, as soon as it began to get light outside, he began to bundle up. I started getting ready. My mom took off her long, heavy stockings and told me to put them on. Then I put on her shawl and pulled my light jacket over that. Taking her headscarf, she tied it around my head and face. When I went out the door after the boy, I felt so hot and tied up I thought I would never get cold. As soon as I slammed the door behind me and climbed the steps, I changed my mind. That awful wind hit with such force that I spun around and almost fell. No matter how I was dressed, there was no way I would stay warm.

Looking through the swirling snow that cut into my face and eyes much like sharp knives, I saw the boy rapidly vanishing through the big open gate. On each side was the high tower Mr. Kunz had found so important. There were no guards. I ran to catch him. That was when he saw me and stopped. "Where are you going?" he shouted, above the rush of the whistling wind, when I got a little closer. He had a tough look on his face. I didn't answer. I just stood looking at him. All he could see was my eyes, but something about his face seemed to indicate he knew who I was. "Wherever you're going," he reached down and picked up a heavy crust of snow, "it's not with me." He drew back his arm as if he was going to bounce the piece of ice off my head.

There wasn't any need to say anything. I was going with him. He just didn't know it yet. Back in the barracks, I had watched the boy. He didn't have a mean face. Maybe, underneath my thin veneer of courage, that was what I was counting on. But there was more to it than that. My little brother and my baby sister Charlotte were always calling my name saying: "Bruno, just a little piece." It wasn't only that I didn't have any bread, it was the way she called my name.

159

I was the one who had gotten her food and she wanted me to get her some more. Sometimes, I heard her call my name when she was sound asleep. Little Egon, who loved to play, spent most of his time sleeping. I knew the heat and light in our barracks had given us new hope for life, but without food, that hope would soon fade. That was what gave me the courage to face the Siberian winter and to stand up to the big boy.

"Go on back," the boy shouted again, and threw the piece of ice in my direction. He made it plain he could have hit me if he had wanted. He took off at a faster pace. I hurried after him. A little way across the snow, he stopped and shook his fist, as though he was going to beat me up. By this time we were out of sight of the barracks. There was no way I could find my way back. What I couldn't figure was how the boy could find his way, since all I could see in every direction was snow. All the roads and underground buildings were covered. Lost or not, the boy was still determined to stop me. By this time we were both covered with snow and I was almost frozen. "Go back," he shouted, real tough like. "I don't want you with me."

That was the instant I felt an overwhelming urge to go back. Thoughts of the warm barrack, out of the wind and away from this boy were strong. If I could have found my way, I might have gone. The problem was, I didn't know how to get there. I had no choice but to bluff him and go along. Maybe he sensed my fear and, at the same time, my determination. He abruptly turned and began walking, only this time a little slower. I stumbled through the snow and caught up. When I got alongside, he kept walking, but looked down at me. "You can go," he said.

I tried to answer, but my lips were too cold to form the words. "O.K.," he said, and slapped me across the back to show we were friends. "Stay close to me. You can get lost out here."

After we walked for a mile or so, I found that I could move my lips and do some talking. The warmth of acceptance by a new friend can do a lot toward warming a person. "How do you know where to go?" I asked.

He pointed overhead. "See that electric line?" I looked where he was pointing. Sure enough, there was the wire that brought electricity into our camp. "That's what we've got to watch," he said. "If we follow that line, it will guide us right into the village. After we get there, we just go from house to house asking for food." He smiled at me. "The people are real good." He glanced up to make sure we were still following the wire. "Then, when we get our sack full, we just follow the wire back to camp."

I was pleased to hear him include me in what he was saying. It didn't take away the cold, but made me feel a lot warmer as the two of us, like snowmen given the power to walk, made our way into a Siberian village to beg for food.

# The Great Whiteness

"Let's go to that house," my new friend Karl called to me above the wind, pointing. I looked, but didn't see any house. We had walked about three or four kilometers, leaning heavily into the wind. The snow, whipping around us in a constant flurry, made it seem that we were by ourselves. I brushed the snow from my face and looked again where Karl had pointed. There wasn't any house! Then, looking more closely, I saw a black chimney sticking out of a roof-shaped mound of snow. The house, I finally realized, was just like our barracks, mostly underground. The entire village was hidden beneath the vast snowfall deep in the frozen earth.

Walking toward the almost hidden house, knowing that Russian people were living there, caused me to think of Mr. Kunz. The little bit of Russian that he had taught me was going to be put to the test, sooner than I had expected. I didn't think I had any reason to learn the Russian language. They had always been our enemies. Maybe it was my usefulness interpreting Polish for my mom that convinced me. It didn't matter. It was good that I had, for now I would use what Mr. Kunz had taught me, as a last effort against starving.

Finding the steps and getting down them was not easy. They were under the edge of the roof, but open so the snow had almost sealed off the door. "We are hungry and cold," Karl said, as soon as the door opened. He spoke Russian worse than I did.

A large Russian woman opened the door a small crack. She stood looking at us for a time, then pulled it open. "Come in," she said. Her flat voice said a lot more to me about hunger, cold and hard times than her words. Even though the weather was heavily overcast and the wind constantly whipped the snow, it was dazzling white outside. Walking into the underground house was like walking into the dark of night. The only light came from a dim electric bulb near the large stove and from a small window under the peak of the roof, at each end of the one long room. As my eyes slowly adjusted to the dark, I saw a man and three children about my age sitting around the stove. They were looking at us without moving or saying anything. I watched as the woman walked to the far side of the room and reached far into a wooden box. She brought a medium size potato to the rough-hewed table and cut it in two equal pieces, handing one piece to each of us and saying something in Russian that I didn't understand. The silent eloquence of giving speaks a beautiful language, all its own.

"Thank you," Karl said in Russian and put a hand to his stomach indicating how good the potato would be.

"Thank you," I repeated, and tried to smile, but my face was too cold. I felt the warm air send shivers racing across my whole body. I couldn't stand still or stop my teeth from chattering. "Let's stand by the stove for a little while," I said to Karl, hoping he would stay. "It's really nice down here."

"No," he answered abruptly, putting his half of potato in his sack. "If we stop now, we won't get enough food before dark. And then," he looked at me as if he knew a lot more than I did, which he did, "we'd just be colder when we went out."

I was not prepared for the intense white waiting at the top of the slippery stairs, nor the cold. Karl was right. Staying by the stove and getting warm would have been a fatal mistake. The wind seemed worse and the sharp sting of ice crystals slashed across my face, but I had half of a boiled potato. All I could think of was getting more and taking everything home to my mom. No power on this earth, even my intense hunger, would make me take a bite of that potato or any other food that might be given to me. What drove me was something that overcomes the cold that doesn't come from a stove.

All that bitter, winter day of whiteness, Karl and I went to various underground houses. Karl tried to remember where he had gone the previous time so he would not go to any one house too often.

Those unknown people of Siberia living in the semi-darkness of their underground houses had opened their doors and taken us in. They gave us the warmth of their stoves and food from their almost empty bins. Not a single person turned us away. Even though we attempted to speak Russian, they instantly knew by our accent that we were German. Although the fighting was over, I was old enough to know that some wars never end. They live on in bitter memories. Somehow those people were able to look beyond our German faces and saw two cold and hungry boys. The women—almost always it was women who talked to us while the men and children stayed on the far side of the underground house—would take a potato, previously boiled to prevent loss from freezing and slice it in half or give us each a half slice of bread. No one sent us away empty-handed. They always wished us well and told us to come back.

About noon, Karl stopped in front of one particular house. The steps led up to the porch instead of disappearing underground. It was a big house and all above ground. "They'll give us a hot meal," he shouted above the wind.

The thought of eating some hot food sounded good to me. "Come in," a woman older than my mom and wearing a pretty dress told us in German after we had knocked. She opened the door so quickly, as though she expected us. There was a big stove in one corner of the huge room and I could smell something awfully good. The house was warm and it was beautiful the way light came through the big windows. "Come over by the stove," she told us. "Are you hungry?" she asked with a knowing smile as we hurried toward the stove. She spoke German, but it sounded different than the other Russians who spoke our language. We were both so cold all we could do was nod our heads while our teeth chattered so loudly that I could hear them. Sometimes you don't know how cold you are until you start to warm up.

Like someone who had known us all our lives, almost as family, the woman told us to take off our snow covered clothes. She wouldn't let us stop with the outer clothes. Everything that had snow or ice had to come off. Then a man, crippled in one leg, came into the room and helped the woman hang our clothes on wooden racks alongside the stove. He was always smiling, saying something in Russian to the woman. They would laugh together as though they were happy and really enjoyed helping us.

Best of all, she told us to sit at a small table and gave us two bowls of steaming soup that even had some chunks of meat along with vegetables. That was the best meal I had eaten since leaving our farm. Then the woman gave us a big chunk of bread to dip into the soup. It was all so good I found it hard to eat. When you want something so badly and you have dreamed of it night and day, your dreams seem real and reality seems a dream. I started to put the bread into my sack. "No. No. You eat." She took my hand with the bread and dipped it into the soup. Then she put an even bigger piece of bread in my sack.

"I told you," Karl said, after we were bundled up and back in the cold. "Wasn't that good?"

We had been in the house for more than an hour getting our bodies warm and our bellies full of hot soup. Our clothes were dry and warm. "How did you know they would give us soup and bread?" I asked Karl, as we made our way through deep snow on the main street of the village.

"Just by knocking on their door," he replied, looking as though I didn't appreciate what they had done for us. "I can't help it if they are Jewish," he said. "They're nice people and they helped us, didn't they? What you got against that?" He sounded mad at me.

I just shrugged. I didn't know they were Jewish people. I could only remember being around Jews one time. My dad and I were passing through a village in Poland about six to eight kilometers from our home. We had seen a large crowd and went to find out what was happening. My dad told me two Jews were being executed for breaking the law. I was frightened and thought it was terrible, but we were told the men were criminals and had to be punished. I looked at Karl. I had noticed that the woman spoke German differently, but that didn't mean anything to me. Her voice was kind and nice. What puzzled me was how he managed to find people who would be so good to us. "Did you notice the big pile of bones in the back yard?" I asked, trying to be friends again.

"How could I not see it?" he replied. "It's big as a mountain."

"Know what they are?" I asked, keeping my head down, but making sure I was staying close to him.

"No, I don't," he answered, but his voice was a little more friendly. "Come on." He turned toward an underground house almost hidden from sight. "Let's try one more place before we head back to camp."

I went several times with my friend Karl into the village to beg food. During those many days my mom, my little brother, baby Charlotte and I lived on what was brought home in the sack. That sack became more important than anything else we owned. Each time Karl and I went to the big house above ground, the woman and the crippled man always gave us hot soup and big chunks of bread. We got warm by their stove and were encouraged by their kindness. They didn't know us, but took us in. That would always remain in my mind—not that they were Russians or Jews, but that they shared. It always inspired me to share with others, not only because of their need, but also by remembering what this unknown couple had shared with me.

As I look back, I remember the beautiful but frightening force of the overpowering Siberian winter. The great whiteness sweeping across the land, blending the earth and sky into one, taking away the horizon. It was a land hidden by continual snowfall. There were no fences, no roads, nothing that separated or identified. All became one. There was another kind of oneness that I discovered during those winter days. Through the kindness of many people who shared what little food they had, I found a oneness with them. That almost became more important than the food they gave me.

After learning the way to the village with Karl, and finally gathering up my own courage, I started making the journey on my own.

We had been in camp long enough that many of the more adventurous ones had begun making food begging trips, as well. Short daylight hours, deep snow and bitterly cold winds were our only guards. On my first trip, I made the mistake of taking my dad's cousin, Klara Kelm, along. She had asked me a lot of times and it seemed a good idea to have someone with me. "Let's try that place," she said, as we waded through the snow. We were in a part of the village I hadn't been before. "I'm real cold," she said.

I was just as cold as she was so I didn't need any encouragement. I followed her down snow covered steps to what we thought was just another underground house. Klara knocked, then knocked again, but there was no answer. So cold that she was bold, my cousin pulled the latch and the door slowly swung open. It was darker than that old train with its doors shut, but we went in anyway. If I had been by myself, I probably would have left, but she led the way and I was cold. Even if no one was there, we had at least found some shelter for a little while.

"Bruno!" She grabbed my arm clutching with all her might, her voice sounding frightened. She backed toward the door, pulling me with her. "Look!" She pointed toward what appeared to be two long boxes on some kind of table. All the time she was getting closer to the door, too scared to turn away from whatever was there, and dragging me along. "Bruno," she said more loudly, as if to let it be known she wasn't alone. "Those are dead people!"

By this time my eyes had adjusted to the darkness. Just like she said, there were two dead people waiting to be buried. The sight of them gave me uneasy feelings, but I wasn't scared. Too many people had died on the train for me to get excited. "I want to go home," my cousin said, in a voice that was hard to recognize. The next instant, she turned and flew out the door and left me standing alone.

Klara never went with me again. I made many cold, difficult trips into the village during those early months of 1946. Those little scraps of food became our main source of life. When others died, we had the strength to survive. As winter turned into spring, more and more of our people traveled into the village. That number greatly increased when we learned that a small bazaar or flea market was held each Saturday in the square of another area village, Yurga (Jurga).

One Saturday morning, I was getting on all the warm clothes we had so I could go to the bazaar. "Get all the food you can," my mom said slowly, taking off her shawl and handing it to me. It was the same shawl I had worn many times in search of food, but this time she said it with special meaning. It was the one item that could be sold any time. A Russian woman didn't consider herself ready to go visiting unless she wore a shawl. I folded it carefully with my clumsy hands and put it in my sack. What surprised me when I looked up was how different my mom appeared. She seemed smaller and almost like a stranger. For an instant, crazy thoughts came racing through my mind. It was as though the small woman standing there was a different person and I had my real mom in a bag to trade her for food. We were down to odds and ends of clothing, but through it all, my mom had been able to hold onto her shawl. I closed my sack, put it under my arm and made my tears wait until I got outside.

The Yurga village square was an open area with a few snow-covered buildings on the far sides. Anyone who had something to sell just took it and waited. Soon people came with money or food to buy or trade. I did well with my mom's shawl. The fine quality and deep colors caught the eyes of all the people. A man, with his wife standing back a little way, quickly examined the shawl and paid me more rubles than I had hoped. As soon as I got the money, I bought a large loaf of round bread, a bunch of garlic and a frozen liter of milk. The bread was for our hunger; the garlic for our health; and the milk for little Egon and Charlotte. Everyone ate as much garlic as they could get. When we were still on the farm, my mom even fed garlic to the chickens so they would stay healthy. Whether it was what the garlic actually did, or what we thought it would do, I don't know. Getting the milk home presented no problem. The Russian farmers poured fresh milk into metal containers, which was soon frozen. When I paid for the milk, the farmer just knocked it out of the container into my sack. In that cold, there was no danger of it melting until I got it back to the big stove in our barracks. Lugging the frozen milk, bread and garlic, I hurried toward camp and more troubles.

"You want to go to the sick building?" I arrived in time to hear my mom speak harshly to my little brother, shaking him to emphasize what she was saying. Both Egon and Charlotte were sick. For some time the Russian authorities had been coming through the barracks each day looking for the sick and the dead. The dead were carried out and placed in a small building until a sleigh came to carry them away. The sick were taken to another barracks. So far we had seen several people taken away to that building, but no one had ever returned. Any mention of the sick building was enough to frighten my little brother to stop his crying. "You'll be better," my mom told him with a hug. "Now go and play with Bruno." She took the food sack and I took off my snow-covered clothing.

From the look on her face and the sound of her voice, we both knew she wasn't asking us to play, she was telling us. Russian soldiers inspected our barracks, the same time every day, so my mom wanted us to look healthy, even if we were sick. My little brother and I began playing soldier. My mom didn't like us to play war, but this time she didn't stop us. Egon's eyes were glazed and his face red and hot, but when the authorities came, we were busy playing and they didn't notice him.

"Bruno," Mr. Oberlaender called me. "This soldier wants to tell you something." I stopped playing with my little brother and stood up. Mr. Oberlaender could speak Russian better than anyone in our barrack, even Mr. Kunz, and he usually talked to the Russian soldiers when they came. Mr. Kunz and I went over. "Where is your mother?" the soldier wanted to know. I didn't answer, but pointed to my mom sitting on our bed holding Charlotte. He walked toward her and I followed. After the soldier got through talking, Mr. Oberlaender told my mom in German that we had been chosen to help him take care of the barrack. "When someone dies," Mr. Oberlaender told us, "you and your son will carry him outside. If there are children left without parents, you are supposed to tell me, so I can report it to the authorities."

My mom didn't say anything. It was obvious why the soldier had chosen us. Everyone else in the whole barrack was either sick or so weak they could hardly walk. It was obvious that my mom didn't like the part about reporting children without parents. She held Charlotte tightly in the tattered blanket so the soldier couldn't see how sick she was. "What will happen to the children who have no parents?" she told Mr. Oberlaender to ask the soldier. She was scared and so was I, but my mom wasn't about to do anything she thought was wrong.

The soldier looked at my mom as though he was going to walk away, but changed his mind after looking at my little brother and me. "They will be placed in an orphanage," he had Mr. Oberlaender tell her, "and raised as Russians." My mom nodded her head to show she understood his orders. She was not saying she would obey. "And one more thing you must do," the soldier made clear before marching away. "You are to report any who are too sick to care for themselves and we will see that they receive care."

The sick were around us everywhere. Even though the authorities had started making deliveries of hot soup once a day, it was not enough. The terrible trip across Russia, the lack of food after we arrived, and the great cold, along with the rats and lice had all taken their toll. The will to survive faded day by day, especially in the very old and the very young. Death, as life in Siberia revealed, can play the waiting game.

From that day, my mom and I began each morning by carrying the dead outside. That was when I learned even more about lice. I had fought the rats with a stick. At least I could see them. I had no way of fighting the lice. There were so many of them sucking the life from all of us. When we took a dead body out of a bunk, the bed would be so full of lice it was like someone had poured living sand across a blanket. Lice, I discovered, will not stay on a dead body after it has become cold. They search for another warm body to help turn into a corpse. We tried to fight them each day and through the night. Grabbing a louse from our clothing or body, especially our hair, we crushed it between our fingernails. But there were so many it didn't make any difference. We dug at our bodies until they bled.

"Cut it off." My mom and I were in front of our bunk, sitting on the floor. She had given me a small pair of scissors and I was kneeling on one knee holding her long, black hair in my left hand. "Cut it off," she said again. "It has to come off." For several days infection had been spreading across her scalp, caused by head lice. I looked at what had been my mom's lovely hair and hesitated. "That's the only way," she told me. "When you cut off all my hair that will get rid of them."

I finally began cutting. As I got close to her scalp, I could see the skin was crusted and raw. The smell made me sick as the broken places oozed a sticky, yellow liquid. In a few minutes, all of my mom's long, black hair was gone. She looked terrible, but I felt good about helping her. I took the hair filled with those little gray specks and threw the whole mess into the fire. In a few seconds all the hair was gone and so were those painful, little creatures. Slowly, in the days to follow, my mom's head began to heal. I kept cutting her hair short and destroying the lice.

"I don't have to worry about combing it," my mom told me, after one of the cutting sessions. After she said that, I was able to smile and I felt better.

# Spring in Siberia

By the end of winter, death had taken a large number of the people who came with us on the train. Life was different. It seemed as though we were waiting for something. The huge buildings that had been so crowded were partially empty. The long lines of people, streaming to the small privies behind the buildings, became shorter and shorter. The pump house, always heated to prevent freezing, was almost deserted. When I went to get water, there were only two or three before me. In the past I had often grumbled about having to wait, especially in line to the privy. And now, to have so few people in that dreadful and lonely place made it seem much worse. It was at the pump house and the toilet where I became the most conscious of our loss.

"Everybody come with me." A Russian soldier, speaking almost understandable German, was striding through our barracks, commanding everyone to go with him. "Bring all of your clothing," he shouted. That last command was not hard to obey. We were wearing almost everything we owned. The only reason anyone had extra clothes was due to the many deaths. The soldier set off at a rapid pace and everyone in our barrack followed. To my surprise, he was walking toward the village that I had come to know so well. Finally, we came to a building that was not as big as our barrack, but it was above ground. When we went up the few steps, then inside, there were big tubs of steaming, hot water waiting for us. The women chattered happily as if they had been given something wonderful. My mom quickly ushered us over to one of the tubs like it was the grandest thing in the world.

"Give me all of your clothes," the soldier commanded. There were about twenty-five women, a lot of children and a few old men in our group. In a few minutes all of us were completely naked. We didn't mind. The deplorable condition of our living quarters had taken away any feelings of modesty. The soldier took our clothes and put them in a small room that was as hot as an oven. I had never seen such splashing and washing. The room was warm, the water was hot, there was soap and it was our first bath in many months.

When our clothes were returned, they were hot and smelled like they had been scorched. It was a while before we could put them on. The happy part was that all lice were killed and the eggs destroyed. For the first time in ages we felt clean. Our clothes were still just as filthy, but the dirt was baked clean and not crawling around, biting as before. About once a week we went to the bathhouse and had our clothes placed in the hot room. After we had been there two or three times, the soldier merely told us we could go. Making sure that everyone in the barrack came along, we made the two or three-kilometer walk. Once again, we were starting to feel good about ourselves. Slowly, the last of the lice disappeared. Many of the women, just like my mom, had cut off their hair because of scalp infection. Now we started healing, but it was too late for many of the old people. They continued to die. Shortly after daybreak, as we had been ordered, my mom and I began our search for the dead. It no longer surprised me that there were few tears when a loved one died. We were borderline people. Every day we lived so close to that land of no return that it was peacefully accepted when a family member or friend crossed over.

Whenever we found a dead person, my mom and I packed the body up the stairs to a small building. There were always two or three dead bodies stretched out on flat, wooden slabs by the time we got there. Whoever brought them took time to fold their arms across their chests. We did the same thing. About mid-morning, a small, white horse came drawing the little, wooden sleigh. The horse looked strange to me. It acted almost wild and had long, shaggy hair. Sometimes all the barracks produced enough bodies for two or three loads. "Food for the wolves," the old man said to me one morning, as we stood watching the loaded sleigh disappear. I didn't say anything. I didn't want to know. The old man, with a woman's scarf tied around his head, looked at me with a grim chuckling sound coming through his wrinkled and puckered lips. He didn't have any teeth and always seemed to be chewing, even when he didn't have anything in his mouth. "You listen tonight," the old man continued. "You'll hear them." He gestured toward the sleigh, almost lost in the morning gray with only tracks to mark where it had been. "No matter how far he goes before dumping them, we'll hear the wolves howl when they feast tonight." He made a sick, sucking sound with his flabby lips.

I turned away so I couldn't hear him and went down the steps. I didn't want to listen. I had heard the wolves. I knew what was happening across the frozen miles. Sometimes their terrible and frightening din had seemed to surround me and felt very close. I always tried to get out to the privy each night before dark. That was not always possible. There were sometimes those unwanted calls that were often so demanding while in the big room, but that dwindled down to nothing while sitting on that very cold hole. It was then that I had heard the clamorous chorus of howling wolves. I knew, but I didn't want to think about it. I didn't want to picture people I had known being torn apart and eaten by fighting wolves. I tried to keep those pictures out of my mind.

The old man followed me down the stairs. He came hobbling along like some stiff-legged bird. "It don't make no difference," he said, seeing my bad feelings and trying to make me feel better. "Once you're dead, it don't matter what happens to you."

"I care," I told him, and he didn't say any more. My dad had a way of ending all talk. That was what I had done, although I hadn't stopped to think about it. The old man and I packed another body up the steps and laid her in the shed. The sleigh would be back in an hour or two for another load. After that, only the living would be in camp.

I quickly returned to our area of the barracks. Some days I had lingered outside to climb a little hill not too far away. On a clear day,

I could see for miles. Besides trying to overcome my feelings about packing dead bodies, I would look to see if anything was moving across the endless miles of snow. Perhaps there would be a wood delivery or they would be bringing soup. I didn't have much hope of that since all deliveries were made late in the night or so early in the morning that everyone was still sleeping. As soon as the men bringing soup yelled, everyone ran to get in line. That day it was different. I was concerned about my mom who was very sick. That was why the old man had offered to help carry the two dead people to the little shed. My mom had managed to nurse both Egon and Charlotte through their sickness. Now, she was down. I was doing my best to see she wasn't taken to the sick building.

When I entered, I could see at a glance that she had not eaten any of the soup I had saved and heated on the stove. She had been coughing for some time and that worried me a lot. I had seen others cough up blood and before long they died. I was trying to see if that was happening without her knowing. When I got close to the bunk, she opened her eyes. Her dark eyes were bright just like Egon's had been when he had been so sick. "Bruno." My mom spoke softly, but I could still hear her. "Bend down," she said. "I want to feel your forehead." That was just like my mom. Even though she was so sick she couldn't get up, she was thinking about the three of us. "You stay inside," she told me, dropping her arm back to the bed as though the effort had completely exhausted her. "Your fever is almost as bad as mine."

I hadn't told my mom I was feeling bad. When you are always hungry and your mind is hardened to what is happening around you, it's hard to know if you are really sick. Watching people die, then carrying their bodies up the snow-covered steps to wait for the little white horse and the sleigh, creates a kind of sickness within, that at least for awhile, hides your own sickness. After my mom told me to stay inside, I did, but it was too late. The sickness had come on me. I fought it in every way I could. I forced myself to eat some of the watery soup brought everyday. I made it go down my throat and then clamped my teeth to make sure it stayed there. To be hungry all of the time, to dream of food every minute, then to have soup and not enjoy its good smell or the taste of it spreading across your mouth makes empty feelings beyond your stomach.

A couple of days later, I walked over to the door and felt the cold draft always blowing there. The air felt good to my face, but I didn't have the strength to stay. I touched my face. It felt cold. How it could feel cold when I felt so hot was beyond me! "You've got the fever real bad," the old man without teeth said, as he walked over to me. "You better go over to the sick building so they can help you." He stood within arm's reach, but I had trouble seeing him. Spots and dancing things went floating across my eyes.

"No," I shouted. What the old man had said scared me. I began running toward the bunk where my mom was resting with Charlotte cuddled in her arm. My little brother was sitting on the floor. All I could think of was the sleigh drawn by the white horse and the wolves waiting across the snow. "Don't let them take me," I shouted at my mom. "I don't want to go." The strange part was that even though I shouted, the words came out in a little whisper. No one heard. The distance from the door to the bunk suddenly became a long way. The dirt floor, hard as concrete, the bunks and all the people began to move as in a great, distorted circle. What I felt, I had seen in others. I had seen them fight the typhus fever with all their remaining strength. I had seen them become weaker and weaker, their eyes sinking into their heads until they were two small balls of fire. I had seen them go out of their heads and talk crazy about all kinds of things. Some had gotten wild and had to be held down. Then, I had seen them die. Those were my fears. All I wanted to do was get back to my mom, to feel her arms around me, and stay right there. I never made it

Slowly, I could feel myself moving through the edge of darkness and into the light. Just when I could see faces looking down at me, the light would fade and I would drift back to the distant darkness. Then the light came strong and stayed. I saw where I was. All around me were rows of bunks filled with sick people. I was in the sick building!

"Are you hungry?"

"Katharina!" The name of a young girl about seventeen or eighteen who had been in our camp in Poland, came to my lips. She was standing by my bunk, looking down at me. She was holding a steaming kettle in one hand and some bowls in the other.

"I've got some hot soup." She smiled at me.

"Where's my mom?" I asked her, forgetting about being hungry. I wasn't going to stay in that building if I could find my mom.

"Well!" She gave me a mysterious little smile. "She's here." Katharina pointed toward the other end of the long building. "Your mom is right down there. She's been sick just like you."

That was the best news I could have heard. I started to rear up as if I could jump out of bed and run to her. As soon as I got my head off the blanket, everything began moving, and that edge of darkness came in waves before my eyes. I dropped back with big drops of sweat running down my face.

Katharina pulled the blanket around me. "You'd better have some soup and wait a little while before going down there." She looked at me with real concern on her face. "I've been trying to feed you for a whole week. Another day or two won't be too long." She poured some soup into a bowl. "Besides," she brought a spoon of warm soup to my lips, "I've told your mom all about you every day."

What Katharina said made me feel better. For three days I was too weak to get up, so I had her deliver my messages. As soon as I got enough strength to raise my hand, I discovered, like everybody else who got typhus that I had lost all of my hair. That was why little Egon and Charlotte had been able to fool the authorities about their sickness. For some reason, they had kept their hair. Then, three days later, with Katharina's help, I got out of bed and went to my mom. "Bruno." Tears were in her eyes. She held out her arms and I fell into them. "It's really you and you're strong enough to walk." She slid over and made a place for me. "Get in," she said holding onto me.

"You're not going back." And that's where I stayed for another three days before I had the strength to get up and put on my clothes.

All the time, we were dreadfully worried about little Egon and Charlotte. Charlotte was so weak, that she no longer walked. With all the sickness and dying, there was only Egon to look after her. Every time someone came by, we would ask about them. No one seemed to know. Katharina, who hadn't seen them since we were in Poland and wouldn't be able to recognize them, was of no help. "Go find them, Bruno," my mom urged, with a frantic sound in her voice, as I got dressed for the first time. "Then come right back and tell me." She was so weak her voice was a hoarse whisper. "I've got to know what has happened to them." She was worried that they might have been taken to an orphanage while we were in the sick building.

The camp had been in continual turmoil since we got off the train four months earlier. Almost everyone had gotten sick; hundreds had died; some had wandered off, knowing they would never come back. No one knew the whereabouts of anyone outside their immediate family and parentless children were taken away by the Russians. I understood the tears in my mom's eyes, so I moved as fast as I could. It had been almost two weeks since my little brother and baby sister had been with us. From all that had happened, there was little hope of seeing them again. And yet, I never felt that way. I was convinced that they had to be alive and waiting for us. We were a part of each other. I would soon know if they were dead or had been taken away by the Russians.

I headed for our barracks. Hurrying to that portion of the bunk where we had slept, I was keenly devastated to find other people there. "Haven't seen any little boy and baby girl around here," the woman said. "We just saw this bed and no one was here so we took it." She looked like she was concerned. "I hope you find them."

After that, I went from building to building, asking everyone if they had seen a little dark-haired boy and a blonde baby girl. Finally I saw some people who had been in the same train car with us. "They're not in this building," a woman told me. She looked hopeful. "They might be in the next building over. She smiled as though there was good news. "Yesterday morning, when I went to the soup wagon, I saw a little boy in line. He went into the building next to this one."

Trembling all over, I thanked her and hurried in that direction. And that was where I found them. No wonder the woman hadn't recognized Egon or Charlotte. They were just skin and bones and each a ragged bundle of filth. If it was possible, Charlotte was even filthier. They were lying in a bunk with a woman I had never seen. She was sick with fever, but conscious. "Egon," I shouted. That was all I could do. I was so happy to see them; I just called his name. He came up out of that bunk like a shot and into my arms. I think he was even happier to see me than I was to see him. He started crying. I was crying. Charlotte was crying and even the lady was crying.

After I had held my little brother for a few minutes, I took Charlotte into my arms. She was almost two years old, but so small and weak she appeared to be a little baby. We were happy enough to make up for all the trouble we were having. I looked down at Egon. He was six years old, all bone and skin, but his eyes were bright pools of happiness. "Who took care of them?" I asked the woman. "How did they get food?"

The woman, so sick she could barely raise her arm, rubbed the tears from her eyes. "You should have seen him," she said, indicating my little brother, who was clinging to me as though he would never let go. "He never missed the food wagon. He was always out there with his pan. After he got the soup and the bread, if they had any, he came in and fed the little one first. He gave her half and ate the rest himself." The woman smiled with real pride at what Egon had done. "That's what he did every day, and that's why they are alive." She made a futile gesture. "I was too weak to help, and everyone else had their own troubles. They were on their own."

I looked around at the people in the big room. She was right. They were sick old people, barely able to move. Thanking the woman with all of my heart for what she had done, I took the two little ones and began the giant job of trying to clean them up. I couldn't do much, certainly not what my mom could have done, but they were in such bad condition that even I was able to bring about vast improvement. Finding an empty bunk after their scrubbing, I got us settled once again. The very next thing I did was run to my mom. "I found them," I shouted, running toward her bed. I told her, just as proud as I could be, about finding them and what Egon had done. That news was the best medicine she could have received. She was happy again. No matter how sick we had been or what we had lost, we were all still alive and together.

My mom and I were as well as could be expected and living in the barrack where I had found Egon and Charlotte. About half of the people had died, leaving nearly four hundred to occupy all of the barracks. That meant there was room for us to live in any of the buildings. When it was too late to prevent the dying, Russian authorities had started bringing more food for us. They brought dried foods, rice, flour and poorly baked dark bread. Our people made the flour into noodle strips and cooked them in hot water. On our way back from the pump house, the old man and I had stopped to talk for a few minutes

"Hear that?" The old man without any teeth had gone to the water house with me.

"Hear what?" I asked him. I knew his hearing wasn't good and I would have heard anything he did.

The old man, dressed in a ragged black coat with a cap covering most of his gray hair, grinned a toothless grin at me. "Spring," he said, with the sound of hope in his voice. "It's all around us."

I must have looked at the old man with my disbelief showing awfully strong because his grin widened. The snow was still six to eight feet deep in places. There wasn't a tree or bird in sight, never had been, and that was what I knew. "What do you mean?" I asked, curious to know what he was talking about. "I haven't heard anything."

The old man, like an old hen cocking her head to listen for a worm, twisted his head to one side, as though hearing something real faint or far away. "Listen," he said. "You can hear it." Caught by his enthusiasm and to please him, I listened. How surprised I was to hear what the old man with the bad ears was hearing, the sound of running water. I smiled at him, and he stood grinning at me. We shared a secret that soon everybody would know. The earth was announcing the return of spring. It was promising that tomorrow would be better. Somewhere, down under the snow, little streams were being formed as the May sun brought warmth back to Siberia. The old man picked up his bucket. "It'll go fast," he said, referring to the snow, "now that the big melt has started. The rivers will run full, and all this snow will soon be fishing water on its way to the ocean." He laughed as he spoke in happy anticipation of summer sun.

What the old man said, proved to be true. The snow vanished more quickly than I could have imagined. As the warmer days came, my old friend had one more bit of wisdom to share. "Things will change when the snow is gone," he said with a mysterious smile, looking up at the towers. All through our winter stay in the barracks, he had held onto the belief that those towers meant something special. Perhaps his memories of spring offensives as a soldier and the persistent belief that we were going to be traded for captured Russian soldiers made sense in his peculiar way of thinking. It was great learning from the old man. He had taught me something special, how to ask for food in Russian; he had taught me to observe the hidden world about me, such as the return of spring; and he had taught me the power of hope, even if I couldn't believe what he knew to be true. That was the last time I was to learn anything from old man who had no teeth. The next day, still early in the morning, several Russian soldiers came into our barracks.

"Reule." A soldier with a list in his hand called our name, indicating we were to stand with a group of about sixty people. Several weeks earlier, about three families had been taken away. Where they were taken, or what they had to do, we didn't know. It was our guess that they had been taken to cut firewood. Now that the weather was better, more of us had been chosen to work. In a way, the old man had been right. With most of the snow gone, changes were taking place. There was work to be done in Siberia, and we were being ordered to do it. My mom and I agreed that about anything was better than sitting in the barracks.

As we walked up the steps of our underground camp, I saw almost everyone was being taken away. The first group walked to a train, waiting on the single track beyond the towers. Our group walked alongside the train. Wherever we were going, it was on foot. I glanced around. My mom was carrying baby Charlotte, and my little brother and I were carrying our few possessions. Everyone was talking and sounded happy. I didn't know where we were going, but it wasn't hard to figure why. The return of spring, as the old man had pointed out, was not only in the air, but in the plans of the Russians as well. My mom knew right away what was happening. "Even if all the snow isn't gone," she told me, "the warmer weather makes it possible for the factories and work places of Siberia to start production. To do that, they need workers." She gave me a look of acceptance. "So, they came for us."

After about two hours of walking, we reached the Tom River. The brisk walk kept us warm, since the sharp, winter wind no longer tore at us with such chilling cold. "Line up." The Russian soldier, who was in charge, told us in understandable German. "You – you – and you." He continued to point to about twenty of us. "Get into the boat." The long rowboat tied to the dock held that number of people. "You row," the soldier said to each of six women. He looked at my mom, but saw she was holding a baby and called on someone else.

My little brother and I liked the crossing. The high swirling water and the large chunks of ice that often scraped against our boat frightened some of the women. Then, about halfway across the river, we came to a small body of land. Getting out of the boat, we walked across the island and got into another boat to complete the crossing. "You will live here," the Russian soldier told us, as we walked to a cluster of houses surrounded by trees a short distance from the river.

Not only were the trees starting to bud, but also the houses were above ground. All of that looked good to us. "Tomorrow you will start work in the brick factory."

We could hardly believe what was happening to us. The houses even had windows where we could stand and look out. The Russian soldier assigned four or five families, depending on the number of children and the number of people already living there, to each house. That meant that every room housed four to five people. There was only one bed in each room, so two slept in comfort and the others on the floor. As for heating, there was one big stove in the center room. But, what we had was a vast improvement over the camp and we had a room of our own. It was then that I learned the strange power of a door. We could go into our room and shut the world out. How beautiful it was. I closed the door and it was as though we had our lives back. By the miracle of nature, we had been released from a dark prison to enter the world of light. We were alive and it was springtime in Siberia.

Working at the brick factory was hard work, but far better than being in the underground camp. Both my mom and I helped to make bricks while Egon looked after Charlotte. We got one day off each week and worked eight or nine hours the other days. Although our pay was irregular, we did receive fifty rubles every two to three weeks. I was extra proud because I got paid the same as my mom. My job was digging clay and putting it in small rail wagons about three and a half feet wide, three and a half feet deep and five feet long. These were pushed on iron tracks to the mixing place and weighed several hundred pounds when loaded. That first payday was really something. The foreman came to where I was working and said, "Here's your envelope." I dropped everything to see what I had. There were the fifty rubles, all in bills. I felt pretty important.

# Thieves of Life

Each morning Russian guards marched a line of us prisoners into the brick factory. The sight of them was a grim reminder that not everything was back to normal. A couple of times, I managed to talk with one of the other prisoners. But he didn't know about any of my family, and I didn't know about any of his. Once on the job, the prisoners worked beside the Russians mixing clay and a grassy material that resembled chopped straw. After the mixing, a large machine pressed the mixture into bricks that were cut into various sizes by means of a wire cutter. The bricks were then stacked three pallets high on another wagon and pushed into electric ovens to bake them. When the oven was opened, there were thousands of red bricks ready for use in building.

"Bruno," my mom said to me the first day we had off, "go to the store and buy some food." We were happy. We had both received our first pay. It wasn't much, but to us it was a fortune. The difference between having something and having nothing, as I came to appreciate, is too great for numbers. Along with our wages, we had been given ration stamps. Credit for food had been given to us from the first day, but now we could pay for what we wanted. The ration stamps made it possible for us to buy basic foods if we had the money. The fact that we had both stamps and money made us feel awfully good. "Get the most you can," my mom told me, taking some rubles from our combined pay that she had safely tucked away. I could tell she was happier than she had been for a long time. "I would go with you, but you understand Russian better and I want to spend more time with the children." She looked at Egon, who enjoyed living in a house, and at Charlotte, who was starting to toddle around the room. They were both sticking close to my mom. "I'll fix something nice to eat when you get back," she promised.

"Going to sell this at the bazaar?" The Russian storekeeper, a tall, stooped man speaking a mixture of German and Russian asked me, referring to the loaf of dark bread I had just bought. Instantly my ears perked up. The storekeeper was standing behind a small counter with scant supplies on the shelves in back of him. One lesson I had learned well was that a chance remark or action might make the difference between living and dying. It started me thinking and I developed a course of action. Tucking the loaf of bread into my sack, along with a few other things, I set off for Yurga and the black market at the bazaar.

"Bruno," my mom said to me in great surprise, as I came proudly into our room. "How did you get so much?"

I was excited to tell her about selling a loaf of bread on the black market. With a ration stamp, the bread had only cost two rubles. I was able to get almost fifty rubles for it on the illegal market. Using the extra rubles, I bought all the potatoes and carrots I could pack home. My mom listened but her happy look changed into grave concern. It made me feel big and important to see how she worried over what I had done. Actually the danger of black market dealings was slight, since everyone, even the soldiers, was doing it. Danger or not, after that first time I was convinced. If it was a choice between starving or having a little more food, then the black market was for me.

Despite our pay, ration stamps and the black market, there still was never enough food to satisfy our hunger. My mom continued to ration us, always making sure we had something for the next day. We were also busy looking around for any natural foods we might find. Once we went into the woods and picked what we thought were edible mushrooms. That was a mistake. We all got sick. But, we did find small strawberries that were extra sweet and tasted good. The days of the early spring of 1946 passed slowly as I learned to deal on the black market and develop a sharp eye for berries or plants we could eat. In the process, our life by the Tom River soon settled into a resemblance of home. We rose each morning before light and a group of us rowed the river, crossed the island, and rowed the rest of the way to the factory. On our day off, I went about my specialty—that of making my best deals at the bazaar.

"Hey kid, where you going in such a hurry?" It was my day off. Before crossing the river the day before, I had been to the store that was just outside the factory. Since it was payday, I had used my pay and my mom's, along with our ration stamps, to buy two loaves of bread, some rice and peas. Then, the next morning, I had taken the bread to the bazaar. For several weeks I had made good trades. The bazaar was located in the middle of Yurga, about an hour's walk from our house. It was open to everyone. If you wanted to buy, you just walked around, looking at what was there and made an offer. If you had something to sell, you found a spot and sat down. There were no booths. It was an outdoor market where each person could leave in a hurry if trouble came. As it so happened, I had been to the bazaar and sold the bread for a good price. But, there were no potatoes for sale. I stuck the money in my pocket and started walking home, wondering all the time where I could buy some potatoes. That was when these two big boys came alongside me. "We're going your way," they said to me, "so we'll just walk with you."

I was pleased to have them. I didn't have any friends, except for my family, since going to work every day took most of my time. It took an hour or more from the time we left home and crossed the river, before we reached the factory. So, it was usually dark when we left home and dark when we got back. My new friends and I talked as we walked along the river. I was proud that two older boys were taking an interest in me.

"You got any money?" one of them asked, after we had walked along talking.

"Sure," I told them, proud of how much I had. "I got a lot of money since there weren't any potatoes for sale." I started to pull the money out of my pocket to show them. That was when I first sensed there might be trouble. As soon as I mentioned having money, a look passed between them that scared me. We were alone on the river road. There wasn't any way I could get away or call for help.

"How much you got?" one of them asked me, no longer pretending to be friendly. He came close and stared hard into my face.

"That's my business," I said, and tried to hurry on, but it was too late. One of the boys got behind me while the bigger one stopped in front of me.

"Give me your money," the bigger one said, "or I'll knock you down." His face was all twisted into a mean look.

I didn't say anything. I just glared up at him with my hands in my pockets, holding onto my money. I was scared, but that money was important. I wasn't going to give it to the likes of them. That was when the boy behind grabbed me. I held my hands into my pockets as long as I could; but with one boy holding me and the other one pulling on my arm, I couldn't stop them. As soon as they had the money, they were gone. I stood watching the two boys run back toward the bazaar, hot tears streaming down my face. That was the second time I had something stolen from me. Just a few weeks before, I had taken a pillow to the bazaar. It was one of the two pillows that my mom had brought with us on the train. I had it in my sack and knew I could get a good price. Finding a place to sit down, I had removed the pillow from my bag and put it beside me. It was pretty nice. My mom had done a lot of fancy stitches around the edges of the cover. While folding the sack, I was busy stretching my neck to see what else might be for sale. I knew the pillow would bring enough rubles for at least four or five buckets of potatoes. My main thought was how to get them home. As it turned out, I didn't need to worry. When I reached for my mom's pillow, it was gone! Someone had snatched it from right beside me. I felt terrible. How was I to tell my mom? But I did. Now, it had happened again. All our food money was gone!

This time I felt worse, perhaps because it was money. The tears were so heavy in my eyes; I didn't even know where I was walking. How could I have been so stupid as to tell those boys I had money, I kept asking myself. It was just like the time that I told where my mom had hidden her wedding ring. I'm so stupid, I thought. Strangers ask me anything and I just tell them, as though they were my life-long friends. It was too much. Alone on that Siberian road, my heart was as empty of affection as my stomach was of food. If anybody acted like my friend, I believed him. I wanted to have friends and to be one. In spite of all that had happened to me, I still trusted people. I wanted them to like me, just as I liked them. I wanted love.

By the time my tears had cleared, I had wandered to the edge of the river. It was running high, as the old man had predicted, caused by the melted snow and ice from the high country. I stood, feeling very much alone, staring into the dark and swirling water. For the first time in my life I felt the terrible despair of having no reason to go on living. I had been so frightened I couldn't move. I had been so sick I would have gladly died. I had been so hungry that food was an all-consuming dream. I had been so cold; it was easier to stay cold, than it was to get warm. I had kicked hardened snow over people I had known and left their bodies in a strange land. All of that was different. I had had those terrible feelings, but at least they had been a part of living.

I no longer had anything. The thieves had taken more than my money. I didn't want to live. I didn't want to go home and tell my mom. I stood atop the steep cliff, looking at the swiftly flowing Tom River until it seemed I was rushing downstream and the water was standing still. My eyes seemed to draw me into the river, to become a part of it. One jump was the thought that leaped into my mind. One jump and it will all be taken care of. I was well aware that from the day we left Romania, we had known hard times. But, what a difference between having hard times and having nothing. That was the moment in my life when I truly had nothing. Living is knowing that someone loves you, needs you, and depends upon you. There were no feelings inside of me reaching for life. I stood tottering be-tween the river and land, between life and death, between thieves who had stolen everything from me, and my mom who was waiting for me to come home.

Perhaps it was my guardian angel, that my mom so often mentioned, that saved me. As the river reached out to take me, a very disturbing thought, sharp and clear as a voice, came racing across my mind: "How will you tell your mom you're not coming home?" Like a broken fever, that grip of empty feelings vanished. I walked back to the road and hurried toward home. Never again would I feel that utter lack of hope and love for life. I was anxious to tell my mom what had happened. Way down deep, I had always known she would be watching and waiting for me—not for the potatoes or even for the money, but for me. That was what took me from the river and caused the thieves of life to disappear forever. That was what brought me home. Even if you have nothing, if someone loves you and is waiting for you, you've got everything.

"Bruno." Egon was whispering, making sure that no one could hear what he was saying. My little brother wasn't so little any more. He was six years old, could speak Polish and German and was rapidly learning Russian. He was also good at taking care of himself and Charlotte, who was two years old. "I know where we can get an egg," he whispered mysteriously, his eyes sparkling bright with pride.

"You do?" I answered, becoming almost as excited as he was. I'm sure my eyes were as big as his were.

It was still morning and a week after my bad encounter with the boys who had taken our money. It was also my day home from the brick factory. Egon and I were playing and looking after baby Charlotte. Food, as usual, was in our thoughts. We were not starving as before, but long term hunger creates a peculiar way of thinking. Between our jobs at the factory and trading on the black market, we managed to have a hot bowl of soup every day. That was what we ate, meal after meal, and were thankful for it.

My mom's potato soup was something special. She was a good cook and that ingredient is almost as important as the food. She also found a particular grass she had known in Romania that grew wild on the small island we crossed every day, to and from work. We always carried a little bag and ripped off enough for our nightly meal. The grass, when cooked with the potatoes, created a slightly spicy, sour taste. "It's good for you," my mom told us. "It will keep us healthy." Perhaps it was really true; perhaps it was just something my mom said to encourage us. It didn't matter. We ate the grass-flavored potato soup. It was good, and we survived.

"There's this chicken," my little brother whispered to me, even though no one was around, "that lays an egg right where I can find it."

We stood looking at each other, gripped by the excitement of having an egg to eat. Strange how life makes rules for us. Those who have known hunger, cold and death make their own rules. My little brother, scarcely half my size, knew that. He had learned it first hand. He didn't believe he was stealing an egg. He had learned that food belongs to empty bellies, and his had been empty for a long time. Egon was a survivor.

"Where?" I asked him. The thought of an egg cooked with potatoes made my mouth start chewing, as though I was eating that good stuff already.

"Come on," he said importantly. "I'll show you."

Everyone we knew in Siberia had been sent there as a punishment. We Germans were sent because of the war. The Russians were sent because of some crime or political belief. In one way, the Germans were better off than the Russians were. We had hopes of going home. The Russian people knew they might live the rest of their lives in that land of endless winters and all-too-brief summers. In spite of such a dismal future, they were a hardy people. That is, the ones that had survived. They had accepted their harsh punishment with a determination to make some kind of a home for themselves. Each family had a couple of animals, such as a pig and a cow. Every spring, they planted potatoes. No food can equal the potato for filling empty bellies. They usually had a few chickens that roamed across the open yards scratching among the manure heaps for worms.

It was one of those independent chickens that my little brother had happily spotted. With chickens, just like people, there is always one that isn't a part of the flock. The one Egon had seen, for reasons known only to her, had made a nest away from the hen house. In some ways, that old chicken made me think of my dad. If he had been a chicken, he would have made his nest wherever he wanted. If someone tried to stop him, he wouldn't have laid an egg at all.

"In there," Egon said, pointing to a tall patch of weeds. He and I had left the house with Charlotte and gone over a small hill. Sure enough, there in a protected area, was a chicken on a self-made nest. Looking at us as though we had no business disturbing her, the hen rose with a loud squawk, shook herself and vanished with great dignity into the surrounding weeds. "Let me get it," Egon said, referring to the beautiful, though slightly soiled, egg gleaming in the nest. He was so proud and eager that I couldn't refuse. That night, when our mom came home, there was the egg waiting for her. That independent chicken produced a lot of eggs for us. Such events brightened our days and it made Siberia a more hospitable place to be.

The warmer days of summer were almost pleasant. We rose early and crossed the river as the sun was peeping over the horizon. The air was cold, but soon warmed and it was good to be alive. Occasionally, we could hear birds singing, and the splash of fish jumping in pursuit of breakfast along the river. Making bricks was hard, but worthwhile work. As with all things I had experienced, that too would change.

"We need workers for the fields." A Russian official, tall and dressed in a brown uniform, came to the factory. It was lunchtime and the manager called us together. The official stood on a stack of bricks. "Some of the crops are ready for harvest," he told us. "We need as many of you as possible to work on the farms."

That was a special opportunity for me. Digging clay for making bricks was hard work. And work in the brick factory could be dangerous. One day when my mother was moving a cartload on the turntable to the kiln room, she was crushed against a wall and severely bruised. She could have been killed. But that wasn't my reason for going to work on the farms. Farming was still in my blood. The attraction to crop preparation and harvest was strong within me. Perhaps even more important was the fact that I would be working with food and saw this as an opportunity to get some for our family. The next day, I crossed the river with my mom, but headed off to the farms instead of the brick factory. I was wearing an old cap and I had carefully made sure the lining didn't have any holes. Then I cut a small, hidden opening. That cap was going to be of real use in the days ahead. That morning, I was assigned to work in the pea fields. It was the kind of work I could really do. The pay was about the same as at the factory, but my old cap provided a bonus every night. Toward the end of the day, I filled the lining with sweet, fresh peas, carefully selected and shelled. When I got home, my mom took those peas and made soup. It was so good; it made all my work on the farm worthwhile.

As the pea harvest ended, it came time to cut the cabbage. One problem about working on the farms was the journey back to the house each night. One of the big farms where I worked was near the camp where our family had spent the long winter. I knew my cousin Annemarie Ziebart, my Aunt Martha's daughter, was still living there and would let me spend the night. Every so often, when I was extra tired, I stayed with her. She was glad to see me and always a little extra happy because I had become good at filling my cap with peas, and later with cabbage. I had also learned how to split a head of cabbage and conceal it up my pant leg. Sometimes my head was pretty lumpy and I had to be careful how I walked, but I never got caught. I had learned to use my head and other parts of me for something.

"Bruno." My cousin called, as I walked beneath the big guard towers of that camp. She seemed anxious to talk to me. It was late in the afternoon, almost dark, and I was tired. There, farm work was less, but I still had found plenty to keep me busy. "You and your family are being sent to Germany."

I looked at her. Tired and dirty as I was, a sudden feeling of great happiness swept over me. I had heard such rumors before, many times. Each one had caused a spark of hope. I had never been to Germany, but I saw it as plainly as my home in Romania. In my quiet dream, I had seen beautiful farms, clean homes with flower boxes in the windows, and big Sunday dinners with long walks through the sunny forest in the afternoon. All that was because of what my dad had told me, and especially from the many talks with the old man on the train. I never stopped to remember what I really knew, that there had been a terrible war. Germany was vastly different than when my dad had gone there to buy prize cows and when the old man had lived there as a boy. All I could think of was a table loaded with food and everyone eating all we wanted each time. As weeks went by and everything remained unchanged, those sparks of hope became cold reality. Dreaming can prove to be very empty. For my own peace of mind, I refused to believe what was said about leaving Siberia. It was too painful to wait with hopes that died a little each day.

"The big commissioner was here today," my seventeen-year old cousin told me. She was too serious for it not to be true. "He said all children and sick people were being sent to Germany."

Annemarie was usually full of life and liked to talk, but now she was quiet and thoughtful. Going back would not include her. She was the right age to work, and the need for workers was too great. Still, it was good news for us, if true! My shoes had gotten so bad that they fell off my feet and I was barefoot. The rest of my clothes were so threadbare that the slightest wind whistled through them. "Are you sure that was what he said?" I asked, my voice trembling by the immense feelings suddenly bursting inside me. I had been disappointed before. Against my will, that persistent spark of believing surged to life once again

"It's true," she answered, her face happy and sad at the same time. The happiness was what she felt for us. She was convinced we were going, and that convinced me. Suddenly, I was no longer tired. I began to run.

"Where you going?" I heard her call after me.

"Got to tell my mom," I shouted over my shoulder, and never even slowed down. I ran as fast as I could. It was dark, but I didn't care. I knew every inch of the way. I had walked it often enough. Now, I had something stirring within me that wouldn't wait. I was running on the wings of that new hope. I wanted to see my mom's face when I told her. It was true this time. I could feel it. I wanted her to know. I wanted her to feel like I felt. It was late and very dark when I stumbled into the brick factory. I was sure my mom was working the night shift, so I began looking for her. A string of electric lights marked the place where she was pushing a wagon filled with clay. "Mom," I shouted, all happy and out of breath. "We're going to Germany."

My mom smiled at me, but kept on pushing the wagon. I jumped between the rails and began pushing with her. "Didn't you hear me, Mom? Annemarie told me the commissioner said all the sick and children were being shipped to Germany. That means we will be leaving."

My mom didn't say anything until we had reached the end of the tracks. Then she stopped, straightened up and stood looking at me. There were tears in her eyes. "Bruno," she said, "are you sure?"

I nodded. She grabbed me in her arms and held me tightly. That was worth more than all of the running I had done to get there. We were happy. The old brick factory no longer seemed so bad or so lonely, now that we would soon be leaving. I stayed the rest of the night and helped my mom. The next morning, at dawn, we crossed the river and went home where my little brother and Charlotte were sleeping. Perhaps, it was a new day for us as well!

# Train West

"I'll miss you Bruno." My cousin Annemarie managed a little smile that was more sad than happy.

A large group of German people was standing by the cattle train. It was just like the one that had brought us to Siberia ten months before. The engine was puffing as if it would be leaving any minute. Everyone was excited and talking at the same time. What my cousin told me about leaving Siberia was coming to pass. A few days later, a Russian official came through and told us to pack our things. We were to report to the landing across the river. It was just a few miles from the place we arrived.

"I'll really miss you Bruno," my cousin said again, glancing at the train. Her face showed how sad she was.

I didn't know why she felt that way about me. We got along all right, but I was too busy working or playing with someone my own age to spend much time with her. It was easy to understand that she was sad about not leaving with us. She would no longer have any family in Siberia. Her mother, my Aunt Martha Ziebart, had vanished while trying to flee the Russians in the long caravan across Poland. Her dad was also missing. Annemarie was pretty sure he was dead. Her brother Paul and sister Leonide were somewhere in Germany, she thought. We were the only family she had left, and now we were leaving. Looking at her face, I realized that leaving takes away much that is unseen. "Me too," I said. I didn't really feel I would miss her until I said it. Then the tears came. We were going to Germany! Feelings swept over me and I was sad. At last our hopes and prayers were about to come true. We were leaving Siberia; and there I was, with tears in my eyes. How foolish and difficult our lives often become.

The Russian official hadn't called our name yet. That was all he had to do—call our names, and we would climb on that old train and be off. A lot of women and children had already gotten aboard. They stood looking out the big doorways. With a last name of Reule, it was no wonder my family was always among the last to be called. I looked at my cousin. There was a strong possibility I would never see her again. Without realizing it, I gave her a hug.

"Olga Reule and three children." I heard the Russian soldier call my mom's name.

My cousin tried to smile. "Better go," she said.

"I can catch that old train even if it starts," I said with a show of bravado I didn't really feel. Then I felt the anger swell inside me. If it only took that smelly train to stop and somebody to call your name for us to leave Siberia, why had it been so hard? Why had we been made to wait so long? Why had we been brought here in the first place? Why had so many been forced to die? Why couldn't everyone leave, now that the train was here?

"Hurry Bruno," Annemarie said, looking toward the train. "Your mom is waving to you."

Giving her one last look, I began running. It wasn't that I wanted to leave my cousin, but the painful confusion inside made my legs run as fast as they could. There weren't any good answers to my questions so my answer was to run. Reaching the train, I grabbed the side railing and scrambled through the big doorway. That was where I stood. My mom was just behind me cradling little Charlotte in one arm and holding Egon's hand. Time passed and the train didn't move. We were used to that. It was always hurry up and wait. Those invisible forces that attempt to control our lives are always marked by certain and unchangeable ways. We had come to expect them, so we stood looking through our tears at the people we knew, waiting to leave. I felt my little brother inch forward and take my hand. My mom laid her hand on my shoulder. We were a family, and we had overcome. Finally, after some shouting and signaling, the train gave a lurch and started to roll. We were on our way west.

"Some things don't change," our mom warned us, as the journey began. "We will be just as hungry going back as we were coming out." In keeping with what she said, once again we lived with hunger. "That's the last of our food," she told us, cutting up a small potato. We had been on the train for several days. "From now on we will have only the food the guards give us." She looked at me with that special look. "And what you can get when the train stops."

I nibbled on my small piece of potato and looked around. Despite the same kind of old train and the same terrible pangs of hunger, our trip back was different. We were leaving Siberia. Every mile brightened the growing hope within us. The October weather was a lot warmer and we were no longer strangers to the Russian people and their ways. As for our food, my mom was just as accurate in her warning about the guards. They were the same, even though they had different faces. We had seen a whole car loaded with food taken from the farm where I had worked. There were crates of cabbage, sacks of potatoes, and great quantities of dark bread, along with turnips and carrots—food that had looked good to me, and even better as my stomach began its usual rumbling argument. But just as before, we saw very little of that food. Except for the occasional soup line when the train stopped for extended times, what little I did see was on the backs of soldiers. Whenever we stopped, at least one of them left the train with a heavy sack over his shoulder. In due time, he came back with several bottles and whatever had taken his fancy. The sack of our food was gone.

"We'll divide what we have," my mom had said the first day on the train. "One piece for each of us and the rest for tomorrow." That was the way she had done it on the way out and now she was doing it on the way back. The most important part of our lives, according to my mom, was always tomorrow. Survival, she taught us, is reaching beyond today.

At first it was hard, harder than I remembered. I had learned to stay alive on very little food and had never forgotten that lesson. What I had forgotten was the indescribable hunger pangs that come when you are not truly hungry. That is when your belly cries out in remembrance of what it was like to eat. That physical hope for food painfully lingers. It's moving beyond those terrible feelings of hunger that is so difficult. Along with our rush into starvation, came problems from long days of inactivity and cold nights. Hours on the train became timeless as we moved slowly across Russia. We tried to sleep, but our rest was more like exhaustion. The constant swaying and rhythmic click of iron wheels drained our minds the same as the lack of food shriveled our bellies.

"We've got to buy food at the next stop," my mom told me. I didn't know how many days we had been travelling or even what time it was. On cloudy and dark days, the mornings and afternoons seemed the same. I never realized how much passage of time is identified by what we do, what we eat and where we go. Time of day and life are shown more by our activities than by the hands of any clock. My mom began looking through our little sack of things. "There has to be something we can sell," she said.

One great advantage on our journey back was that the train stopped in villages for water and fuel. Great numbers of people came to talk and especially to trade with us. I saw buckets of potatoes, carrots and cabbage all being traded by the villagers for whatever clothing or other items we Germans had. Since we were in desperate need, the price was high, but at least there was food. It was again the black market that kept us alive, and at the same time took every possession we had managed to accumulate.

My mom examined the few ragged clothes in our sack. "There is nothing we can sell," she said, completely discouraged. We both knew that. We had searched before. I looked at my mom. Suddenly her face brightened, as though an idea had come to her. I was ready to do whatever she told me. "You will have to sell your jacket," she said.

It made sense. We had to have food. Yet, thoughts of selling my jacket made me feel a different kind of emptiness. My mom knew how much I needed the quilted coat I had been issued at the brick factory. I felt the warmth of it around my shoulders. Ever since I had lost my dad's big fur lined coat, I had been without something warm to wear. Cold was an all-embracing companion, and one I never learned to accept. I had become attached to my jacket and quilted pants, living in them day and night. Once again, the cold nights would keep me awake through endless hours. Although Egon and baby Charlotte had grown in the past year, their only set of clothes had not. They were too small and in tatters. My mom had patched her only dress so much that you could no longer see the original material.

The expression on my mom's face told me how much she hated selling my jacket. But, without food, none of us would have a need for clothing, no matter how cold it got. At the next stop, I jumped from the train and made my way toward the far end of the platform. Since we had been warned not to sell our issued clothing, on penalty of being sent back to Siberia, I wanted to go as far as possible from our own people. Some of the Germans were so strict about following orders that no matter who gave them, if they saw me sell the jacket, they would feel it was their duty to turn me in. That was something hard to understand. The very people who shipped us clear across Russia to Siberia and starved us, could make rules and some of our own people felt duty bound to keep those rules. I decided that keeping or breaking a rule depends more on who made the rule and why, than the rule itself.

"Want to sell your jacket?"

I hadn't even reached the end of the platform. The jacket was still on my back. Usually, when I wanted to sell something, I carried it in my hands and held it in front of me. The people were always so anxious to buy that I could strike a bargain in no time. "Sure," I said and slipped it off so he might look at it.

The Russian man, small of size with wrinkled, leathery skin, turned the jacket inside out, checking for holes or tears. Satisfied, he handed it back to me. "How much?" he asked.

"Three hundred and fifty rubles," I said, knowing the price was high. My thoughts weren't on the jacket, but on the vegetables I could buy. Whoever had those vegetables was going to charge me a hundred times what they would bring on the legal market.

Give you three hundred," the man replied, reaching into his pocket. He had that look in his eyes of wanting, a look I knew well.

"No. I've got to have three hundred and fifty," I told him.

The man was not a whole lot bigger than I was, and yet I knew he was stronger. He could have taken my jacket and pushed me aside. There was no one to help, and I didn't have it within me to distrust him. Maybe my trust was more than just being young. Maybe it was my way of attempting to make everything normal.

"Three hundred," the man said again, but with less spirit. "That's all I got."

"O.K.," I said, more because I could feel how badly he wanted the jacket than thinking of the extra money. "Three hundred."

Just then a rough voice sounded beside me. "Did you say three hundred and fifty rubles, kid?"

I looked around to see a bigger man reaching out to give me the money. "I'll buy it for that."

I looked at the smaller man who stood with one hand still in his pocket where he had the three hundred rubles. It was one of those times when I didn't think; I felt my way into an answer. "I've already sold it to him," I said. That was that. Later, walking back to our wagon, carrying potatoes and carrots, I thought about what had happened. I realized that life often brings tears of wisdom instead of laughter, I had learned how to sell a jacket for less money than what I could get. I always hoped the small Russian found my jacket to be as warm as I had. At least I still had the pants.

Food on the black market was so expensive that our three hundred rubles were soon gone. The next article of clothing to be sold was my mom's slip. "Sure is something," my mom said, taking the slip off in the semi-darkness of the boxcar, "selling our clothes while they're still warm."

My mom was right. I jumped from the train and began walking along the platform, holding the slip in front of me. Before it was cold, I had the rubles in my hand. "Here's your slip," I told her later, holding out a sack of dirty carrots.

Those carrots looked awfully good to us. We had eaten almost nothing for several days, and those few vegetables were more valuable than pure gold. I could have eaten the whole bunch, but my mom rubbed them clean and gave us each one. That was her way. Something for right now and most of whatever we had for the future. I didn't know where she learned so much, but it was her way of doing things that had brought us through our Siberian captivity and would get us to Germany.

"The border is next! The border is next!" Word went from car to car and buzzed from person to person inside our wagon. I was scared. So was my mom. The Russian authorities had told us that without the padded jacket and pants to turn in when we reached the Polish border, we would be sent back. There was almost none of the issued clothing left on the whole train and absolutely no money. We had spent all of our money and eaten the clothing right off our backs. The closer we got, the more frightened we got. What did help was the fact that if they kept their threat, almost everyone would be shipped back to Siberia. To make matters worse, my mom had a bad cold deep in her chest. She coughed a lot and sometimes the pain was so bad, she didn't even want to eat. . She tried to hide it from us, but I knew about it

When the train stopped at the Polish border, all I could think of was being shipped back to Siberia. I looked around to see how many people would be going with us. I got the foolish thought of being forced to spend our lives going back and forth across Russia on a cold train. Fearful of what could happen, I still had one strong hope that I could count on. Most authorities do whatever is most convenient. What is said or done in one place, especially when that is far away, is seldom followed in another place, unless there is a profit to be made. Boundaries established by bullets, as in time of war, may be clearly marked, but all other affairs are muddled. Despite reasoning that my dad had taught me, I was still scared.

There was a lot of frantic and confusing activity when we reached the border, but none of it had to do with our clothing or the lack of it. We began by getting off the Russian train. After the usual hurry-up-and-wait, we crowded into a Polish train to begin the last part of our trip to Germany. Once we were out of Russia, I began to think of the Germany that my dad, and especially the old man, had known. I wondered about people walking in the forest and singing and about Sunday dinner. In spite of those hopeful thoughts, there was a part of me that refused to believe. Deep down was the knowledge my dad and the old man were dead. It was far easier for me to believe that the Germany they had known had died with them.

"Out. Everybody out." Only a German officer can open a door in such a way that it jumps at his command. The train had pulled into the rail station at Frankfurt on the Oder. This time I was mistaken. The person in charge was not a soldier. It was a woman with the Red Cross. "You will get off the train," she ordered, "and follow me." That was our welcome to Germany.

Once again we began the process of following someone running our lives. So many men had been killed that it was now a woman in charge, but it was still the same to us. We followed her to a row of single story buildings. Quickly and efficiently she divided all the people from the train into several groups. We became part of more than a hundred women and children that went into one of the buildings. Each room was filled with the usual hard bunks. Once again we were in a room with only a bunk space to call our own. Poland, Siberia or Germany, it was all the same. Then something nice happened. We got called to eat supper and there was plenty of soup—all we wanted. My mom warned me to eat slowly and not to each too much, but the temptation was too strong. It was rich soup with lots of vegetables and something we had not seen for a long time, thick pieces of meat. Some of the meat was heavy with fat, but I was too busy eating to chew, let alone take notice of what I was eating. Within a short time, I was so full that I was sick. All of that beautiful soup was coming up the hard way. My mom called one of the nurses to come and take care of me. I wasn't the first one, she told my mom. Most of the children and a lot of the adults had gotten sick after their first real meal

The third day, we left for Treuenbritzen, which is close to Berlin. This time, we went in style. The train had seats and we got to ride just like passengers who had bought tickets. Once again the Red Cross people met us. The bands on their arms with red crosses were by now a welcome sight. After about a forty-five minute walk from the station, we came to four, four-story buildings surrounded by a fence. All of us who came on the train from Siberia stayed in one building. Beyond the fence, I soon discovered, was the hospital.

"This will be where you stay," the Red Cross woman told us.

I immediately began looking around. It seemed we would never escape our life in Siberia. There were double size bunks stacked two high against each wall. Our family and two other women were assigned to one room. In one of the other buildings I soon discovered a kitchen, deserted, but usable. To my delight, the stoves were electric, not wood. It would be a great place for cooking potatoes, if I had any, which I didn't. I didn't have to guess anymore what Germany was to be like. I remembered my happy feelings when we were told we were leaving Siberia. Why had I been so happy if this was what waited? I discovered that it is hard to arrive, only to discover you never left.

"Just sign right there." We were standing in a long line and had finally reached the table where an officer was sitting. "These are not to be sold," he told us, not bothering to look up as he signed four food cards. He placed them in a neat little stack and pushed the cards toward us. His long, slender fingers took the form my mom had just signed, as if it were some great document. He directed all his attention to the papers, never really looking at us. I had feelings we were not people to him, but some kind of walking numbers. "Now," his voice was brisk, hurrying us along, "when you get food at the commissary, you must present these cards so they can be punched."

"Is there a charge for the food?" my mom asked. Her voice didn't express any greater respect for the soldier than he was showing us. Her attitude had come out of a long and difficult journey; his must have come from being in a position of power too long.

The officer didn't answer. He carefully laid the form my mom had signed in the neat stack beside his right arm. The table was very tidy. The unsigned forms were beside his left arm, and the food cards were arranged in front of him. He was very efficient. "No," he answered, after his little table chores were done. He directed attention for the first time at my mom. I watched the man's thin, military face. It had not changed or wavered in the slightest, and yet he had changed. It was as if he were seeing us for the first time. All I could think of was that he was a soldier. We were not soldiers. We were what war leaves behind—old men, sick women and starving children. As long as this man could concentrate on forms and cards, he could be a soldier. When he saw us, the soldier part of him marched away and his true self appeared. "Twice a day," he said sharply, "there is hot soup given to all people in the camp." He looked at his neat stacks of cards and forms and went back to being a soldier. "Next," he said to the table. My mom picked up the cards and we walked away. We were hungry, but at least we had food cards. I looked back at the busy, efficient soldier. Head down, quickly working with forms and food cards, he represented men in faraway places filling out papers that carry the sentence of life or death.

"Everyone line up for health inspection." We had been in camp two days. There had been ice on the ground when we left Siberia. By now, early winter winds would be sweeping across the miles and miles of Siberian plains, and snow would be stacking higher and higher. The people we had left behind would be staying more and more indoors. Those in underground houses would be sitting in quiet darkness around warm stoves, waiting for spring. We were more fortunate in East Germany. October had brought chilly mornings and cold nights, but some of the days had been sunny and bright. During those two days I had become acquainted with every place I could.

Also, I made it a point never to miss lining up when the soup was given out. The third day was different. A man in a white coat and a large woman dressed like a nurse, with a mean look on her face, were standing in the middle of our big room.

We lined up as commanded. No one thought of doing differently. The four of us stood there waiting. I looked at my mom and felt my heart sink. Her cough had not gone away, as she had said. Just the opposite, it had gotten much worse. The last few days on the train west had been especially bad for her. "It's only a chest cold," she had told us, over and over. "As soon as we get to Germany, everything will be all right." For the first time, I had a strong feeling it wasn't going to be all right.

I watched with growing feelings of dread, as the health inspector moved down the line of people toward us. He seemed to know exactly what he was looking for. Maybe he had heard my mom coughing. Placing one end of his earpiece against her chest, he told her to cough. I watched his face closely. He looked grim. What he was hearing wasn't good. "You will have to go to the hospital right away," he told her. He looked at her with a friendly, but sad smile. "You should have been there a long time ago."

I looked at my mom. Tears came to her eyes. Maybe it was the doctor's orders; maybe it was the line of people wearing rags for clothes; maybe it was the many sick, some with a short time to live; maybe it was a lot of things, but right then something important happened. Suddenly, I was looking at everyone, especially my mom, with a different pair of eyes. For the first time, I saw them as individuals struggling to live, to be themselves. Above everyone else, I saw my mom as a person. I saw her not as my mother, not as someone whose total purpose in being was for me. I saw her as a person with a life of her own. It was then that I became dreadfully aware of how frail and run-down she was. To me, she had always been so strong, so able to handle whatever came. Now, beside the well-fed inspector and nurse, she was all bones with bright, burning eyes; eyes that I had seen so many times on the train. She was so little; she was so weak. I looked around. We were all the same. Everything was the same. I looked again at the inspector and nurse. They were wearing stiff, white coats. If we had any starch in Siberia, it wouldn't have gone into our clothes. We would have eaten it. It was then that I felt the full impact of what had happened to us since leaving Romania. It had taken strangers to make me see the reality of ourselves and to discover my mom as a person.

Egon and Charlotte saw the tears in my mom's eyes, they started crying. "It will be better if you go now," the stout nurse said, taking Charlotte into her arms. She put her other arm around my little brother. I looked at her. The stern face that she carried about was totally different than the soft, gentle voice with which she spoke. "The hospital is beside the camp," she told my mom, to comfort us. "You will be just a little way from your children."

We helped my mom get ready to go, then waved goodbye to her from the doorway of the big building where we had been housed. What we thought was a chest cold turned out to be tuberculosis. It was the contagious type, so we weren't allowed to go see her. From that time on, I tried my best to care for the two little ones.

"I'm still hungry." My little brother had just finished the last drop of soup in his battered bowl. His face was downcast. Egon wasn't talking to anyone in particular. He was just announcing to the world that he was still hungry. Sometimes it is good to say what is felt, even if no one is listening. Twice a day we lined up for the small amount of food that was given to us. It was always the same, thin potato soup. The problem came because the small amount we were given kept us hungry. There are basic differences in starving. A very small amount of food, or none at all, makes you weak; and before long it is easier to die than it is to live. A little more food takes you longer to die; and is so painful because your belly lives in perpetual hope, while it shrivels into emptiness. That was what we had— too much food to die, and not enough to live.

It was then, when my little brother said he was still hungry; I made up my mind to start stealing again. I didn't want to steal, but my eyes were always looking for food and my mind always gave me ideas how to get it. Once again, it was time to take my blue bucket and do what I had learned to do so well.

# The Orphanage

As soon as I thought about stealing food, I remembered the potato fields, not far from camp. When I saw fields, something clicked in my mind and I remembered. The next question was how to get the potatoes out of the ground.

"I'm hungry Bruno," my little brother said again. In the quietness of our darkened room, his whisper sounded loud. Since our mom had been taken to the hospital, I slept in the upper double bunk; Egon and Charlotte were sleeping in the lower. The two women in our room slept in the two double beds fastened to the opposite wall. We were on the third floor of the four-story building and baby Charlotte had just fallen asleep. Sleep comes slowly when your stomach is wide-awake. My little brother wasn't crying. He had been hungry almost all of his life and could handle the pain. Instead of saying "Good night" because he was thinking of pleasant sleep and the good things tomorrow would bring, he was telling me why he couldn't sleep and why he was turning this way and that.

"There will be enough food tomorrow," I whispered to him. "Now go to sleep and dream about having all the food you want."

Earlier that day, the two women had asked me if I knew the way to a potato field. They were just as determined to find extra food as I was. That's why I didn't try to go to sleep, but lay there, waiting. The almost silent hours of night passed slowly, but I was used to that. Long after others had fallen asleep, I waited. Stealing was dangerous. A guard or farmer, who had some kind of gun, didn't look favorably on potato thieves. With my mom in the hospital, it would be terrible for Charlotte and Egon, if something were to happen to me. When I felt the time was right, I slipped from under the covers and prepared to go. Dim light in the hallway reached through the open door, casting dark shadows across the big room. I moved quickly and softly, but even then someone was awake.

"Don't be gone too long," my little brother said.

I didn't answer, but reached back and touched him. Stepping lightly, I headed toward the door where I was joined by the two women who had agreed to go with me. Through the door and silently down three flights of open stairs and into the darkness, we left camp, following the edge of the road toward the fields. Reaching the place I had marked in my mind, we left the road and made our way along a hidden path where I believed the potatoes might still be in the ground. Guided by something inside of me, I began to dig. Using a stick to break the topsoil, I was soon going at it with my bare hands. The ground was not frozen, but cold and hard. It wasn't long before I encountered the familiar feel of potatoes. One hill was all I needed to fill my blue bucket. The women had also found potatoes and moved just as fast. Taking care that none got away, we hurried back to our beds.

"Did you get them?" my little brother whispered, as I climbed into the upper bunk. Cold and exhausted, I pulled the cover to my chin. "Go to sleep," I told him. I was proud he had waited for me. "We'll have all we want to eat come tomorrow." Then we slept.

"Your name Reule?"

I was in the big, empty kitchen, boiling the potatoes I had stolen the night before. My little brother was watching Charlotte. I turned quickly. There wasn't any way I could explain the potatoes. Despite that impossibility, I was thinking up some big lie, even as I turned. It was a young man from the camp. "Yes," I answered. "I'm Bruno Reule."

"Your dad's outside looking for you," he said with a smile.

"My dad!" My heart leaped as if it would jump out of my chest. "What are you talking about?" My dad was alive? It was too good to be true.

He smiled as if he was real sure. "Go out and see. It's your dad and he's looking for you."

I didn't wait to ask any more. Running toward the door, I burst outside and began looking around.

"Bruno!" The voice sounded like my dad's. I was so excited, I couldn't breathe. I spun around. There stood Uncle Otto, my dad's brother. "Bruno," he said again and threw his arms around me. "You made it back!"

I felt the spinning world come to a sudden stop. My moment of joy had passed. Brushing the tears away, I stood stiff against my crushed feelings. The world was still the same. It would always be the same, I thought. When I could talk, I told my uncle about our coming back and that my mom was in the hospital.

He listened, then asked hopefully, "Have you seen any of my family?"

I told him that the last time I saw them, they were in the wagon caravan, trying to make it out of Poland to Germany. "They must have been caught by the Russians, just as we were," I said. What little hope there had been faded from his face. "We didn't see them in Siberia," I told him. Seeing his disappointment, I tried to be a little more cheerful. "Maybe they are still in Poland." Uncle Otto nodded his head without saying anything. We both knew the chances of them still being alive were not very good. Since leaving our village of Friedenstal in Romania, at least one in every family had been killed; and many entire families were dead or had disappeared.

"I meet every train that comes in from Russia and Poland," he said grimly, giving a shrug of his shoulders to show the sadness he felt. "I don't feel that they are dead." He looked at me with a wistful smile. "That's why I hurried here. Someone told me my family had arrived."

We talked until the potatoes were done, then he came into the other building and up the three flights to say hello to Egon and Charlotte. "You look awfully little," he said to Egon, while holding baby Charlotte. The train trip had been hard on Egon, and especially on baby Charlotte. She no longer had the strength to walk. Born in March of 1944, she was two and a half years old, but only about half the size of a normal baby. Egon wasn't in much better shape. "How would you like to come out to the big farm where I work and help me?" He gave a deep chuckle as he spoke to Egon. "I'll see that you get all you can eat."

The thought of getting all he could eat made such an impression that his mouth popped open. He could never remember being in such a place. A big smile came to his face and he said one word, "When?"

Uncle Otto patted him on the head. He was pleased to see how eager Egon was to go. "Is today soon enough?" he asked. All Egon could do was nod. Uncle Otto looked at me. "Is your mom in the hospital next to this building?" he asked.

I nodded.

"I'll just go see her before I head back. That way I can tell her you three are doing fine. She'll be glad to know that two of my sisters, your Aunt Erna Sauter and Aunt Olga Schuett, are living in West Germany." He handed me little Charlotte. "At least part of our family is getting back together. I sure wish I could find my wife and children."

True to what he had said, Uncle Otto came back after seeing my mom and took Egon to the farm. I wanted my little brother to go, and yet, I was upset over his going. To be on a farm and have all the food he wanted would be good. What was bothering me was that every time we had been apart, something bad had happened. I was most concerned about Egon, but almost concerned about telling my mom if something should happen to him.

That night and the next several days passed slowly. Late afternoon, about a week later, Uncle Otto came into the building with Egon clinging to his hand. "I got sick, Bruno," he said, running and throwing his arms around me.

"I guess I let him eat too much," my uncle said, his voice showing how sorry he was. "I took him to the doctor and he's all right now."

Egon began sobbing. "They stuck a tube down my throat and took the food out," he said between sobs.

My uncle looked unhappy. "I feel real bad about the whole thing," he said. "I didn't know. We thought all that food he was eating was good for him and that he was just making up for the days he didn't have anything to eat." He looked at the floor. "We didn't realize the food wasn't working right inside of him."

After our uncle left, the two of us walked around the grounds, carrying Charlotte. Getting sick made Egon feel he had been gone much longer than a week. He was glad to be back, and we were all happy. He had a lot to say about the farm, but not once did he mention food.

As soon as I got permission, I went to the hospital every afternoon to see my mom. I knew she was awfully sick because she didn't say a thing about my dirty hands or my clothes being torn. She just lay there so weak that she could hardly talk.

"Bruno." I was on my way into the hospital when one of the nurses stopped me. She did a good job looking after my mom, so I liked her. "The doctor is making arrangements for you and your brother and sister to stay in a home for children," the nurse told me.

Go to an orphanage! The terrible feelings that suddenly gripped me must have shown in my face.

The nurse walked into the room with me. "You talk to your mom about going. It might be the right thing to do."

There wasn't much talking with my mom. She said we should go and that was that. Even I could figure the reason we were being put in a home. The doctor and nurses didn't have any hope my mom would live. Going to an orphanage was bad enough, but I didn't know how we would manage without her.

"Are you Bruno Reule?" It was a few days later and soon after my little brother had gotten back from the farm. We had just gotten over that unhappy time. I looked up from our bunk where I was sitting with Egon and Charlotte. A woman, younger than my mom with dark, straight hair and an extra-white face, stood looking at us.

"Yes," I said, standing up, suddenly fearful about what was wanted. By the way she looked and acted, I knew she was some kind of government official; and I was sure she was from the orphanage.

"Are they your brother and sister?" She looked at Egon and Charlotte.

I thought for a minute before answering. There wasn't much I could say, since everyone in the building knew they were. I nodded yes.

"I am Director Krause," she said briskly, "Superintendent of the home for children. You three children are to come with me!"

I remembered Siberia. When the parents died, the children were placed in a state orphanage and made into Russians. I couldn't stop the tears from coming as bad thoughts jumped into my mind. "Is my mom dead?" I asked.

The woman smiled one of those smiles that I like. She wasn't laughing, but smiling because she didn't have any bad news. "No," she said, and I liked her. "Your mom is coming along fine. She is showing improvement. But," she looked at me very closely, "she is still very sick, and it will take a long time for her to get well." There was no doubt the woman was seeing everything about us, my dirty hands grimy with field dirt from stealing potatoes, to the layers of filth on Egon and Charlotte. "You do need some looking after." She smiled again. "Don't you?"

I couldn't agree more. The weather was getting colder, the potatoes were getting hard to find; and before long, the ground would be frozen. Besides, we were missing our mom terribly and feeling very lonely. In a few minutes, I had gathered what belongings we had, and we were ready to go. It was good for us to get away from the camp and its soup line. The woman took Charlotte into her arms, while I held my little brother's hand, carrying our few possessions in the other. Reaching the door, I did as my mom had always done, and looked back. There by the empty bunk was my blue bucket. It had traveled with us into Siberia and out again. Each time it had been worth a lot. Letting go of Egon's hand, I ran back to get it. Until I was more certain of the future, I was going to hang onto that old, blue bucket.

That was the way we left the camp in Eastern Germany. I never returned. As life has taught me, there are some places you would rather not see again. Not that the camp had been a bad place, it hadn't. It had been a waiting place. And life doesn't exist in waiting places.

The orphanage consisted of two large buildings. The one where we went first, was the activity and dining area, along with a big kitchen and office. The other building was our sleeping quarters. Each room had four double bunks. There were about fifty children, none over fourteen years of age. I was twelve. The best part, there was plenty of food. It turned out to be a good place for us, although it didn't seem that way for me at first. "The first thing we've got to do," said another woman, who had come into the office when we first arrived, "is to get you cleaned up."

I looked at Charlotte and little Egon. They were sure dirty. I didn't think of myself standing there barefooted, clothes in tatters and my skin so dirty it seemed to be my natural color.

"You too!"

Suddenly I realized that she was going to give me a bath just like my little sister and brother! The woman marched off and I stood. I looked around. Charlotte and Egon had gone with yet another woman. I looked at the director who was seated behind a desk. She didn't say anything, but seemed to be very busy with official looking papers. There wasn't much I could do so I walked slowly toward the woman, who was waiting at the door. I had a feeling the director was watching me.

"Take off your clothes and jump in the tub," she said.

We had gone into the washroom where a big tub of hot water and a large bar of soap were waiting. The woman paid no attention to me, but what she was doing certainly got my attention. She was laying out a shirt, a pair of pants, and best of all, a pair of shoes and socks. I'd have taken two baths for those shoes. The weather was way beyond barefoot time. Even though I had been without shoes since summer in Siberia, my experienced feet were starting to complain. I've never forgotten that first bath at the orphanage—the big tub, the clear water and how quickly it became dirty. Nor will I forget the feeling of being almost clean, since it was several baths before my skin got back to its original color. Best of all, I remember putting on clothes that were clean and in one piece. My feet protested against the confinement of shoes.

In a short time, I felt at home in the orphanage. My family had been through a pretty bad time, but memories of what we had suffered were softened somewhat by talking to the other children. Many of them didn't even know if their parents were dead or alive. Some knew. They were dead. At least our mom was alive and we awaited the day when she would come for us.

There was one activity that I enjoyed more than any other at the orphanage. That was working in the garden in back of the buildings. The vegetables were delicious; I had spent many hours harvesting carrots, beets and, above all, potatoes. And yet, I was lonely. I was missing my mom. Each day I became more and more determined to see her, even if I had to run away. One morning, after working in the garden, I went into the office. Director Krause was working at her desk. "I want to go see my mom," I told her.

She looked up at me and thought about it for a minute. We both knew there weren't any locks on the doors. I could run away any time. But, I knew my mom wouldn't have been proud of me if I ran away. And that was better than any lock. "That's a very good idea," the Superintendent said. "Do you know the way?"

"Sure," I said, surprised I was given permission. "The hospital is beside the camp."

It didn't take long for me to be out the front door and gone. The walk took about an hour. "Hello, Mom," I said, sauntering into her room, as though I was a big shot. That didn't last long. She gave me a hug and I was in tears.

"Bruno," she said, surprised as only moms can be. "How did you get here? Is anything wrong?"

I had a great time visiting with my mom. The problem was that of my many visits, she never seemed to be any better. We talked, and I told her all about Charlotte and Egon. I tried to find something good to say. But my mom had a way of asking questions to learn the truth. Baby Charlotte was so weak that she was cared for in a small baby bed. Egon was in pretty good health, having learned how to eat all over again, but missed her so much that he often cried himself to sleep. I guess she could tell how much I missed her every time I left the hospital. Separation, in many ways, was worse than being in Siberia.

"Bruno," my mom told me, during one of my visits. "I've gotten letters from two of your dad's sisters, Aunt Olga Schuett and Aunt Erna Sauter, in West Germany." They were the part of our family that Uncle Otto had mentioned earlier. She smiled, and for the first time, I saw a little hope in her eyes. "They want us to come and live with them."

All the way to the orphanage, I thought about my two aunts. The chances we could get out of East Germany were slim. Even I knew about the military border between East and West Germany. The Russians soldiers were on constant guard to prevent any escapes. Worse than the soldiers were my mom's sickness and Charlotte's weakness. There was almost no chance we could make the trip, even if my aunts did have a place for us.

I couldn't let myself believe this was possible. The disappointment would be too great if we couldn't get there. Still, I never erased the thought from my mind. Without a reason for hoping, I spent my days watching and waiting. This time I wasn't disappointed. In December after lunch on a cold, windy day, I had gone to the playroom. Baby Charlotte was in her small bed and Egon was taking a nap. For some reason, I glanced up from playing with the other children and looked toward the door. There stood my Aunt Erna. I felt my heart pound. She was small in size with dark hair, but she was big to me that day. "Bruno," she said. I jumped to my feet and ran to her. She gave me a big hug. "How would you, your mom, Charlotte and Egon like to go home with your Aunt Olga and me?"

I threw my arms around her. There wasn't anything I could say. When something you have prayed and hoped for with all your heart really happens, there aren't any words. It seemed too good to be true.

"You get ready," she said, as excited as I was. "I'll go after Charlotte and Egon."

It didn't take any time for me to get ready. I was always ready. It was just a matter of saying goodbye. Even then, the winter darkness was settling over the orphanage and lights were being turned on, as my aunt and the three of us stood in Director Krause's office. "This is not our recommended way of releasing children," she said to my aunt, as though assuring her the orphanage had strict rules and regulations. "But," she gave a little sigh, "with so many families separated and attempting to find each other, how can anything be done as it should be?"

That was the way we left—Aunt Erna carrying Charlotte, with Egon and me hurrying beside her. The night wind was cold, as we walked toward the rail station. Few people were on the streets; and those that were, hurried by as though warm homes were waiting. Despite the cold, I was happy. At last we were on our way to a place where we were wanted. At the station was my Aunt Olga, a large woman with freckles, but the grandest surprise of all was my mom. She looked tired and weak, but the excitement of being with us and hopes of leaving East Germany had given her special strength.

"How did you get out of the hospital?" I asked, after the hugging and kissing had stopped.

"The doctor let her go because I am a nurse and can look after her," Aunt Erna told me. Even as dumb as I was, I knew there was a lot more to it than that. I was smart enough to be thankful and not ask any more questions. I learned later that the doctor didn't think my mom was going to live and he didn't have any medicine to make her dying easier. If she stood any chance at all, it would be in the West where there was better treatment available.

We rode the train all night. At first I was too excited to sleep. There were a lot of people on the train and from what I could gather, most of them were planning to escape across the border just as we were. Putting my head against my mom's shoulder, I watched the people around us. Some paced up and down the aisle, as though they had to keep moving, but couldn't go any place; others sat whispering in low voices, making sure no one overheard. Since it was mainly women and children, many of the small ones were stretched out on their mothers' laps or wherever they could find room.

"Bruno." My mom was shaking me. "We've got to get off the train." I wasn't aware that I had fallen asleep. I rubbed my eyes and looked out the window. It was still dark, but the train had stopped and people around us were moving. I didn't know where we were, but guessed the border was only a few miles away. I was scared. I knew it was forbidden to cross the border without permission. And we certainly didn't have permission. There were no walls or fences, but constant surveillance by Russian patrols. If we were caught, we could be sent back. If we tried to get away, we might be shot.

"Not too fast, Bruno." Aunt Olga warned. She was carrying Charlotte. Little Egon was holding my mom's hand. I was carrying some things in my blue bucket, but was so excited I didn't think how heavy they were. The closer we got to the border, the more scared I got. I had always been frightened of Russian soldiers. Knowing they were patrolling the border made me so nervous that I couldn't walk. I had to run. I watched the sky. It was almost dawn. Soldiers, guns and daylight would not be a good combination for us. "We don't want to be first," my aunt explained to me.

"Why not?" I started to ask, thinking the faster we crossed the border, the better. That was when I heard gunfire. A large group from the train had walked some distance ahead of us.

"Wait," my Aunt Olga commanded. We stood in the early morning light and waited. I listened, but didn't hear any more gunfire. That didn't make me feel any better, since I knew that just ahead were Russian soldiers, who had apparently shot or captured the first group. "We'll go this way," my aunt said.

It was past dawn when made our way across a frozen field. All eyes, and sticking close to my mom and two aunts, I wasn't mindful of the cold December wind tearing at us. All I could think of was the Russian soldiers and what had happened to those other people. We had been walking for about an hour when we saw the first sign indicating we were in West Germany. Even that didn't take away my fears. I had been conditioned to feel fearful and would remain that way for a long time. Tired and hungry, we finally came to a small town. We walked to the rail station where a lot of people were waiting for trains. They had crossed the border illegally, the same as we had. There was no questioning the happy feelings of my two aunts. It had been especially dangerous for them, since they had gone both ways. Now it was over. We were safe. Once again the Red Cross was helping people, so we got on the train for Bremerhaven with full stomachs.

Settled onto a seat, I looked at my mom. As soon as we got on the train and found a place, she had fallen into a heavy sleep. I thought of the long and terrible journey to Siberia and back. Our luck had finally changed. We were no longer under Russian control and could start building our lives again. We had no idea how hard that would be.

# School Days

By train to Bremerhaven, then by bus to Aunt Olga's house, and our journey home would be complete, or so I thought. It was almost Christmas when we arrived at the house where Uncle Emanuel and Aunt Olga Schuett lived. They worked for a farmer and lived in two upstairs rooms of a big old farmhouse. They had three boys and three girls. Elfriede, their eldest girl, was gone when we arrived, Gerhart and Elvira were near my age, Erwin and Bernhard were several year younger and Annemarie was the baby.

The farmer, who lived downstairs, was not pleased to have us there. Two days later, after stewing around with an unhappy look on his face, he finally gave permission for us to live in one of the spare, upstairs rooms. Once again, when we got settled, I was anxious to explore. In Siberia I acquired the skill of knowing how to scout out an area and look for things I might want. In one of the unused rooms I found stacks of old letters. I had a great time removing the stamps and starting a stamp collection.

"We can't stay here," my mom told us after she and Aunt Olga returned from the mayor's office. I could see disappointment all over her face. I didn't understand why. The war was over and everything still seemed mixed-up. The authorities in East Germany would shoot us to make us stay, but in West Germany they wanted us to leave. It would be nice to find someplace in this world where people would let us come and go as we pleased. "They're calling us Russian refugees," my mom sounded bitter. "Our home was in Romania; Hitler sent us to Poland and the Russians captured us so that makes us Russian refugees." She was starting to sound like my dad.

"It's all politics," my Aunt Olga said. "The rich people elect the mayor, and they don't want refugees bringing in all their problems."

Despite the government's refusal to let us stay in northern Germany, we continued to live in the upstairs room of the farmer's big house. We were told that Russian refugees had to settle in southern Germany such as in Bavaria or Baden Wuerttemberg, if they could find a place to stay. There were almost no rooms to be rented there, and we didn't have any money so the future looked bad for us.

The last days of 1946 were cold. For once, I was prepared. I had shoes. The brightest part of my stay at the orphanage had been getting warm clothing and shoes. During those cold days we did a lot of skating on a small pond near the house. I didn't have any skates, but I could run along and slide across the ice on my shoes. Then, just before Christmas, Gerhard and I went into the forest to cut a tree. It wasn't a big, beautiful tree, since the forests of northern Germany are not as productive as those in southern Germany; but it looked good to me. On Christmas Eve we gathered around the tree and sang carols and ate cookies. We didn't have any presents, but we wished each other a Merry Christmas. Our greatest present was being together, being warm and having enough to eat. As we sang, I remembered that Christmas Eve on the train when we were being taken to Siberia. Not even this Christmas Eve at Aunt Olga's, was as joyous or filled with such sacred meaning as that time. In that freezing cattle car, not knowing where we were going or what might happen to us, I experienced my Christmas for a lifetime.

As the new days of 1947 slipped by, it became clear that we had to leave Aunt Olga's. My mom's health was becoming dangerously worse. Without permission to stay in northern Germany, she couldn't go to the hospital. There was no way we could get medical help, and there was no way we could help her ourselves. Then, when everything looked the darkest, we got a letter from Aunt Martha Ziebart. She was my mom's half-sister who had taken care of Egon and me back in Poland when Charlotte was born. During that frantic wagon caravan across Poland, she had gotten concerned about us. She had left Uncle Gustav with their wagon, and went searching for us. In all the confusion, she never found him again. That fruitless search may have saved her life. She made her way to Germany, but never saw her husband again.

During the war years, her son Paul was in Hitler Youth stationed in Bavaria and her daughter Leonide taught kindergarten. The three of them were living together in Unterkochen in southern Germany. She invited us to come and she would help us find a place to live.

It was a cold, windy day in mid-January when we left the big house and farm where Uncle Emanuel and Aunt Olga worked and lived. I took one last look at the small pond where we had done so much skating. Again I felt that familiar tug at my feelings because we were leaving. At least I could take my shoes with me. We caught the bus to Bremerhaven and went by train to Stuttgart, Aalen and finally to Unterkochen.

"Are we there, Bruno?" my mom asked, waking to look out the window as the train reached the Unterkochen depot. It wasn't hard to see that our all day trip had exhausted her. As her sickness got worse, she grew increasingly weaker. We got off the train, but there was no Aunt Martha to greet us. The cold wind sent us hurrying along the main street, searching for Rieger and Dietz, the chain company. We discovered much rumor and legend connected with Unterkochen and the chain factory. It was commonly said that Unterkochen was not bombed because the factory had strong connections with the Americans; Aalen, about four miles away, had been severely bombed. The plant made tire chains, cow chains, tow chains and industrial chains. The company had been under full production during the war; and the need for workers had been so great that they brought in forced laborers from conquered countries such as Poland. Now, with the war over, prisoners were gone; and German refugee families like Aunt Martha's were using the barracks, where they lived.

People on the streets gave us directions to Rieger & Dietz. The plant was about a mile from the train station. Stretched around the perimeter was a seven-foot fence topped by barbed wire placed at a slant. Immediately through the large metal gates were two dull wooden barracks, separated by a driveway. A large wooden bridge crossed the River Kocher to another barracks and a building that stored a large pile of coke. Beyond them was the plant consisting of several more buildings.

"Come in. Come in." My Aunt Martha was all aflutter as she opened the door and ushered us into the one room where she and her two children lived. Leonide was about twenty-five years old and Paul was about seventeen. "We'll find room," she said, graciously hugging each of us. "You're hungry," she said and began dishing potatoes that had been cooking on a small stove in the corner.

I looked around the small room that seven of us were to occupy. The barracks had eight rooms on each side of a long hallway, with a family to each room. Aunt Martha had located another bed, so now three bunks rested one on top of the other. There was about enough room to turn around, if everyone held their breath.

Next day, my mom and Aunt Martha went to see the mayor. They were discouraged to find things the same in Unterkochen as they had been in Bremerhaven. Many displaced people were looking for family members and seeking permission to stay. We didn't have a place of our own or any employment. We still had no money. No matter where we went or what we did, life remained the same.

"You need medical attention, and you're going to the hospital," Aunt Martha told my mom, a few days later. She knew something had to be done right away, or it would be too late. Every day my mom had grown weaker, and her painful cough sounded awful. The next day, Aunt Martha took her to the hospital in Stuttgart. Knowing my aunt and the way she felt, the lack of official papers wouldn't stop her. All of the families living in our barracks were from Friedenstal. Although we were extremely crowded there, the place seemed empty without her.

Whenever I could, I went exploring around the factory. Charlotte went to the kindergarten where Leonide taught; the basic requirement was that each little one had to be out of diapers. With

Charlotte being cared for, Egon and I had plenty of time to roam. Since there were many children living in the barracks, we did not lack for companions. Gradually, Egon chose playmates of his age and I became best of friends with Erich and Erwin. Our favorite place to play, especially on cold days, was the big boiler room where heat was generated for the plant. From there, we often went to the hills behind the factory. We played in the woods or slid down the snowy slopes. One day we found a bunker across the road from the barracks. It was covered with underbrush and snow, but we found the entrance. It had been built as a bomb shelter for the factory workers. We also discovered, to our delight, that this was the place where Mr. Rieger kept his apples and potatoes.

By the end of January, Aunt Martha was telling me what I already knew. My mom was extremely sick. Until she got well, and I remember Aunt Martha emphasizing the word "well," it would be better if I went to stay with my mom's sister, Aunt Maria Albrecht in Aurich. Despite my aunt's talk about my mom getting well, I had terrible feelings. I felt she was really saying there was no hope.

Once again we were separated. My mom was in the hospital in Stuttgart, Charlotte and Egon remained at the barracks in Unterkochen and I was taken by Aunt Martha to live with the Albrecht family about 30 kilometers outside Stuttgart. "You are welcome to our home," Uncle Michael told me. He pointed to a bed in the corner of the large room where we were standing. "That is yours," he said.

I looked around. He, Aunt Maria and their five children—Emil, Elvira, Alide, Waltraud, and Helga—all lived in this one room. It was about thirty feet long and twelve feet wide, in the upstairs of the Lutheran parsonage. The pastor lived across the hall. Downstairs was a large meeting room, opening into the church. The church held about three hundred people. Aurich was a strong Lutheran town of about one thousand people, mostly farmers who raised wheat, potatoes and beets. There was no industry of any great size.

From my first day, I could see that I was going to have a problem with Alide. She was about a year younger and quite bossy. Monday morning Aunt Maria walked me three blocks up the main street and enrolled me in school. The schoolhouse was a small building with two classrooms on the ground floor. Upstairs was a small apartment where one teacher, Mr. Schlosser, his wife and their two daughters, lived. They were nice girls and often helped me with my schoolwork. Classes began at seven a.m. and were over at noon. That gave me all afternoon to help my uncle and work for the surrounding farmers.

Uncle Michael was a little like my dad. He liked the outdoors and had a great love for working with horses. When running from the Russians across Poland, he had been more fortunate. He made it to Germany with his wagon and best horses. At first, he had gone to Unterkochen, but not wanting to work in a chain factory, he went to Aurich. He immediately found work, plowing fields in the spring and cutting wood in the fall. One great advantage was that he was paid in meat, potatoes, and grain, along with hay for the horses. That was the best kind of pay.

Throughout the early winter of 1947, I was busy chopping wood and helping to pull trees to the road for cutting. I spent a lot of time on one end of a two-man saw, and delivered firewood, which also meant unloading and stacking it. As spring came, I worked with my new family in weeding potatoes and thinning beets. It was a pleasant time, and once in a while something would cause me to think of our farm in Bessarabia. Those thoughts quickly faded, as though too much time had gone by. Too much had happened for my memory to linger for more than an instant in that distant place. Toward the end of summer, all of us went into the woods to collect beechnuts to make cooking oil. About every seven years there is a good crop, and this year it was exceptional. I liked the great forest and the fields, but school remained a hard affair. Even with help, spelling remained my downfall. The truly happy times were when I got to visit the hospital and see my mom. At first, it had been very painful. She looked so much worse than when we had been in Siberia or even on the train. Then week by week, she got better. After that, it made me happy to catch the train to

Stuttgart and see her. In September, nine months after going to the hospital, she got to go home. That was the happiest for me because I could go back to Unterkochen and be with my family.

Home, or what was to be our home, was a storage room filled with greasy chains, broken machinery and stacks of wood. Once again, Aunt Martha had come to our rescue. She had gotten permission from Rieger and Dietz for us to clean out the room and make it our home. Once again, fortune and misfortune, like a pair of mismatched twins, came our way. We had a place to live. That made us happy. Working hard, we did our best to push, shove and carry away the dirt and clutter. The misfortune was baby Charlotte. She had gone blind. At first her eyes had been watery and filled with a yellow infection. Then, while I was at Uncle Michael and Aunt Maria's, she had completely lost her sight. But even blindness could not stop her from wandering about the barracks. "The little blind girl," she was called. Groping her way along the long hall, she would knock on the doors calling out, "That's me."

Then Uncle Leonhard Funk joined our family. That was really good. He had married my dad's sister, Else. While fighting as a soldier in France during the war, he was captured and shipped to England, and then sent as a prisoner of war to the East Coast of America. When he returned to Germany, he began searching for his family, only to discover through the Red Cross that his wife Else, and two of his children, Emil and Annemarie, had died of hunger and related sicknesses while prisoners in Russia. His oldest boy, Heinz, had been placed in a Russian orphanage. With no family to keep him in Germany, he had applied for immigration to America, but the waiting list was too long. When I returned to live at the barracks, he was staying with his sister and working at Rieger and Dietz. That was a blessing for us. He helped us cover the walls of our room with roofing paper, and we soon had a more comfortable place to live. But it was a lot more than that. Someone, at last, was taking an interest in us.

There was no reason why we qualified to have a room in the barracks. We had no money, and no member of our family worked for the factory. It was only through kindness. The man who gave us permission to stay was Otto Rieger. He was the oldest of the four Rieger brothers and seemed to be the boss. Because the town was mostly Roman Catholic, Mr. Rieger, who was also a Protestant like all the refugees living in his camp, furnished the mess hall for a chapel on Sundays. The services were well attended. They were more than just religious services. Just as it had been in Friedenstal back in Romania, the church served as the center of life in our little barracks village.

All things considered, life was starting to look up for us. Charlotte, with some medication and tender care by my mom, regained her sight within a few months. Our home was small, but snug and warm. We didn't have an overabundance of food, but enough. Then, just when everything was leveling out, my mom started talking to me about school. "There's no future for you without some kind of education," she told me. Of course, I knew that. I was thirteen. I could read small words in large print if there were not too many of them. And I could write my name if I wasn't too hurried. Perhaps no one could read it except me, but I could write it.

She smiled at me and then looked around, as I had seen her do so many times, in those narrow places not measured by walls. "We can't live here forever," she said. I knew she was thinking of the hundreds of times that I had brought in food or water, so we might go on living. Now she was telling me that when we left the barracks, it would again be partly my doing. That made me feel pretty proud. If we could overcome capture by the Russians, a freezing trip into Siberia and the terrible conditions there, then together, we could overcome the obstacles of getting an education.

School and I were on a German-Russian level from the start; that is, we never saw eye to eye. Walking with my mom and little Egon that first morning was like leaving Romania all over again. The walk of two kilometers took us through the town and to a hill where the three buildings of Unterkochen School were located. The first building was for higher grades, which I would be attending. In two years when I turned fifteen, I would have to leave school, whether I had graduated from the eighth grade or not. There was no time to waste. I felt the need to hurry, but didn't know how. Perhaps those feelings were responsible for what little education I managed to absorb.

After meeting Mr. Hermann, who served as both teacher and principal, my mom went back to the barracks. Egon went to one of the buildings higher on the hill where the lower grades were taught. And I walked into trouble. As soon as I opened the door to my first class, I knew hard times were back. The way the kids were dressed and the way they looked at me—it all added up to another war.

"You good at fighting?"

I looked up from my can of hot cereal. Erich, my friend from the barracks was standing in front of me. Part of my equipment for coming to school was a cardboard backpack for books and an empty quart can with a bail and spoon that fastened to one side of my pack. That lunch pail, as I was soon to discover, was worth its weight in gold and good for more than eating. It was a little after ten in the morning. I had found an isolated corner in the schoolyard to eat my "Hoover" food named for the American aid program after the war.

"If I have to," I answered."

"You have to," he said.

"Who says?" I spouted. Although Erich and I had always gotten along well, he was a little cocky and trouble seemed to follow him around. "They don't even know who I am."

"Won't take them long to figure that out," he said, looking at my clothes.

I already knew that, but didn't like the way he was telling me. There were no girls in our classes, just boys. "I've been fighting my way home from school just about every afternoon," he paused and sort of mumbled, "and losing." He turned his head so I could see the bruised places on his face.

"Maybe you better learn to run a little faster." Immediately I could see I had said the wrong thing.

"The day I run from those damn b———, I'll be dead." He took a big bite of his cereal and banged his spoon against the can. "For every one that hits me, I hit three."

"Is there enough of you to go around?" I asked, thinking of the damage to the side of his head.

"Listen." Erich's voice was mean. "I'll outfight them, I'll outlast them, and I'll make them sorry they ever jumped me."

"How you gonna do that? It looks like they've got the better of you."

"It's because there's no one to cover my back." He looked at me and I could see he was sizing me up as a fighter. "I've got to have a friend who will stop them from jumping me from behind." He put his fingers into his quart can and fished out an American raisin. "Either you fight with me or you fight alone. They're gonna get you just like they try to get me, and maybe worse."

I looked at him for a minute, thinking. "Why would they get me worse?" What Erich was saying and what I had seen in the classroom, all went together. But, I wanted to know more.

"You think when I bash them and get away, that they're gonna let you walk home like you're something special?" His lips curled into a mean look. "They're gonna jump you something fierce."

We sat in silence, eating our cereal. "Who are we fighting?" I asked, with emphasis on the "we."

"The school is divided into four camps." Erich became a lot friendlier when I said I would help. He began counting the groups on his fingers. "First, and meanest, are the Center Kids. They all live in the center of town. Second, there are the Blacksmith Kids. They live east of town and are not quite so bad. Then, there are the Frog Pond Kids. They live in the south of town. And finally, there are the Barracks Kids. That means you and me."

"Won't anybody help us?" I asked.

Erich laughed. "The Center Kids are too many and too tough. Sometimes the Blacksmith Kids pick on me, but usually they just watch. Never had any trouble with the Frog Pond Kids."

We stood up. The food break was only fifteen minutes and Mr. Hermann didn't tolerate anybody being late. There weren't many boys in the yard. Some had gotten their food and gone back into the building. The ones who weren't so poor had brought their own, not liking to take handouts from America.

The rest of the morning was a total loss as far as listening to the teachers was concerned. I was too busy spotting the Center Kids and which ones were tough. Erich used strong words to describe some of the kids. It was obvious he didn't take anything from anyone. I just hoped he was as tough as he talked.

As we agreed, Erich and I left the schoolhouse together. There wasn't any danger, as long as we were within sight of the school. Mr. Hermann managed to keep order at the school. Once we were out of sight, we were on our own.

"Here they come," Erich yelled.

Sure enough, about fifteen Center Kids came running after us as soon as we were over the hill.

"Hey you refugee kids. Don't you know you're too dumb to be in our school?"

"Dummies," some of the others shouted. "Why don't you go back to those old barracks and hide with your mommies?"

I could see Erich bristle. He was mad, but a lot calmer than I had imagined he would be. I was getting used to bad names. I knew them in Polish and also in Russian. I didn't like it, but fighting fifteen kids, several of them bigger than we were, wasn't my chosen way of spending an afternoon.

"Hey barrack pee-ers. I see you got your pot with you."

That was when Erich began the battle. As I learned later, any reference to him being a dummy was easily shrugged off. He was probably the smartest kid, and the laziest, in our school. As for hiding behind his mom, Erich was never concerned about showing how brave he was. But, to be called a barracks pee-er—that did it.

The big kid who had taunted us about being barracks pee-ers had made the mistake of running in a little too close. Faster than I had thought possible, Erich came around with his quart can. The dull clunk of head and can, colliding, was quickly followed by two more clunks. Before the boys could regroup to grab him, he was back to me.

"Cover my back," he shouted. "I'll show those d--- b------- how much of a pee-er I am. I'll knock the s--- out of them."

That was the way we walked the next two to three hundred yards, covering each other so the Center Kids couldn't slip up behind us. Luckily, most of the fight had been knocked out of them and our constant swinging of lunch pails kept them at distance.

"You wait until tomorrow," they yelled, breaking off and letting us go. "We'll get you good. Pee-ers, pee-ers," they shouted, running away with at least two of them holding their heads to stop the flow of blood.

"You did real good, Bruno," Erich said, laughing at the Center Kids as they ran away. He didn't bother yelling at them. It was obvious we had held our own. I had completed my first day of education, but Erich had another lesson for me to learn. He held out his dinner pail for me to see inside. "Tomorrow make sure you put a good sized rock like this in your bucket. It makes that pack of rats keep their distance."

When I got home, I was bursting to tell my mom what had happened at school, but as soon as I saw her, I forgot all about it. Her sickness was back. She was lying down, barely able to turn her head and look at me. Fixing our home had taken all of her energy. Once again that upward turn had reversed itself and we were headed down. My mom had to go back to the hospital. This time, it wasn't only the problem of her being sick and in the hospital; the three of us were left at the barracks with no money and no food. I could go out and steal as before, but this time it would be different. It would really seem like stealing, since we were among our own people. That was when my Uncle Leonhard Funk looked after us. He made arrangements to pick up a hot meal at the employee's kitchen and bring the food over to our home. Then, when I got home, I would fix it for the three of us. Since the big meal of the day was at noon, it was possible to survive in good shape.

For the next three months, my mom was in the hospital at Aalen with open tuberculosis. As the days got colder, I went into the woods and cut down trees to help supplement our limited wood supply. Our stove was very small, holding sticks only about six to eight inches long; but it did a good job of heating. On Saturday or Sunday afternoon, I walked the five kilometers to Aalen to visit my mom. Gradually our life adjusted to what was happening. Even school became a routine for Erich and me—classes all morning, including Saturday, and fighting our way home. The educational process, as we were experiencing it, was a means of keeping our minds sharp and our feet quick. Only once did trouble with other students come into the classroom. That was the time another teacher had come to see Mr. Hermann. The two of them had stepped out of the room.

"Hey barracks pee-ers," a tall Center Kid called to Erich, "you can't run fast enough to get away today." That was all he needed to say. Before he could lean back with a smug look on his face, Erich landed a book upside his head. That was when war began. The air was filled with books; most of them aimed at Erich and me. Of course, the more that came our way, the more ammunition we had to return. Right in the middle of a good offensive by Erich and me, Mr. Hermann came through the door. I was launching one of the larger books when his commanding voice stopped us in mid-assault.

"You will come to attention!" No one has truly been a student until a former German army officer gives a command. The gravitational pull of books dropping to the floor was slow compared to the changed atmosphere of the room. In the silence that paralyzed us, we waited for the wrath of our teacher. At first he didn't say anything. He stood seeing the entire room, and somehow looking into the eyes of every one of us at the same time. The power of our teacher gripped us. "You will stand by your seats." We were swift and we were silent, forty boys standing, knowing that punishment was coming. Our teacher slowly took a long, slender stick from his desk.

"You will come forward, one at a time, and extend your hands." He looked us over in that very calm way, that made everything so much worse. "Beginning with that row."

The punishment began. It was not only the swish of the stick across the palms of our hands that was so bad, but the wait to go up to his desk. Then, there was the almost irresistible temptation to jerk just as the stick began its downswing. To do so meant double punishment. Sometimes I wished Erich had been a little slower to fight when someone called him a barrack pee-er.

Our school days passed with the two of us fighting the rest of them. It wasn't a question of being tough or even winning. It was survival; and that, of necessity, fashions its own rules. Erich and I also learned an ancient lesson that came the hard way. When he and I had a falling out, and it only happened once, we went home separately and got beat up. From then on, it was the two of us together, back-to-back, slugging our way home.

There was also a woman teacher, Miss Moniger, and getting in trouble with her one morning was quite by accident. It was like blundering into some kind of trap and not being able to get out. She had lost her spectacles. First, she asked the class, half suspecting that one of us had hidden them. Then the search began. Being good at spotting things, I saw the missing glasses almost hidden by the hair on top of her head. If I had had any sense, I would have told her. But, the sight of her searching for glasses perched on her head was too much. When she wasn't looking, I nudged Erich and pointed to the glasses. Soon all the boys were laughing, and our teacher was looking bewildered. That bewilderment didn't last long. Her hand flashed to her head and pulled off her glasses; and when she looked straight at me, any laughter I had, along with my heart, sank clear to my toes. This time it wasn't Erich and me against the world. I went alone to face the enemy.

I've been told that education comes from personally knowing your teachers. I learned painfully to know them from Poland to Siberia to West Germany. I've been told that education is developing personal and intimate relations. I became well acquainted with the people about me, but it was hard for that relationship to be intimate when it often consisted of the sharp toe of a boot aimed at my behind. I've been told that education is preparation to face the obstacles and opportunities of life. In that, I consider myself a graduate of the greatest schools this world has ever produced.

# Epilogue

At the end of June 1949, when I turned fifteen, I had to leave primary school. Almost three years after our return from Siberia, our family was still living in the barracks. Egon had just completed second grade and entered the third grade in the fall of 1949 and Charlotte was five years old and her health had improved. In the fall of 1950, she entered the first grade. My mother's health continued to improve; but she sometimes spent long sessions, up to six months at a time, in the hospital during the coming years.

As information slowly arrived concerning our extended family, we learned that Uncle Otto's wife and children had also fled before the advancing Russians in Poland. They had been stopped and turned back as we had. They were never taken to Siberia, but continued to live in Poland. With the help of the Red Cross, Otto, his wife Emilie, and four daughters—Elfriede, Elvira, Gertrud, and Waltraud—were reunited. After a difficult struggle to find housing, they finally settled in East Germany.

My mom's parents, Samuel and Dorothea Funk, also tried to escape the Russians. When captured, Grandpa Funk vanished, never to be heard from again. Grandma Funk and her son Herbert, returned to what had been their farm and continued to live there for about two years. Determined to leave Poland and Russian domination, Grandma Funk and Uncle Herbert saved all the money they could. When the time was right, they took the train to East Germany and illegally crossed the border into West Germany. Eventually they settled in Unterkochen, with Uncle Herbert finding work at Rieger and Dietz.

My dad's parents, Johannes and Maria Reule, also fled the Russians and were captured. During the return trip to what had been their farm, Grandpa Reule was forced off his wagon by Polish people, and then beaten and left for dead in a ditch. Later, Grandma Reule and my dad's sister, Aunt Else were shipped to Siberia where they and two of Else's children died. Grandpa Reule, unconscious in a ditch, was found by a Jewish family in Poland and nursed back to health. He continued to live with the family for about five years. After that, he went to live with his daughter, my Aunt Olga Schuett, in West Germany where he died.

My cousin, Annemarie Ziebart, who had been with us in Siberia, finally managed to leave two years later in 1949. She lives in Stuttgart, Germany, is married and has three children.

Because I had received so little education during all those years and there was too little time to catch up before having to leave primary school at age fifteen, I was unable to meet the requirements for higher education in Germany. I decided to serve a trade apprenticeship and was accepted as a trainee by the Woehr Company in Unterkochen, specializing in metal fabrication. My three-year contract provided token payment in return for my training. The work-study program took about 53 hours a week. The heavy construction work included high rises, bridges and heavy equipment, such as conveyers. Every three months, I was transferred to a new department. I completed my training in 1952 and became a journeyman.

My mother started receiving widow and disability pensions, which helped our financial situation; and Mr. Rieger helped Uncle Leonhard Funk secure a building lot. We pooled our resources and that same year our extended family was able to move into our own house. Uncle Leonhard later married my mom, so he became my stepfather, as well.

Now that life was getting happier and easier for my family, I began to think about striking off on my own. Emanuel Krueger, a distant relative in America, visited our family in 1953 and this influenced my decision. I applied to immigrate to America, but there was a delay when x-rays showed spots on my lungs. Finally in 1955, I received my papers.

The Lutheran Church provided me with a $200 ticket to sail on a former U.S. "Liberty" troop ship. Mr. Krueger sponsored Uncle Herbert Funk as well, and we arrived in Lodi, California, that November.

Uncle Herbert went to work for a rubber company and later had his own machine shop business. He remained in Southern California where he married and has four children and three grandchildren.

I was hired by a building contractor, but when things slowed down and I was laid off, I didn't realize that this was a temporary situation and common in my new country. I thought I had been fired for unsatisfactory work.

I moved to Portland, Oregon, in the spring of 1956 and entered the metal trade until I was drafted into the American army and sent to Germany. I found the barracks in Unterkochen were gone. I also learned that our forced exile to Siberia had been a terrible case of mistaken identity. The Germans from Bessarabia had been incorrectly identified as Germans from Russia.

I returned to Portland and stayed in the metal work trade until my retirement. I married Isolde Schlaps, also Bessarabian German and we have a married daughter, Ramona and a grandson.

My brother, Egon, is a retired schoolteacher living in Gaildorf, Germany. He has three grown daughters. He still is bothered by his fingers, which were frostbitten when we arrived in Siberia, and has other medical problems that probably stem from our poor living conditions during that very difficult period.

Charlotte's blindness lasted only a few months. We consider her current good health to be almost a miracle because of malnutrition and lack of milk during those important early years. She lives in Buchen, Germany, is married and has one daughter. She and her husband translate business materials.

Charlotte and I returned to Poland in 1999 and visited my old schoolhouse and the farm where we lived. The house, barn and water pump that our father had built over half a century earlier were all in good shape and much as we had left them. The Sobczak family still lives in the area, and Henryka, who had been our hired girl, remembered us clearly. It was an emotional meeting for all of us. Charlotte and I plan to return to Poland and take Egon with us next time.

# Chronology

## 1940

**June 26, 1940**—Russia demands the return of Bessarabia and Bukowina regions of Romania, which it lost in 1918, following World War I. Hundreds of villages, many settled by ethnic Germans, are affected. Hitler invites ethnic Germans to return to the Fatherland.

**September 29, 1940**—The first group of 737 villagers leaves Friedenstal. Their first stop is Chilia (Kilija) near the Black Sea.

**October 8, 1940**—The Rueles leave by bus for Galatz (Galati), where they stay briefly before boarding a large riverboat on the Danube to Zemun (Semlin), Yugoslavia, outside Beograd (Belgrade). Bruno comes down with measles and is in a coma, having to stay in a Zemun hospital for weeks. He joins his family, living in a former schoolhouse in Liboch. (This Sudetenland region of Germany is now in the Czech Republic.)

## 1941

**Late summer 1941**—The Reule family leaves by train for Waldhorst and Kutno in German-occupied Poland. They are issued a run-down farm in the village of Stefanov.

## 1943

**Spring 1943**—A baby girl is born and dies shortly after; Gotthilf is drafted into the military.

# 1944

**March 1944**—Baby Charlotte is born; word arrives that Gotthilf is dead.

# 1945

**January 1945**—Stefanov village is caught between advancing Russians and retreating Germans. The Reules flee by horse-drawn wagon, but are turned back. A Polish family already occupies their house.

**May 7-8, 1945**—Germany surrenders, but it takes months to work out the complicated terms.

**November 1945**—Ethnic Germans of Stefanov receive word that they are going to Germany.

**December 1, 1945**—After the villagers board cattle cars, they discover that their destination is east through Brest-Litovsk (now Brest), on the Russian border.

# 1946

**January 1, 1946**—The freight train of villagers arrives in Siberia at an isolated prisoner of war camp near Yurga (Jurga) on the Tom River, between Novosibirsk and Tomsk.

**October 1946**—The Reules leave the Siberian camp by boxcar, heading to Frankfurt on the Oder in Eastern Germany.

Gotthilf Reule's independence and spirit served
as an inspiration throughout Bruno's life.

Gotthilf Reule (second from right, back row) played the French horn in the church band in Friedenstal.

Caravans of hourse-drawn wagons carried household goods from Friedenstal to the gathering place in Galatz.

The tent city in Galatz was their temporary home after leaving Friedenstal.

For nearly a year, the Reule family shared a room with several other families in a Liboch schoolhouse in Sudetenland.

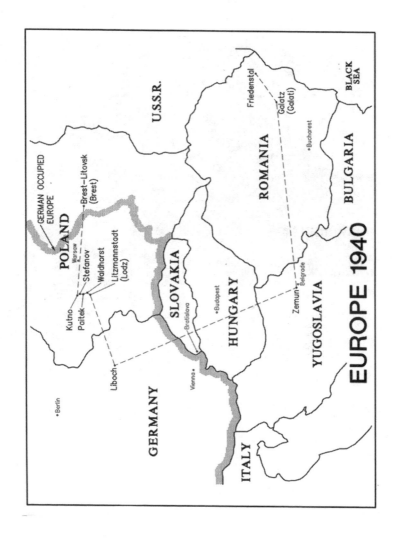

EUROPE 1940

GERMANY · Berlin

POLAND
GERMAN OCCUPIED EUROPE
Warsaw
Stefanov
Kutno
Paitek
Waldhorst
Litzmannstadt (Lodz)
Brest–Litovsk (Brest)
Liboch

U.S.S.R.

SLOVAKIA
Bratislava
Vienna ·

HUNGARY
· Budapest

ROMANIA
Friedenstal
Galatz (Galati)
· Bucharest
Zemun · Belgrade

YUGOSLAVIA

ITALY

BULGARIA

BLACK SEA

Gotthilf Reule constructed the house and barn at their Stefanov farm.

Gotthilf Reule's skill at trading on the black market provided scarce goods such as bicycles during the war.

Gotthilf Reule didn't live to see his baby daughter
Charlotte, here with Bruno.

The Reule family made an unsuccessful attempt to flee Poland
in a horse-drawn wagon such as these.

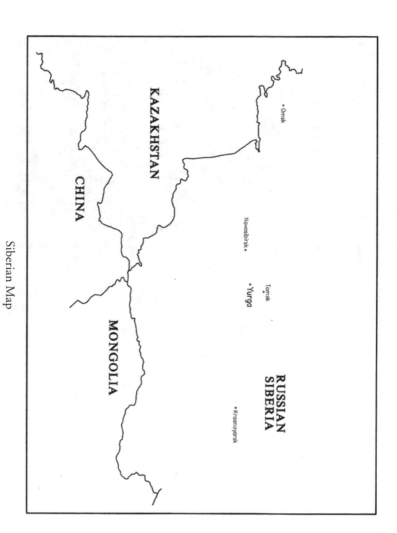

Siberian Map

Refugees in post-war Germany carried special identification.

The house and barn built by Gotthilf Reule in 1942
are still solid, more than half a century later.

Members of the Sobszak family, who befriended the Reules
during the war years, still live in the Reule house.

# The Authors

After almost a year in Siberia, the Reule family's odyssey took them by boxcar to East Germany. They managed to escape to West Germany, where refugees received abusive treatment. Because the war years had robbed Bruno of a formal education and there was insufficient time to catch up, he entered the metal fabrication trade. He came to America in 1955 under the sponsorship of a distant relative and settled in Portland, Oregon, where he still lives with his wife, Isolde. He has a married daughter and one grandson.

The endless chain of tragic events, in the early life of Bruno Reule, captivated the Reverend James Estes, former minister of Rivercrest Community Church in Portland, Oregon. He was convinced that this spellbinding saga should be shared with others. And so, the two began the long, tedious task of parishioner pouring out his past and Estes recording it, and turning it into this moving tale of survival. Estes died in 1999.